Working-Class Rhetorics

Critical Media Literacies Series

Series Editor

William M. Reynolds (*Georgia Southern University, USA*)

Editorial Board

Peter Appelbaum (*Arcadia University, USA*)
Jennifer Beech (*University of Tennessee – Chattanooga, USA*)
Eleanor Blair (*Western Carolina University, USA*)
Ana Cruz (*St. Louis Community College, USA*)
Venus Evans-Winters (*Illinois State University, USA*)
Julie C. Garlen (*Georgia Southern University, USA*)
Nicholas Hartlep (*Berea College, Kentucky, USA*)
Mark Helmsing (*George Mason University, USA*)
Sherick Hughes (*University of North Carolina – Chapel Hill, USA*)
Danielle Ligocki (*Oakland University, USA*)
John Lupinacci (*Washington State University, USA*)
Peter McLaren (*Chapman University, USA*)
Yolanda Medina (*Borough of Manhattan Community College/CUNY, USA*)
Brad Porfilio (*Seattle University, USA*)
Jennifer Sandlin (*Arizona State University, USA*)
Julie Webber (*Illinois State University, USA*)
Handel Kashope Wright (*The University of British Columbia, Canada*)
William Yousman (*Sacred Heart University, USA*)

VOLUME 9

The titles published in this series are listed at *brill.com/cmls*

Working-Class Rhetorics

Contemporary Memoirs and Analyses

Edited by

Jennifer Beech and Matthew Wayne Guy

BRILL

LEIDEN | BOSTON

Cover illustration: Artwork by Ryan Cooper Carl

All chapters in this book have undergone peer review.

The Library of Congress Cataloging-in-Publication Data is available online at http://catalog.loc.gov

Typeface for the Latin, Greek, and Cyrillic scripts: "Brill". See and download: brill.com/brill-typeface.

ISSN 2666-4097
ISBN 978-90-04-50149-2 (paperback)
ISBN 978-90-04-39591-6 (hardback)
ISBN 978-90-04-50150-8 (e-book)

Copyright 2021 by Koninklijke Brill NV, Leiden, The Netherlands.
Koninklijke Brill NV incorporates the imprints Brill, Brill Nijhoff, Brill Hotei, Brill Schöningh, Brill Fink, Brill mentis, Vandenhoeck & Ruprecht, Böhlau Verlag and V&R Unipress.
All rights reserved. No part of this publication may be reproduced, translated, stored in a retrieval system, or transmitted in any form or by any means, electronic, mechanical, photocopying, recording or otherwise, without prior written permission from the publisher. Requests for re-use and/or translations must be addressed to Koninklijke Brill NV via brill.com or copyright.com.

This book is printed on acid-free paper and produced in a sustainable manner.

Contents

List of Figures   VII
Notes on Contributors   VIII

Introduction: Defining and Defying Common (Mis)Understandings of the Working Class   1
  Jennifer Beech and Matthew Wayne Guy

PART 1
Memoirs and Personal Essays

1   Social Class and Sociolects   15
    Irvin Peckham

2   Becoming "Gente Educada": Navigating Academia as a Working-Class, Multiply-Marginalized Student   26
    Christina V. Cedillo

3   Rhetoric: From a Community Yet to Arrive   39
    José Manuel Cortez

4   Five Miles and a World Away: A Memoir   44
    Edward J. Whitelock

5   Feeling Like an Imposter at College   55
    Nancy Mack

6   (Un)Belonging in Liminality: Garage Stories   65
    Phil Bratta

7   Book Smart AND Street Smart   78
    Valerie Murrenus Pilmaier

8   "Remember the Spartans"   90
    William Thelin

9   Honest Work   107
    Katherine Highfill

PART 2
Critical Essays

10 Bodies in the World of Labor: Class, Affect, and Rhetoric in IWW's "What is What in the World of Labor?" Poster   119
   Phil Bratta

11 Mind on Heaven: Working-Class Rhetorics in Serpent-Handling Rituals of Southern Appalachia   134
   Heather Palmer

12 White Bread as a Working-Class Symbol   148
   Kelli R. Gill

13 "Put Some Flowers in the Graveyard": The Gloomy Fate of the Working Class in George A. Romero's *Land of the Dead*   159
   Philip L. Simpson

14 Working Class on the Small Screen   180
   Sarah Attfield

15 #ActorsWithDayJobs: Geoffrey Owens, Job Shaming, and the Ideology of Work   195
   William DeGenaro

16 (Literal) Self-Exposure: Celebrity "Activism" during Covid-19   208
   Abby Graves

17 Returning to Van Buren Street: A Photographic Essay   216
   David Engen

Index   233

Figures

Figures

5.1	News Sun photo, by Scott Kissell.	61
10.1	"What Is What in the World of Labor?" (Jospeh A. Labadie Collection, University of Michigan).	120
12.1	"Growing up Poor" (internet meme, public domain).	149
16.1	@joshgondelman Tweet, March 19, 2020 (https://twitter.com/joshgondelman/status/1240642905947148289).	212
16.2	@writtenbyahmad Tweet, March 19, 2020 (https://twitter.com/writtenbyahmad/status/1240625861801447433?ref_src=twsrc%5Etfw).	213
16.3	"We're All in This Together." Offkey Comics (instagram.com/offkeycomics).	214
17.1	7400 Block of Van Buren Street.	216
17.2	7461 Van Buren Street, Engen family home.	218
17.3	Neighbor Pat's place.	219
17.4	Kenny Engen's garage.	221
17.5	Neighbor, Paul Kroska.	222
17.6	Car on Van Buren Street.	224
17.7	Home on North End of Van Buren.	225
17.8	Woodcrest Elementary School, Van Buren Street.	227
17.9	Dick and Barb's old place, Van Buren Street.	228
17.10	Driveway of Engen family home.	229

Notes on Contributors

Sarah Attfield
comes from a working-class background and grew up on a high-rise social housing estate in north east London, England. She now lives in Australia where she lectures in the School of Communication at the University of Technology, Sydney. Her research interests are focused around working-class representation in TV, film, popular music, the media and literature. She is the editor of the *Journal of Working-Class Studies* and the author of *Class On Screen: The Global Working Class in Contemporary Cinema* (Palgrave, 2020).

Jennifer Beech
(Ph.D.) is Professor of English at the University of Tennessee at Chattanooga, where she teaches a variety of rhetoric and writing courses. In addition to her book *White Out: A Guidebook for Teaching and Engaging with Critical Whiteness Studies* (Brill | Sense, 2020), she has published in numerous edited collections and in such journals as *College English*, *JAC*, *Pedagogy*, and *Open Words*. Since 2004, she has co-chaired the Working-Class Culture and Pedagogy Standing Group of the Conference on College Composition and Communication. Having grown up in a rural working-class community in Alabama, she considers herself multi-classed.

Phil Bratta
is an independent scholar whose work focuses on rhetorical theory, culture, digital-visual rhetorics, and embodiment in everyday, socially-engaged practices. He has published or has forthcoming work in several edited collections and journals, including *The Journal of Multimodal Rhetorics, Rhetoric Review, College Composition and Communication, Computers and Composition, Enculturation, Feminist Teacher, Visual Culture and Gender*, and *The Journal of American Culture*.

Ryan Cooper Carl
(cover artist) teaches art at Chattanooga Preparatory in TN. Working in large and small mediums, his murals appear in restaurants around town. Visit his Instagram: cooperdome.

Christina V. Cedillo
first realized she came from a working-class family when she was a kid being coached on how to not sound working class by a parent. Currently, she is an Assistant Professor of Writing and Rhetoric at the University of Houston-Clear

Lake. Her research draws from cultural rhetorics and decolonial theory to focus on embodied rhetorics and rhetorics of embodiment at the intersections of race, gender, and disability. Her work has appeared in *College Composition & Communication, Rhetoric Society Quarterly, Composition Forum*, and other journals, and in various edited collections. Her current project examines the multimodal rhetorics of 20th and 21st century women of color activists. She is the lead editor of the *Journal of Multimodal Rhetorics*.

José Manuel Cortez
is Assistant Professor in the Department of English at the University of Oregon. His writing appears in *Philosophy and Rhetoric*; *Rhetoric Society Quarterly*; *College Composition and Communication*; *Journal for the History of Rhetoric*; and *Rhetorics of the Democracy in the Americas*.

William DeGenaro
is Professor of Composition & Rhetoric at the University of Michigan Dearborn where he has taught first-year and creative writing for fifteen years. His scholarly work includes *Who Says? Working-Class Rhetoric, Class Consciousness, and Community* (University of Pittsburgh Press, 2007) and essays in *The Journal of Basic Writing, Rhetoric Review, WPA: Writing Program Administration,* and elsewhere. He is a two-time Fulbright Scholar. His introduction to working-class studies came via seminars with Professors Linda Strom and Sherry Linkon at Youngstown State University.

David Engen
is Associate Professor of Communication Studies at Minnesota State University, Mankato. He is the author of *The Wagon Wheel Project* (with photographer John Cross, Minnesota Heritage Publishing, 2012) and co-producer of *The Finding Your Place College Podcast* (with Robert Jersak and six outstanding students (Apple Podcasts, 2019). Dave was trained in documentary studies at Duke University's Center for Documentary Studies. His more discipline-based education comes from Bowling Green State University (Ph.D.), Auburn University (M.A.), Minnesota State University, Mankato (B.S.), and, not far from Van Buren Street, Anoka-Ramsey Community College (A.A.). For 15 years he hosted *Listen to Your Folks*, an Americana radio show on KMSU Radio in Mankato, Minnesota. He teaches courses ranging from Public Speaking to Communication and Community. He has also led several community workshops on audio storytelling.

Kelli R. Gill
is a rhetoric and composition scholar completing her Ph.D. at Texas Christian University, with emphasis in women and gender Studies and new media. Her

research interests include multimodal composition, cultural rhetorics, and food studies. She grew up in Whitton, a rural farming community in East Texas, where she first learned how much food can bring communities together.

Abby Graves
is a graduate teaching assistant at the University of New Mexico, and will receive her M.A. in Rhetoric and Writing. She received a B.A. in Rhetoric and Professional Writing from the University of Tennessee at Chattanooga, where she was named the English department's Outstanding Graduating Senior, and received the Sally B. Young professional writing award.

Matthew Wayne Guy
earned his Ph.D. in Comparative Literature from Louisiana State University, and teaches literary theory and criticism, literature, and pop culture studies as Associate Professor of English at the University of Tennessee at Chattanooga. He has published and presented on a range of topics, from pop culture, phenomenology, and ethics, to the works of Emmanuel Levinas.

Katherine Highfill
is the daughter of an English teacher and a concrete contractor. She grew up in rural Wyoming learning the appropriate feminine arts of baking and sewing alongside hunting, fishing, and finishing concrete. Kate's scholarly work examines power and dissonance in the field of Rhetoric and Composition. She advocates for the acceptance and support of mental illness in the university and society at large. Kate is currently ABD at the University of Houston English program with a concentration in Composition, Rhetoric, and Pedagogy.

Nancy Mack
is Professor Emeritus of English at Wright State University and the author of *Engaging Writers with Multigenre Research Projects* (Teachers College Press, 2015) and two volumes about teaching grammar with poetry. She edited a special issue of the *English Journal* about bullying and has published several articles and chapters on memoir, emotional labor, working class, and teaching writing. She still stops at yard sales, bargain hunts, and has trouble throwing anything away.

Heather Palmer
is Associate Professor of Rhetoric in the English and Women's Gender and Sexuality Studies Departments at the University of Tennessee at Chattanooga. She teaches graduate and undergraduate classes in the History and Theory of Rhetoric, Queer Theory, Women's and Feminist Rhetorics, and has taught

courses on Animals and Rhetoric, Embodiment, and Comparative Rhetoric. Her research interests include the posthuman turn in the humanities, digital feminisms, and affect theory in religious archives. Recent publications include work on the affects of teaching Queer Theory in the South, biopolitics in the naked protest group FEMEN, and she is currently working on a book monograph, *The Spell of the Serpent: Affect in the Digital Archive* on affect in the religious rhetoric of the serpent-handling archive at the University of Tennessee at Chattanooga.

Irvin Peckham

(Ph.D.) grew up in rural Wisconsin. He understood middle-class as the Clarks, who lived down the road and had an indoor bathroom. He attended a one-room schoolhouse and was salutatorian in his eighth-grade class of two. He improbably got into college and became a writing teacher. Now retired, he had been teaching writing at the high school and college level for forty years – in Morgan Hill, CA; the University of Nebraska, Omaha; Louisiana State University; and Drexel University. He writes about social-class relationships, personal writing, and writing assessment. He has been involved in social justice and anti-war movements ever since he first got a letter telling him to report for duty in Viet-Nam. He keeps a blog at personalwriting2.blogspot.com

Valerie Murrenus Pilmaier

is Associate Professor of English, Humanities, and Women's and Gender Studies at the University of Wisconsin – Green Bay. Although trained as an Irish literature scholar, she found that teaching in the Two-Year system for a decade quickly informed her research interests. A First-Generation student herself, she has been focusing on interventions for First-Generation students via SOTL work since 2010. She has previously published articles on composition studies, grief, George Bernard Shaw's plays, female friendship in *Anne of Green Gables* and the gendered nature of SOTL work in Academia. Current projects include effective pedagogy for teaching Holocaust literature and history in the digital environment and best practices for trauma-informed pedagogy . She is the first person in her entire extended family to attend college, and she ardently believes that there is no such thing as "street smart or book smart" as you can be both/and.

Philip L. Simpson

is the son of university-educated professionals; he grew up in a small, working-class village (population under 250) in central Illinois in the heart of the Midwestern "Corn Belt." He received his bachelor's and master's degrees in English from Eastern Illinois University and his doctorate in American

Literature from Southern Illinois University. He currently serves as Provost of the Titusville Campus and Eastern Florida Online at Eastern Florida State College and worked at the college in other administrative roles and as tenured professor of Communications and Humanities and Department Chair of Liberal Arts at the Palm Bay campus. He is immediate past President of the Popular Culture Association/American Culture Association, additionally serving as Co-Chair of the Stephen King Area for the Association and Editorial Board member of the *Journal of Popular Culture* and *Journal of American Culture*. He is the author of two books, *Psycho Paths: Tracking the Serial Killer through Contemporary American Film and Fiction* (Southern Illinois University Press, 2000) and *Making Murder: The Fiction of Thomas Harris* (Praeger, 2009). He co-edited *Stephen King's Contemporary Classics: Reflections on the Modern Master of Horror* ((Rowman & Littlefield, 2014)) and The Walking Dead *Live! Essays on the Television Show* (Rowman & Littlefield, 2016). Finally, he has published numerous journal articles and book chapters on film, literature, popular culture, and horror.

William Thelin
earned his Ph.D. at Indiana University of Pennsylvania. He has worked as a professor since 1994 and has held various administrative positions, such as writing center coordinator, writing program director, and department chair. He has written over 30 articles in his career, published one textbook, and co-edited two scholarly volumes. He currently works at the University of Akron, where he teaches graduate courses in Composition Studies, introductory literature, and first-year writing. He takes most pride, though, in being a grandfather to Hailey, who is now two.

Edward J. Whitelock
was born in Upland, Pennsylvania, and eared a Ph.D. from Indiana University of Pennsylvania. He is co-author (with David Janssen) of *Apocalypse Jukebox: The End of the World in American Popular Music* (Soft Skull Press, 2009) and is a Professor of English at Gordon State College in Barnesville, Georgia.

INTRODUCTION

Defining and Defying Common (Mis)Understandings of the Working Class

Jennifer Beech and Matthew Wayne Guy

When the editors and contributors conceived of this collection, we could not have anticipated the global pandemic that we were about to face—a pandemic that suddenly made apparent that many citizens were just one or two paychecks away from bankruptcy, a pandemic that brought into contrast the very differing responses from various countries to provide for the health and economic safety of the country, of big corporations, and of ordinary citizens. Upon the writing of this introduction, the Institute for Public Policy reported the following telling statistics on June 4, 2020:

> U.S. billionaire's total wealth surged by over $565 billion, an increase of 19.15 percent, since its low point near the beginning of the pandemic, according to calculations to update a report by the Institute for Policy Studies (IPS). The figures date from March 18—the rough start date of the pandemic shutdown, when most federal and state economic restrictions were in place. During the same 11 weeks, 42.6 million US workers filed for unemployment (1.877 million in the last week). The number of workers receiving jobless benefits is holding steady at 21.5 million, according to *The Wall Street Journal*.

It's getting harder and harder to hold to the common myth of the United States as a classless or middle-class society. Back in 2012, Michael Zweig argued in *The Working-Class Majority: America's Best Kept Secret*, that most Americans are working class, even if they do not claim that affiliation. Zweig locates class not simply in money—despite the country's ever-widening gap in income distribution from the small minority at the top to the majority of our citizens at the bottom.

Instead, Zweig locates it in power: power in the workplace, in politics, and in culture. Recent figurations of class as based upon a gradational scale of income also make clear a large working-class citizenry. If the populist rhetoric employed in our last Presidential election from both sides of the aisle had indicated that it was beginning to be a prime time for students of rhetoric, politics, and American culture to revisit and gain a greater critical literacy with respect to social class, the economic disparities made starkly clear in the wake of shutdowns have brought that exigency home. This collection seeks to reintroduce class from a neo-Marxist perspective with the aim of increasing critical literacy in the fight for equitable distribution of income and class power. This literacy and advocacy are necessary to maintain democracy and to help readers consider the role that discourse plays in shaping notions of power and empowering folks from a range of class backgrounds to use rhetoric to mobilize for social justice. Our collection is especially aimed at the following audiences: (1) academics from the working class who often find themselves caught in liminal spaces, (2) professors who have working-class students and colleagues, and (3) anyone interested in how class is presented or even misrepresented in various forms of discourse (memoirs, the media, and pop culture) and the role that rhetoric plays in shaping and reshaping those representations.

Class theorists in general disagree with how to define class, and our contributors—particularly those in the memoir part—have found that as class has played out in their daily lives, no single definition of class has been adequate for making sense of their experiences. Consider, for example, the following ways of defining class that folks who are even willing to acknowledge the existence of class will find themselves grappling with:

1. Gradational—based upon income, wealth, or social status. Once, most people referred to class in one of three ways: the rich, the middle class, and the poor. Now, of course, we find more and more distinctions and gradations being made concerning class in America. Academically, social stratification has been classified in numerous ways, one of the most popular and lasting being the model put forth by sociologists Dennis Gilbert and Joseph Kahl. Rather than relying solely on wealth and income, the Gilbert-Kahl model locates six distinct classes in America: the upper or "capitalist class," the upper middle, the middle class, the working class, the working poor, and the underclass. For the most part, "working class" usually refers to the last four classes, though as we point out in this collection, all classes participate in the rhetoric of the working class, it being so ingrained in American culture.

2. Relational—based upon the position one has in the power structure at a given time. That last qualification is important: "at a given time." Rather than an essential identity, class, as many neo-Marxists argue, has more to do with one's relation to others within the operations of capital. Class within the whole of society is thus more fluid, more contextual. Therefore wealth accumulation and the economic exploitation of others operate more effectively in society than do the effects of holding a certain social

status. Think merely of your middle managers everywhere demanding more and more from the workers underneath them, all the while staying late in the office to "catch up on some work" without overtime compensation. Is this manager a tool of or a victim of capitalist exploitation? The fact that one would probably say both points to class as a relational, rather than an essential phenomenon.

3. Cultural—based upon habits, pastimes, beliefs, and social practices. Class is not so much an identity as it is an ideology, a "mindset" initiated in the midst of certain political speech, advertising, forms of entertainment and the like. The culture of class politics and identities can be even more fluid than the relational or gradational ways of defining class. Class can be an offensive or defensive weapon at times, used to belittle others or lift up one's esteem. Class can be sneered at or worn as a badge of authenticity. Class can determine certain choices at the grocery store, shopping mall, high school cafeterias, or even wedding days. Class can also help one make sense of a rough upbringing, a sheltered life, a sense of privilege or a lack of fulfillment.

These ways of defining class point to an implicit assumption: most academics are more comfortable thinking of class as a fluid, rather than stable, category. Or, put another way, class—especially the category reserved for "working class"—should be seen through the lenses of experience, be they personal or observational, rather than through a checklist of certain defining elements. No one feature of class nowadays can be said to define the categories of class.

This extreme variability is where the study of rhetoric comes in. As a fluid and situational experience, class needs to be understood as a linguistic construct in the broadest of terms. Studying the rhetorical situation, the meanings of things as they are enacted within a specific instance and experience, brings the elusive features of class politics to the forefront to be assessed, studied, and understood. Rhetorical investigation can thus bring about a deeper understanding of how class determines meaning much more than the charts, graphs, surveys and polls of other disciplines.

The experience of class was therefore important to both editors when we gathered the works for this collection. We sought out academic writing that operated more as memoir, critical yet personal testimony of the experience of class, especially from writers with working-class backgrounds. Many times, just achieving a role as an academic can itself be enough of an experience. As bell hooks (2000) notes, in *Where We Stand: Class Matters*, folks often cannot anticipate the "psychic turmoil" that obtaining a college education puts one and one's family through. As pressure is put upon us, or as we put pressure upon ourselves to assimilate to the more middle-class ways of academe, we find more than simply our knowledge changing. College changes not just our chances for a middle-class income. College changes our habits of mind, our decorum, and our ways of being in the world—often in ways that displace us from belonging with those back in our families and home communities. Yet—as the memoirs in the first part illustrate—we often still do not fit in with our colleagues from middle-class backgrounds. Often suffering from imposter syndrome and an inability or lack of desire to "act middle-class," we don't fit well into academe either. Hence, the importance of us working as rhetors (those who practice rhetoric) to share stories and locate other working-class academics that we may mentor and support.

From the mid-1990's to the mid-2000's several edited collections of memoirs by working-class academics were highly popular—two particularly popular ones were *This Fine Place So Far From Home: Voices of Academics from the Working Class* (1995) and *Reflections from the Wrong Side of the Tracks: Class, Identity, and the Working Class Experience in Academe* (2006). Those memoirs are still relevant but do not always reflect more recent experiences contemporary to those of our students and of newer postgraduates. Recently, members of the Working-Class Culture and Pedagogy Standing Group of the Conference on College Composition and Communication released the collection *Class in the Composition Classroom: Pedagogy and the Working Class* (2017); our collection complements, rather than competes with, that book. A number of monographs exists by scholars interested in class—bell hooks' (2000) *Where We Stand: Class Matters* and Joanna Kadi's *Thinking-Class: Sketches from a Cultural Worker* (1996, now out of print)—and several of our contributors cite these in their work. Thus, we hope our collection works from those earlier traditions while also depicting how class continues to play out in the material conditions of everyday life.

We open the first part of our collection with Irvin Peckham's chapter, "Social Class and Sociolects," because he speaks directly to our student audience and because his easy style makes rhetoric, notions of what it means to be educated, and theories of class accessible while still capturing their complexities. Drawing upon the work of French sociologist Pierre Bourdieu, Peckham explains the important concept of habitus, and—by relating his family's history and his own story—makes clear how family habits often work to reproduce social class structures. His chapter is valuable, as well, for his discussion of the various subjectivities and conditions that intersect to form social class distinctions. With several theories under their belt, students can move on to read Christina V. Cedillo's "Becoming 'Gente Educada': Navigating Academia as a Working-Class, Multiply Marginalized Student"—although her discussion of how a person's working-class background "intersects with race, gender, and disability" stands up well on its own. Like Peckham, Cedillo applies theories of rhetoric, explicating and enacting the position of a cultural rhetorician, while simultaneously making use of socio-linguistic theories (like code switching) to make clear the role that language plays in social class formation. Cedillo, who identifies herself as "a multiply-marginalized individual, a disable woman of color (Chicana) raised by working-class parents in the U.S.-Mexico borderlands of South Texas," draws on the work of Gloria Anzaldua in ways that will introduce students to important concepts like "epistemology switching" and dwelling in "in-between spaces." Next, in "Rhetoric: From a Community Yet to Arrive," José Manuel Cortez, an American citizen who also has familial ties to Mexico, recounts a trip with his father and uncle in 2006 to settle a land dispute on the family farm in Florencia de Benito, Jaurez. As so often happens with memoir, the process of recreating memories is not a simple act of transcription, but rather an opportunity for reflection and connection to larger stories and dilemmas of humanity. Writing in 2019, Cortez overlays onto the stories of his family and others who have sought to come to the states a quote from Donald Trump (in which the then Presidential candidate equated Mexican immigrants with rapists, drug dealers, and generally bad people)—posing a problem for us as readers, thinkers, and working-class rhetors: "How do we begin to practice a new nomos of community that accommodates those who have nothing—those whose stories cannot be rendered within the technology of a narrative order?" Like Cedillo's piece, Cortez's reflections give us fodder for contemplating the limits of narrativization for those writing the diasporic, working-class experience. Together, these three skillfully written opening chapters help students get a hold of key concepts in both rhetoric and social class theory.

Tension makes for a great story: right? But it also makes for a fraught adolescence. It's what makes us grow into the adults we become. The memoirs that make up Chapters 4 and 5 model how a good story can get at class in poignant ways that polemic or even academic research cannot. Fans of nostalgia will likely enjoy the memoirs of Whitelock and Mack, which give us glimpses into what it was like to come of age during the late 1960's and 70's. Edward J. Whitelock's "Five Miles and a World Away" draws readers in by mixing thick cultural and era detail with the classic tale of the misfit youth displaced by a family move. Stigmatized as a working-class out-of-towner with ill-fitting clothes, Whitelock became an early observer of social labels, like "gear heads" and "burn outs" that so many ethnographers of social class (see Eckert and Bettie) have observed in schools across the country and through the decades. The terms may change with the locales and era, but the sting of being an outsider remains. Drawing upon the famous study by Jean Anyon in which she observed that schools often and even inadvertently reproduce social class through pedagogies that tend to teach some students (primarily working class) to be obedient and other students to be future leaders (middle and elite classes), Whitelock finds himself woefully underprepared for the pedagogy enacted as his new school. His tale is not one of the scholarship boy who overcomes tension by simply relying on his smarts; without spoiling it for you, we'll just say that things get pretty shaky (even suicidal) before they get better. Nancy Mack's "Feeling Like an Imposter at College" further demonstrates how clothes—in her case, different shoes—can operate as a metaphor for class and for trying and failing or rebelliously not trying to look the part of the successful academic. Anyone who has ever met Nancy Mack will appreciate how she infuses humor into her memoir, and that's part of her point: humor can be wielded as a weapon against those who purposefully or even unwittingly attempt to deny working-class folks access to empowering education; humor can also provide catharsis. Mack's chapter also provides a useful chart delineating the major pitfalls of the imposter syndrome harbored by so many of us academics from the working class. Further, her chapter demonstrates writing as an act of resistance and highlights the importance of sharing such personal stories with other academics.

What does it mean to work? How do tensions between differing definitions of work interfere with one's ability or desire to take on academic work? To accept academic work as "real" or to have one's work valued by members of one's working-class family and home community? In Paul Willis's famous study *Learning to Labor: How Working Class Kids Get Working Class Jobs* (1977), he observed the disdain that working-class school lads had for academic labor, a disposition they picked up from their fathers who held disdain for their middle-class bosses; indeed, they did not see intellectual endeavors as work at all. One common experience related by academics who come from working-class backgrounds and by those who have conducted ethnographic studies of various working-class students is that of a disjunction between how work is defined and valued in working-class communities versus the types of work that get done and valued in academic settings. Like so many memoirs, Phil Bratta's "(Un)Belonging in Liminality: Garage Stories" highlights the recursive nature of memory work. Recounting a conversation with his grandmother, Bratta toggles to his experiences in graduate school and his introduction to the work of Sara Ahmed's *Queer Phenomenology* (2006), who opens her book by asking, "What does it mean to be oriented?" Like Ahmed, the memoirs of Bratta and Valerie Murrenus Pilmaier further render visible how rhetoric is embodied in the interplay of any number of competing subjectivities and existential dilemmas—be it those of class, race, gender, disability, sexual orientation, orientation to work and place, etc. Relating the liminality that so many of our authors inhabit, in "Book Smart AND Street Smart," Pilmaier opens by noting that her working-class family feels that she betrayed them by seeking and achieving a Ph.D. Making a pop-culture allusion, Pilmaier bemoans that since childhood, she has lived in the "Upside-Down": as a bookish child and now a professor, she has never fit in well with her family, and now around her academic peers, she suffers from imposter syndrome, constantly fearing that her middle-class façade will be unveiled. Much like Nancy Mack, Pilmaier hopes her ultimately successfully, yet complicated, story will serve as support and inspiration for first-generation and working-class students.

The final two pieces in this part underscore the impact of mental illness on social class standings and affiliations. Class is not simply about income, and working-class students are not always first-generation college goers. Further, class can be said to be fluid, rather than a static category, so that even when one achieves a certain gradational marker—like income or education—that might denote one as officially having "moved up," one may still retain various working-class habitus, attitudes, and attachments. The son of a judge, William Thelin might seem like an odd person to write a personal essay about how class-related anxieties have plagued him from his childhood into his more recent days as a full professor. However, as he relates in "Remember the Spartans" as a result of his mother's hording and obsessive-compulsive disorder, he developed an early distrust of wealth accumulation, along with a desire to emulate what he viewed as more traditional working-class orientations to work and habits of self-presentation. His chapter is helpful for thinking about the possibility that a person could be multi-classed (as opposed to simply occupying a single class positionality). The end piece in this part rests somewhere between personal essay, memoir, and rant—a compelling argument for the need for genre innovation when it comes to working-class rhetoric. In "Honest Work," Katherine Highfill is even more brutally honest than William Thelin about her fraught relationship with academe. Highfill is an adjunct professor—THE working-class of academe upon whose back rests the corporatized university. Highfill, who has Major Depressive Disorder, has difficulty affording the medical treatment she so desperately needs because adjunct laborers do not often qualify for full medical coverage, but that's not her sole beef with academe. Drawing upon the work of Foucault, Highfill observes how university cultures replicate larger systems of power to let in just enough members from beyond the hegemonic group to appear meritorious while simultaneously ensuring that they know their place. Neither rage quit lit nor a Pollyannaish scholarship piece, Highfill's chapter is an important explication and provocative pondering on the two terms in her title.

As rhetoricians, those who study rhetoric, we assert the importance of acting in critical dialogue with culture, as opposed to being passive objects of it. Hence, the second half of this book includes critical studies of the many places working class rhetoric operate: social media, television, film, political posters, religious rituals, food, and even suburban streets. We gathered up essays that investigate hidden assumptions, politicized themes, and overt pandering to the notions of the working class, in all of its implications, from praise to calumny. Some operate rather academically, while some are as unorthodox as the channels into which they pursue their critical approach.

The second part of the collection opens with essays that look into traditional areas of working-class ideology, even though in some unusual approaches. First we have Phil Bratta's essay on visual rhetoric, "Bodies in the World of Labor: Class, Affect, and Rhetoric in IWW's 'What is What in the World of Labor?' Poster." Bratta looks at the historical and rhetorical situation of a mid-twentieth century poster put out by the organization, Industrial Workers of the World, whose members came to be known as "Wobblies." The poster, as Bratta argues, serves to focus knowledge about labor, value, and the relationships formed amongst individuals within the world of the working-class. Activism and political consciousness is the goal of the poster, but it approaches this goal in a very clever way, by referencing the four suits of common playing cards. Within the very simple rhetoric of this poster, a good deal of which is expressed by symbols, lies a coherent argument about power, exploitation, and the necessity of organizing labor to be a more productive player in the game of capitalism.

Working-class identity does not stop at the factory or the labor union hall, of course, and as Heather Palmer's essays shows, it even continues into the pews of churches on Sunday morning. Her essay, "Mind on Heaven: Working-Class Rhetorics in Serpent-Handling Rituals of Southern Appalachia," posits that the snake-handling rituals of certain religious sects operate as rhetorical stances which assert and even uphold the working-class identity of its followers. Important to these rituals are the assumptions that such identities are under threat, inasmuch as the regional economies, cultures and communities themselves are under threat. Labor, property, wages, and regional identities come together in the meaningfulness of rituals designed to show that having the Lord's protection is inherent in one's identity.

Identity is also inherent to one's possessions, or even, one's objects of consumption, no matter how mundane. Kelli R. Gill's essay, "White Bread as a Working-Class Symbol," stands as a clever combination of the personal and observational that we have pursued for this collection. Culturally, white bread was once the status of the upper-class, for it was an object that went through refinement and softening, much like the elites that consumed it. The rough, often adulterated, wheat bread was for the peasants, while the labor that the refining and bleaching of white bread needed added to the price and thus the status. Here in the twenty-first century, things have changed. Gill's goes into the origins, representations, and moralization of a staple of working-class kitchens for almost a century.

The remainder of the essays look at presentations and even subtle politicizing of working-class ideas within the media. Philip L. Simpson gives an in-depth analysis of the critique of capitalism in one of the great zombie films of all time, 2005's *Land of the Dead*. His essay, "'Put Some Flowers in the Graveyard': The Gloomy Fate of the Working Class in George A. Romero's *Land of the Dead*," discusses the zombie apocalypse in the film as a metaphor for capitalism's class warfare, consumer culture, and exploitation of communities. Simpson opens the essay discussing one of the film's more clever moments, when the lead actors seek to distract the zombies with fireworks, a sly criticism on Romero's part concerning the pairing of patriotism and consumerism.

We turn from film to television in Sarah Attfield's essay, "Working Class on the Small Screen," which discusses how members of the working-class are represented on what was at one time inarguably the most influential element of everyday life. Nowadays, though, social media could be vying for more influence, as television has turned to following trends on social media rather than the other way around. Still, television is the center of the cultural universe even today, and whether we are watching Homer Simpson, or keeping up with the Kardashians, or watching people get voted off of an island, the vices and virtues of working-class identities permeate what we consume. Attfield argues that for the most part, even when having fun with the stereotypes, as in *My Name is Earl*, for example, television shows rely on a rather shallow representation of the working class. Issues of exploitation, insolvency, or even unemployment may be presented but never confronted.

The other essays pursue the more subdued features of working-class rhetoric in the area where it perhaps is most dynamic, that of celebrity culture. William DeGenaro gives a wonderful investigation into a more recent "viral" video of actor Geoffrey Owens working at a grocery store bagging groceries. The event sparked off with a lot of what can only be called gloating over the supposed fall of a one-time celebrity, but was followed up with some rather good, healthy debate about working-class values. DeGenaro's essay, "#ActorsWithDayJobs: Geoffrey Owens, Job Shaming, and the Ideology of Work," reveals how the viral event touched upon certain myths and stereotypes concerning the working class, but also myths and stereotypes about the world we don't examine, such as the myth that once you "make it," the hard work is over. Or, the myth that working hard is rewarded within the system of meritocracy. The person who took Owens' picture posted it with a mild mockery, which was followed by more "job shaming" from others on social media (we know, hard to believe, right?), but was also followed up with plenty of "shame-shaming," if you will, criticizing those who were debasing a person who was actually working hard to support a family. DeGenaro, though, goes deeper into how the event actually showed the actual vulnerability of most workers, but also perhaps more subtle ways in which discrimination, race and status operate a bit more malevolently within such social media spectacles.

Abby Graves looks into the odd feature of celebrities wanting to "do their part" recently. Her essay, "(Literal) Self-Exposure: Celebrity 'Activism' during Covid-19" gives us an academic, yet humorous, analysis of one of the more hideous moments of the whole "lockdown" months in America. Celebrity Gal Gadot decided to gather up other celebrities to sing bits of John Lennon's song, "Imagine" for a video. It went viral, of course, but not for the reasons that perhaps the celebrities themselves had hoped for. The video and the celebrities themselves were panned for being insensitive, contrived, and self-indulgent, for "virtue-signaling" while the majority of Americans worried about finding toilet paper and food. As most people online saw it, while people were laid off and holed up in their houses, or working double shifts as "essential workers," celebrities took it upon themselves to sing from their mansions a song that criticizes wealth and status. Graves looks at the underlying rhetorical situation of the video and the response to it, one in which millions of working-class people experienced true economic despair and deprivation, and will feel the effects of such instability for years to come. The rhetoric of the video, the celebrities, the viewers and the people who "called them out" permeate with assumptions about class politics and identity.

We conclude the collection with David Engen's "Returning to Van Buren Street: A Photographic Essay." The essay is part memoir, part visual rhetoric, part collage of nostalgia and academic insights. Engen, like many of us, is as much of his working-class family and neighborhood as he is an English professor. Well, actually, as he admits, he usually says "teacher." As he puts it in the essay, "I assume I'll look arrogant if I say I'm a *professor*." The aversion to the term "professor"? "That's Van Buren Street talking some."

Engen's aversion could also be that "turmoil" bell hooks references which we mentioned early in this introduction. It's a very apt word, actually. For most, it conjures up psychic distress, or confusion. We say "economic turmoil" to describe a recession, or refer to the "turmoil" of politically tense times. The word, though, most likely comes from the French "tremouille," the word for the mill hopper that swayed back and forth, spreading the grain on top of the mill stone. So, it's a working-class term, for sure. It is also not as quite "hectic" or vigorous in its original meaning. Primarily, it simply described an action that was back and forth, not static, but rather fluid, constant only in its capacity to change, much like the very ideas of class and identity that the works in this collection focus on, and, to be frank, much like many of the contributors to this collection who find themselves living, struggling, and even researching those very elusive working-class elements to their own lives.

References

Bettie, J. (2014). *Women without class: Girls, race, and identity*. University of California Press.

Billionaire wealth surges by over half a trillion dollars during the pandemic. (2020). Institute for Public Policy Studies via Common Dreams. https://www.commondreams.org/newswire/2020/06/04/billionaire-wealth-surges-over-half-trillion-dollars-during-pandemic

Carter, G., & Thelin, W. (Eds.). (2017). *Class in the composition classroom: Pedagogy and the working class*. University of Colorado Press.

Dews, C. L., & Law, C. L. (1995). *This fine place so far from home: Voices of academics from the working class*. Temple University Press.

Eckert, P. (1990). *Jocks & burnouts: Social categories and identity in the high school*. Teachers College Press.

Gilbert, D. L., & Kahl, J. A. (1982). *The American class structure: A new synthesis*. Dorsey Press.

hooks, b. (2000). *Where we stand: Class matters*. Routledge.

Kadi, J. (1996). *Thinking class: Sketches from a cultural worker*. South End Press.

Muzatti, S., & Samarco, C. V. (Eds.). (2006). *Reflections from the wrong side of the tracks: Class, identity, and the working class experience in academe*. Rowman & Littlefield.

Romero, G. A. (Director). (2005). *Land of the dead* [Film]. Universal Pictures.

Willis, P. (1977). *Learning to labour: How working class kids get working class jobs*. Columbia University Press.

Zweig, M. (2012). *The working class majority: America's best kept secret*. Cornell University Press.

PART 1

Memoirs and Personal Essays

∴

CHAPTER 1

Social Class and Sociolects

Irvin Peckham

I want to open this essay by situating myself within the rhetorical situation in which I am writing and with a little luck, read and responded to. I hesitated to use the phrase, "rhetorical situation," because that's the kind of language you are going to hear only from academics—the sort of people who teach and write to each other about subjects that are of little interest to anyone other than themselves. Although we often pretend to, we don't, for instance, write directly to students as I am doing here to you.

 I am a rhetorician by training, someone who studies the part that writing plays in our culture. As rhetoricians, we use "rhetorical situation" to refer to a host of relationships that surround any speaking or writing event. In this situation, for example, there is my relationship to my subject (writing and social-class relationships), your relationship to that subject, where this essay might appear (a collection of essays specifically addressed to students in college writing classes), your relationship with the teacher who may have assigned this essay to you, the specific physical scene within which you might be reading it, the fact that you might rather be doing something else—one could go on. It's actually interesting to study this kind of flotsam because writing is so much more than simply transferring thoughts from one's mind onto a page or screen.

1 Writing and Social Class

As a first-year student at the University of Wisconsin in 1962, I thought writing was simply that: a matter of corralling my rambling thoughts and getting them onto paper so that my essay would make sense to whoever might read it, almost always a teacher who was going to grade me. I was uncomfortable with most writing situations. In high school, I usually had managed to get B's from my English teacher, a tall, willowy, platinum blonde whom I adored. On occasion, I got an A or a C. At Wisconsin, I usually came in one grade lower, my grades hovering between Bs and Cs with an occasional A when I accidentally hooked into a subject that fascinated me. Mrs. Ghastin would be shocked that I decided to become a writing teacher—and even more that she might have been the reason for my obsession with teaching writing.

I suspect that most of you are entering the university knowing more about writing than I did, and probably about the part your background plays in what you know. Entering college, I had no idea that my social-class origin might have something to do with how difficult writing was for me. I didn't even know I had a social-class origin. I thought there were some rich kids in town and others who lived on the proverbial other side of the tracks with my family being somewhere in the middle.

My background was rural, working-class. By rural, I mean seriously rural: rich to my family meant people who had running water, like the Clarks up the road. Our one-room schoolhouse in Rockbridge, Wisconsin had an outhouse with two sides, one for the girls, one for the boys. We raised our hand with two fingers extended to ask for permission to go to the bathroom. Before going outside, we had to write our name on the blackboard, in case, I suppose, we got lost in a blizzard. In winter, we didn't stay out there long.

My father was a farmer and mechanic—a mechanic to subsidize our eighty-acre dairy farm, which was going under. My father didn't like books. He thought teachers belonged to the group of people who screwed those who actually worked for a living—by which he meant, worked with their hands. He came from a long line of Wisconsin farmers, his great-grandfather having settled in Southwest Wisconsin shortly after the Black Hawk War. My mother was a secretary. She, however, had come on her mother's side from the educated class. Her mother had graduated in 1912 from Ripon College, an unusual circumstance for a Wisconsin woman at the turn of the 20th century. My grandmother never forgave my mother for marrying an "uneducated" farmer. I had to put uneducated in scare quotes (they are called scare quotes to scare the meaning of the word away from the person who uses it) because I don't think one is educated only by going to school and learning from books. Farmers, for instance, are educated in the way the land and animals work. Blues musicians are educated by playing their instruments and fitting their songs within a long history of others'. Many of the best blues musicians, like Leadbelly, didn't finish grade school. I hope you get my point: "educated" as a value judgment means different things to people from different social classes.

My parents' backgrounds explain in part how I managed to make it through college, which is generally designed to weed out students like me, that is, students who grow up in the working classes, speaking working-class English, and learning working-class habits. A famous sociologist named Pierre Bourdieu calls the constellation of habits that characterize different social groups *habitus*. Our *habitus* includes such things as the ways we speak, think, eat, dress, entertain ourselves, the sports we play, the TV programs we watch, the music we listen to, the friends we have, and so on. We recognize which social group we belong to by our *habitus*. You probably know what I mean. In my high school, we called them groups—or perhaps if we were trying to sound high-minded, cliques. Cliques are slightly different from social classes, but they function in the same way: you know who is in and who is out. In a large part, a clique is determined by the social class of the members. There are ways, however, for someone from a "lower" clique to get into an "upper" clique. A boy might become the quarterback. Back in the sixties, a girl could become a cheerleader. Lord. References to social classes make people in the United States nervous because our nation was supposedly founded on the assumption that "all men are created equal." Some will argue that Thomas Jefferson and his friends meant all people were created equal, but it doesn't take much research to discover that not only was "men" gender specific, excluding women, but also race and social-class specific. In general, only white males with property were allowed to vote until the mid-19th century. With some differences according to the state in which they lived, women were not allowed to vote until 1920. Even now, the structure of our voting system is predicated on an assumption of ignorance among people from the working classes. As Alexander Hamilton claims in "The Federalist Papers No. 68," only people (white men with property) from the higher social classes have the requisite ability to discern truth from flim-flam and should thus be allowed to vote for president. That's why we have the electoral college. We elect representatives who then vote the way they see fit, guided by the results of the popular votes in their states.

Social classes are mostly in our heads: that is, they are not real as diamonds are real; but they are close to it, functioning to regulate who goes to college, who marries who, who gets what kind of job, who gets elected to run our communities, states, and country. This kind of regulation is studied closely by stratification researchers. They study how organizations like educational institutions, legal systems, club memberships, taxation systems, and electoral colleges function to keep the children of those at the top at the top and those at the bottom at the bottom. The maintenance of this system of social positions across generations is called social reproduction, resembling the ways in which organisms reproduce themselves. To varying degrees, cultures allow some leakage such that a small percentage (about 8% in the United States) of people from the working classes move into the middle classes and virtually never into the stratosphere of the elite (Kerbo, 1996).

In the United States, it is particularly important to have some movement across social classes to maintain the illusion of the possibility of going from rags to riches, memorialized in *Ragged Dick*, a famous book written by Horatio Algers Jr., who, although pretending in his pseudo autobiography to have been born in poverty, was born rich. The point of *Ragged Dick* was to sustain the hard-work myth, that if you work hard enough and are smart enough, you will make it. You might even become President. Politicians—like Elizabeth Warren,

Joe Biden, Chris Christie, or Marco Rubio (the list is virtually endless)—are fond of recounting how their parents were poor and that their rise to wealth and prominence is proof of the American Dream.

2 Reproduction of Social Class Privilege

Depending on the social class, race, and gender into which people are born, they react differently to this kind of social-class analysis. People born into the higher social classes will be disinclined to believe social reproduction theory, whereas people from the lower social classes will nod their heads and say, of course. This difference in reaction is understandable if you compare it to what is known as white privilege. When you are the one benefitting from the privilege, you tend not to see it. I, for instance, needed to have my privilege as a white male pointed out to me a few decades ago when I was a graduate student at the University of California, San Diego. I won't go into all the benefits I inherited by being a white male in a male-, white-dominated culture, but I have them.

It is to my benefit *not* to see my privilege. I prefer to think that my social and professional success has been a consequence of my intelligence and work ethic rather than a consequence of having been born male and white. Similarly, if I had been born into the wealthier classes, say, in the upper-middle class, I probably would not have been aware of all the advantages that came from being a member of the higher social classes. I would prefer to think that everyone has an equal chance to succeed.

Cultures have various ways of keeping people from the different social classes in their places. About thirty years ago, I wrote an article in which I analyzed how social-class characteristics affect our academic performances in college. At the end of the article, I ended a discussion of cultural literacy with a comparison between the literacy of a student from the ghettos in South Omaha, where I was living at the time, to that of my daughter, who was about to enter college:

> Working class students, for example, will not be acquainted with Bartok, Duke Ellington, or Van Gogh. If knowledge is predicated on experience, working-class midwesterners won't know what the ocean or mountains really are, because few of them will have traveled far from home, and working-class New Jerseyites won't know the Mississippi from the Platte. Working-class students will not really know about airplanes, about the differences between the east and west coasts, much less the difference

between Wisconsin and Greece. Many professional/managerial class students will know about these things from personal experience. They will have been to plays. Many will have been to concerts, operas, and ballets. I compare my daughter, a high school senior, to children who have grown up in South Omaha, the ghetto of white working-class children. My daughter is familiar with Puccini, the Weavers, and Moody Blues. She knows more about literature and painting than I knew when I was a senior in college. She has frequently been to Mexico, twice to England, and once to Switzerland, France, Italy, and Greece. She has lived in a rural community in northern California, in San Diego, and now lives in Omaha. She is used to flying across the country by herself ... Coming up against the likes of my daughter, those kids in South Omaha don't have a chance particularly since the educational system is *not* predicated upon equal education for all but upon competition with professional/managerial class students starting from the fifty and working-class students starting from the zero yard line in the one hundred yard dash. And then working-class students are told the reason they didn't win was because they were slow. (Peckham, 1995, p. 274)

My prediction of academic success for my daughter was accurate, a consequence of the social-class codes my wife and I, college graduates with postgraduate degrees, had imbued in her. Simply said, we had taught her how to display unselfconsciously the codes expected by her professors, most of whom had likewise been raised by parents with college degrees, very few of whom had ever heard the word "ain't." My daughter completed her BA at Smith in four years, her PhD from Yale at twenty-nine, and was a full professor at thirty-nine. We gave her the codes that would help her fit in—not seamlessly, I might add, but she was recognized as someone who belonged.

For the most part, parents naturally pass on the codes of their social class to their children, which codes the children absorb the way the earth soaks up rain. This was certainly the way in which my wife, who grew up in a professional/managerial (Basil Bernstein's label for the middle-middle and upper-middle classes) household, passed on the class codes of her childhood to our daughter. By contrast, I was passing on not the codes of the social class codes into which I was born but the social class into which I had married. I knew that by passing on my secondary codes, I was helping to prepare my daughter for success in the middle-class world. Because I had crossed the borders separating social classes, I was more aware of them than was my wife, who had always lived in the middle classes.

3   Um ... Social Class?

I have referred to the classes in the plural, e.g., the working classes rather than the working class. Stratification researchers have various names for sub-classes of the working, middle, and upper classes, such as the homeless, the poverty class, the working poor, the professional/managerial class, the corporate class, or the elite, but we can usefully break the working, middle, and upper classes each into three subclasses, like the lower working class, the middle working class, and the upper working class. A common misconception is that these classes and sub-classes are marked by wealth—how much money one makes in a year and the value of his or her assets. Digging slightly deeper, people associate classes with how much education one has received. The longer one has gone to school (without failing), the higher one's social class. Some people crassly refer to the educated and the uneducated classes; in fact, standard "educated" English is frequently used to distinguish "correct" from uneducated English, the latter referring to the language used by those who have not completed college. Bourdieu describes different social classes according to the kinds of *capital* people possess: economic, social, educational, symbolic, and linguistic. People's social classes, then, are mapped by wealth, who they hang out with, degrees obtained, control of symbol systems like titles, and command of "correct" language. Here I will distinguish between "language" and what sociolinguists (people who study the relationships between cultures and language) call sociolects. A language generally refers to a collection of dialects, characterized by a geographical area, and to sociolects characterized by a social group.

In addition to describing a social class by these kinds of capital, Bourdieu imagined two poles, which he called fractions, for each class—the economic and cultural fractions. Thus, you could have the economic fraction of the upper-middle class (e.g., bankers, high level managers, investment brokers) or the cultural fraction (e.g., professors, artists, musicians, actors). The economic fraction would have more wealth and the cultural more culture. Bourdieu frequently referred to these classes as social spaces, a nod toward members' habits of hanging out in particular physical locations marking the territory of the group, e.g., the group of people you would see at an opera verses the group you would see at a Townes Van Zandt performance.

Before exploring more fully the sociolect codes and their effects on writing ability, I want to explore the hot issue of the values associated with the different social classes and their aligned codes. In general, we can say the higher your social class, the more your privileges and status. Social reproduction works by convincing members of the culture that markers like salary, working conditions, titles, how much you travel, what kinds of music you're familiar with, what your wear, how often you go out to dinner, and so on really matter, that is, how much you are "worth." Looked at from a different perspective, say from a humanistic or religious perspective, your value may be marked instead by the good you do in the world, by how you treat others, by what you give rather than by what you get from your community. From this alternative perspective, one might say that the working classes and their codes have more value than the moneyed classes. For instance, a hoarder, a multi-billionaire who has made his or her wealth (a conventional marker of worth in our culture) by trading stocks for a living is of far less value than a carpenter who builds real rather than paper houses.

But our culture trains us to value the markers of higher social classes more than the markers of the working classes. Consequently, the middle-class (i.e., "educated") sociolect has more value than working-class sociolect. If you want to get a good job with high salaries and prestige, you have to learn the sociolect of middle-class culture. That's the A, B, and C of it. This analysis suggests a critical picture of the middle classes and the ways in which middle-class professors discriminate against students speaking and writing in working-class codes. We do this, labeling the working-class codes as "incorrect," with the implication that the social classes marked by these codes are "incorrect." But we middle-class professors, even those of us who came from the working classes, are conditioned to this way of thinking just as working-class students are. The educational system, starting from about grade three on up, teaches us the correct/incorrect perspective on language use (we generally get a free pass in kindergarten and grades one and two). Like other working-class students going to college, I bought into this frame.

4 Slipping through the Cracks

Because of my mother, I managed to slip through the cracks. The cracks, while not impassable, are not wide. Twenty-five percent of working-class students make it through college compared to ninety-percent of middle and upper-class students (Estep, 2016). The filtering system, an important element of which depends on one's linguistic capital, is how social reproduction works.

Although my mother never finished college due to a pre-marital pregnancy, she was an avid reader. She read aloud to my siblings and me when we were young, brought tons of books home from the library, and took a lively interest in our education. In spite of our father, books were all over our home. Because my father was in a German prison camp and a VA hospital for the first three years of my life. I was heavily influenced by my mother. I became a reader. I loved reading the World Book Encyclopedia, novels, and biographies.

By the time I was a sophomore in high school, I had unrealistically decided I wanted to be a writer. I remember the exact moment when I decided. I was lying on my bed on a late Sunday afternoon. I was near the end of Dumas' *The Count of Monte Cristo*. Dantes and Mercedes were meeting in a cave for what I expected would be the last time. I didn't want to finish the book.

I decided then that I wanted to write novels, being simultaneously the reader and writer, not knowing what the next sentence would bring. Sixty years later, I am that kind of writer. To reassure you as a reader, I have, in addition, learned how to rewrite. I am more of a rewriter than writer. If I am writing something to publish, I will generally rewrite it more than a dozen times, usually with feedback from friends and editors. How I have become, in spite of my father, a writer/rewriter is the core of this story.

As much as I adored her, Mrs. Ghastin tried to dissuade me from my dream. I can't remember from this distance the point of her corrections, but I think many of them were connected to my father's working-class grammar. It took me years of teaching and reading books on education to realize that "correctness" is a social construction designed to privilege people in the dominant social group who speak and write that way.

Although my mother and Mrs. Ghastin were probably forever correcting my "ain't's," most of my relatives and friends were ain'ters. The corrections collectively wore me down. Fear of being corrected migrated into a fear of writing—at least school writing, which spilled over into writing in general. Because I hated to write papers, I drifted into the sciences for the first three years of my undergraduate career. But I nursed my underground desire to write, taking creative writing course on the side.

I changed my major from pre-med to psychology, to philosophy, and finally to English in the second semester of my junior year. Writing school papers was still difficult for me, but I managed to keep an A/B average in my English classes, wiggled my way into the MA and later the PhD program at Wisconsin largely by memorizing a trove of CliffsNotes.

I remember a time when I was sitting in a seminar while I was a graduate student at Wisconsin, probably about fifteen students sitting around a table with Professor Lenehan leading the discussion about some readings in our Modern American Literature course. I wondered how others could so confidently speak. I was nervous about speaking because I was afraid of tangling my sentences. If I had something to say, I would rehearse my comment in my head so that I would speak in complete sentences. By the time I had worked out the comment in my head, the conversation had moved elsewhere (Bourdieu calls the lag phenomenon "hysteresis"). I simply didn't know how to say what I was thinking. I didn't have confidence that the words would come out right. A few layers down, I thought people would know I had grown up poor (even at that time, I didn't know being poor was being working-class).

After one semester in the Wisconsin PhD program, I went to Canada rather than Vietnam. In spite of my fear of writing and speaking out in class, I had a solid GPA in graduate school. I consequently received a fellowship for the PhD program at Macmaster University in Ontario.

At Macmaster, I was still plagued with unease about my writing ability and sociolect. In my seminar on Spenser, Professor Cain (may he forever be haunted by the ghost of the Red Knight), returned my seminar paper to me with page after page of intemperate comments on my inability to write coherent sentences.

His comments may not have been the last straw, but they were close. I decided the academic world wasn't for me—or better put, I wasn't for it. I don't remember the precise sequence of events, but I do know that in the following summer, I studied grammar non-stop. I read Wariner's and several other grammar books cover to cover. I studied grammar the way I had studied CliffsNotes.

My self-prescribed course on grammar gave me what I needed. I never again had to worry about being "corrected." The change didn't happen in a summer, but by knowing my grammar, I was more able to write with confidence. The transformation was as simple as that: I became a reasonably good writer. That is, I was able to write naturally without Mrs. Ghastin or Tom Cain hanging like The Ghost of Christmas Past over my shoulder.

5   Takeaways

There are takeaways from my story. First, it's my story; it may not resemble yours. If you come from the working classes or from other social groups whose home sociolect has little overlap with the academic, middle-class sociolect, you may have had your writing corrected until you were blue in the face. Your teachers may have told you they were only correcting your writing, not you, but that's bullshit—and you probably knew it. Or you may have been lucky and had teachers who knew the difference between "correct" and "appropriate."

Correct, to put it mildly, is wrong. No sociolect is "correct" or "incorrect." Sociolects are simply different habits of language that are common to people who belong to specific social classes. We can, however, talk about language uses that are "appropriate" to specific kinds of writing or speaking situations (my reference to "rhetorical situations" in the first two paragraphs of this essay). Your professors have been trained to expect you to use an educated, middle-class sociolect. In middle-class business situations, you will likewise be expected to use middle-class language in which one doesn't say "he don't go there." If you use "ain't" in one of your college essays, it will generally be considered inappropriate. People who don't know very much about language use will imagine that use as "incorrect."

If you came from the middle classes, you probably didn't have to worry about these distinctions because your parents didn't say "ain't." You may have faced some degree of correction such as with your awkwardly written sentences or poorly supported arguments, but your home sociolect was closer to what your teachers thought was the "correct" way of writing. We teachers have other tricks up our sleeves to make you think you're wrong and we're right (and thus, control you), so you haven't gotten off scot-free. But you will have had a better chance than your working-class friends of sliding through school.

If you came from the academic middle-class, that is, if one or, even better, both of your parents were doctors, lawyers, or PhDs, you have an even better chance of not having had to pay a scot. Your parents will probably have taught you not only how to speak and write "correctly" but also how to think and frame your arguments as your teachers do. A's come as easily to you as songs to a nightingale.

And if you came from the elites, the notorious 1%, your sociolect and habits of thinking simply didn't matter. Whatever they were, were right.

6   Multilinguality

I hope you will have given me some slack while you have been reading this. I have generalized, and any generalization is bound to be as full of holes as Mao's umbrella (worth looking up). Still, some of what I have said might catch rain. I have described one of the ways in which schools function to reproduce the social structure in which they are embedded. Put simply, the children of parents who are wealthy and highly educated will have a much higher chance of doing well in school than the children of parents who are poor and did not go to college. There is far more than language habits to social reproduction, but I have described how social reproduction works through language. Underneath this script lies the assumption of right and wrong, correct and incorrect when what teachers really mean is themselves and others.

If you want to do well in school, to some extent you have to play the game; you have to learn the sociolect of the "other." The real trick is not to be taken in by the game of "correct." The "other's" sociolect is just different. Like another language, like learning how to speak French if you're German. In a sense, you're richer when you know how to speak several languages.

References

Alger Jr., H. (1910). *Ragged dick: Or, street life in New York with the boot-blacks*. The John C. Winston Co.

Bernstein, B. (1971). *Class, codes, and control, I*. Routledge & Kegan.

Bourdieu, P. (1984). *Distinction: A social critique of the judgement of taste*. Harvard University Press.

Estep, T. M. (2016, October). *The graduation gap and socioeconomic status: Using stereotype threat to explain graduation rates*. American Psychological Association. apa.org/pi/ses/resources/indicator/2016/10/graduation-gap/

Hamilton, A. (1788). *Federalist No. 68. The federalist papers*. United States Congress.

Kerbo, H. R. (1996). *Social stratification and inequality: Class conflict in historical and comparative perspective* (3rd ed.). McGraw-Hill.

Peckham, I. (1995). Complicity in class codes. In C. Law & B. Dews (Eds.), *This fine places so far from home: Voices of working-class academics* (pp. 263–276). Temple UP.

CHAPTER 2

Becoming "Gente Educada"

Navigating Academia as a Working-Class, Multiply-Marginalized Student

Christina V. Cedillo

This chapter[1] is part explication, part personal narrative, all story. Here, I want to provide a candid discussion regarding the effects that academic norms can have on a person from a working-class background, particularly as that background intersects with race, gender, and disability. Story is an important methodology for articulating what I wish to share, because story reminds us that there are always real people behind the words we use; as methodology, story also illustrates why specialized accounts can only come from those who *know*. From experience, from a lived understanding.

I begin this way because I am a cultural rhetorician, or scholar of cultural rhetorics (CR), a field that asks us to ethically acknowledge our relationships with others, especially those we write to and about. CR instructs us to build knowledge with people, not over them and at their expense, even when we are talking about our own communities. Thus, cultural rhetoricians explicitly declare what "intersecting, shifting, and variable methodological and theoretical frames and relationships we bring to our scholarly and teaching practices," and we acknowledge that "where someone is located culturally, socially, historically, and physically is significant to the ways that s/he makes meaning" (Cultural Rhetorics Theory Lab, 2014). We do this because the stories we learn at home are very different from those we learn at school, but that does not make them any less authoritative or significant. Those of us marginalized are often told we must renounce our homegrown knowledge, but they can prove powerful technologies for countering systemic injustice. Whether sitting at your abuelita's table, surrounded by your cousins and aunties, or hanging out with friends, stories help us know who we are and allow us to claim that version of the world that we alone can know. As an academic methodology, story is a vital "counter-hegemonic scholarly practice" that allows us to contradict generally accepted and standard/ized beliefs about us, our communities, and our lives using our own lived experiences (CRTL, 2014). Consequently, you're reading my story here because I'm hoping that the knowledge I gained in navigating the complexities of the U.S. educational system as a multiply-marginalized person can provide you with insights useful in your own journey.

1 Academic Difficulties

People in my field (rhetoric and composition) who examine working-class rhetorics may focus on histories (DeGenaro, 2007), localized spaces and cultures (Lindquist, 2002), and identity and/in writing and discourse (Linkon, Peckham, & Lanier-Nabors, 2004; Zebroski, 2006). This essay considers these areas of attention by focusing on people who are multiply-marginalized, or people whose diverse identities and associations with particular communities converge to make the academy especially inhospitable. Teachers and students who are multiply marginalized according to class, race, and so on must study privileged histories and stories that are not their own to be considered "educated." We must also become experts at associating spaces with specific ethoi, impressions of identity in communication, in order to get by or fit in. Along with pathos and logos, ethos is one of the elements of that reliable rhetorical triad we encounter in first year writing and tends to be defined as credibility, but it's rather more complicated. As Jacqueline Jones Royster explains, ethos is "the formation and development of a writing self" (2000, p. 10), highly dependent on one's "sense of self in society" (p. 58), and influenced by how we are seen and how we see ourselves. Multiply marginalized people must contend with social perceptions that may be "deeply compromised" by prejudices and stereotypes (p. 64) to achieve the desired outcome in any rhetorical context, particularly when addressing audiences outside our home communities.

As a result, we tend to become adept at code switching across contexts, finding on account of our educational experiences that we're supposed to shake off certain languages, dialects, and registers as we take on those that mark us as gente educada. We accept this expectation without realizing how it relates to DuBois' concept of "double consciousness," the way a racialized individual living in a racist society always feels an internal conflict among their identities due to how they are perceived by those in power.[2] Writing about code switching pedagogies, Vershawn Ashanti Young explains that teaching students to believe that Black English and Standard Written English are "equal" but maintain "prestige in their respective, separate sites" simply reaffirms the segregationist's mantra of "separate but equal" by substituting language for race (Palmer Baxley, 2012, p. 55). He argues that "what's really wrong with code switching is that it seeks to transform double consciousness, the very product of racism, into a linguistic solution to racial discrimination" (p. 56). Code switching does not account for the various histories of exclusion that we bring with us to scholarship and their influences on our writing and speaking. Furthermore, code switching advocates overlook how the practice asks us to also alter our behaviors, identities, and epistemologies.

Such expectations can exact a heavy price. On finding that his goals didn't resonate with those of his department, Orville Blackman writes, "I recall Goffman's 1959 work where the author opined that we are all actors on stage, presenting a façade that we want others to believe is the true representation of self. We become who we need to become for the purpose of presenting the best face to the audiences to whom we are playing" (A. Smith, 2013, p. 39). When a university deploys a simplistic notion of diversity, talk of diversity actually "individuates difference, conceals inequalities and neutralises histories of antagonism and struggle" under more comfortable neoliberal rhetorics of inclusion (Ahmed & Swan, 2006, p. 96), stealthily affirming privileged norms instead of accommodating difference. Already marginalized individuals who refuse to conform to these norms may find themselves ostracized by administrators and their peers; those who do conform may soon grow weary under the pressures of this burdensome performance. Thus, members of marginalized communities face a "Faustian bargain" when we enter the academy, an institution that was created without us in mind and never quite inclusive of us. Because we are ostensibly welcomed in, academia frames us as proof of its striving for diversity, but academia also renders us proof of a whitestream, "objective" way of being that suggests we need correcting if we do not fit its norms. And, those elusive norms change depending on the program, department, and discipline.

Within institutions that pride themselves on fostering diverse environments where all are welcome, individuals can experience gaslighting—intentional or unintentional "psychological manipulation that forces the victim to question [their] sanity and a product of normalized ways of being" (Wozolek, 2018, pp. 319–320). Gaslighting relies on "gender-based stereotypes, intersecting inequalities, and institutional vulnerabilities" to mark victims as irrational, cutting them off from needed institutional resources and exposing them to "epistemic injustice" (Sweet, 2019, p. 852; McKinnon, 2017). That is, even self-declared allies may discount an affected person's grievances if they don't align with their own privileged perspectives. A school's own discourses of diversity can promote gaslighting when "diversity and equality become forms of capital within organisations" (Ahmed and Swan, 2006, p. 98). Used as a trademark, diversity can subsume human beings under an institution's commercial brand, erasing the reality of those framed as embodying its benefits.

Making matters more complicated, academia often promotes isolation, making it difficult to find real allies or establish solidarity with others having similar experiences. Perhaps we can trace this tendency toward isolation to deeply ingrained beliefs regarding academia's ends. In *Women and Minority Faculty in the Academic Workplace: Recruitment, Retention, and Academic*

Culture, Adalberto Aguirre explains that academics tend to see themselves as "need[ing] distance from the everyday world" to think through their "obscure theories" or to develop "creative ideas for dealing with social and environmental problems" from which they are nevertheless removed (Aguirre, 2000, p. 22). This idea that a proper scholar should be divorced from the realities of everyday life easily translates into a refusal to acknowledge problems like harassment or any ensuing health concerns in one's academic sphere lest one seem weak or unfit, or a reluctance to seek assistance even outside of one's intellectual community.

2 The Importance of Stories

In writing this chapter, I aim to let you know that you aren't alone; many of us have experienced these problems and actively seek to combat their foothold in the academy. I write this story as someone familiar with these difficulties. As a rhetorician, I examine the stressful relationships between academic norms and the body, namely, how academic expectations dictate what is socially acceptable and how they attempt to discipline us into proper form. As a multiply-marginalized individual, I know that these relationships prove daunting, causing us to wonder when things get rough who really are allies, what counts as good enough to get by, and what benefits might accompany "selling out." For these reasons, I use a combination of research and personal narrative to share, and draw attention to, the experiences faced by many marginalized people through the lens of my own. Minerva S. Chávez (2012, p. 344) discusses the use of *testimonio* as a way to "[call] attention to the impact on the ideological roles that educational institutions play in the sorting practices that influence the formation of particular identities." Using *testimonio* as a critical race theory methodology, Chávez reminds us that we can invite the voices of excluded people—including our own—into scholarship by employing the academy's preferred communicative mode (publishing) to inscribe our experiences.

In addition, by using story, we can strategically repurpose academic spaces and practices that fit the conventional mold but speak to Othered ways of making meaning. By sharing our stories like we might do at the kitchen table, we can redeploy our experiences as useful resources. Typically discounted as the mere background to "real scholarship," our stories can provide a kind of "feminist/womanist transformative mentoring" for those who need us but are not necessarily close by (Powell & Mukavetz, 2015). Here, I want to provide support in the form of information and counsel regarding academia's effects on our identities and how it demands their reorientation and reorganization in sometimes violent ways. However, I also wish to show how our texts, practices, and embodied experiences can be used to enact the strategic reframing of accepted methods and tools and contest harmful academic norms.

3   Entre Amigxs/Between Friends

I am a multiply-marginalized individual, a disabled woman of color (Chicana) raised by working class parents in the U.S.-Mexico borderlands of South Texas. I grew up in Laredo, Texas, a city on the Mexico-Texas border. Statistically and financially, my upbringing would probably be deemed lower middle class. However, the values with which I was raised were characteristically working class. Our stories were those of the hardships endured by my parents' families, who knew how to make do with scarce resources. My family often utilized credit to "escape" working class status, but even now our relationship to capital remains a complicated one. Class identity isn't something you just step out of when you decide to go to college. As MIT economist Peter Temin argues in *The Vanishing Middle Class: Prejudice and Power in a Dual Economy*, it takes almost twenty years with nothing going wrong for people to escape poverty or move up a class bracket (White, 2017). It's too easy for something to go wrong without factoring in additional obstacles facing working class BIPOC, including the racism of the carceral system and the effects of cultural and class prejudices on job hiring practices.

In academia, being raised working class means you may not readily fit in with savvier, more affluent peers who have been prepped for college or graduate studies for a long time. Part of the learning curve involves what we might term "epistemology switching," being made to take on a foreign worldview than that shared by members of your community in order to engage in a particular space. Steve Parks and Nick Pollard (2010) explain how, when they invited a group of writing students to write for real-world labor scenarios, the assignments did not necessarily connect to their lives. The students "were writing within a logic and set of experiences that did not intersect with the primary representational logics within the course … Yet changing the representational logic that dominated the classroom required such connections if the working-class student voices were to gain power 'in numbers'" (p. 486). The instructors were trying to "empower" students based on a set of underlying values that did not align with those that students brought with them to the classroom, even in a space supposedly built on and for class-based camaraderie.

As someone who grew up on the border and is therefore tricultural (United-Statesian, Mexican, and Chicana), the pressure to "switch" involves toggling between a mix of English, Spanish, and Spanglish, and between aggregative and linear thinking. Some things are just better expressed in one language than another—or maybe we're just used to certain expressions—and we attach memories and emotions to certain terms. Spanglish is perceived as a working-class (read "lower-class") dialect among many Latinxs seeking to climb the social ladder, a source of shame as it supposedly bastardizes proper English and proper Spanish. Yet it remains the dialect of home, family, and affection for many of us. Whitestream expectations of monolingualism force us to scour the thesaurus searching for just the right word to convey an experience that doesn't exist in English. Some experiences simply cannot be translated because borderlands consciousness runs contrary to academic reasoning; borderlands logics are characterized not by either/or thinking but both+and, meaning you see the world from a multitude of vectors. Gloria Anzaldúa explains this epistemology in terms of nepantla, a Nahuatl word for "in-between space" (Moraga & Anzaldúa, 2015, p. 8). In this space of spiritual, physical, and material liminality, change is a constant; new things are always in the process of becoming in this land of linguistic and cultural bricolage. You learn to focus on fluid and ephemeral connections between things rather than fixed categories, and on what could be rather than what is. Such thinking does not jibe with academic rigidity.

Unfortunately, attempting to establish solidarity with working class peers outside of ones ethnoracial or cultural community can prove challenging, given that class is a highly ambiguous notion. Some scholars assume that class is a matter of self-identification, while others argue that class classifications have a lot to do with power and agency. According to Richard Ohmann, class "is more deeply a matter of decision-making power, particularly in relation to where and how one works ... [distinguished] by the conditions and terms under which one works in order to live [and] the degree to which [individuals] do or don't manage the work of others" (Welch, 2011, pp. 225–226). In other words, one climbs the class ladder by gaining authority and autonomy in decision-making in one's workplace and one's community.

Race complicates this process by rendering social mobility more accessible to some groups over others. Jennifer Beech reveals how race influences class constructs and vice versa. Speaking of white stereotypes like the "redneck" and the "hillbilly," like Ohmann, Beech explains these as terms related to power, namely, whether one is the object of the gaze or the one who gazes. This objectification is racialized. Beech states that "terms like redneck and hillbilly are regularly constructed as racial terms that work to identify for mainstream whites other white people who behave in ways supposedly unbecoming to or unexpected of whites" (2004, p. 175). Nevertheless, it's important to remember that class and race are not fungible terms of oppression. In an effort to build class solidarity across racial lines, some people equate the two and in so doing, erase the very real racial oppression that keeps BIPOC in poverty and debt at higher rates than white people (Office of the Assistant Secretary, 2016, p. 26). At the same time, this thinking ignores a crucial point: working-class whites maintain racial privilege over their BIPOC counterparts, meaning they may ignore or downplay complaints about racial discrimination and microaggressions made by BIPOC peers to center class oppression.

Scholarly definitions of working-class identity and its qualifiers are still open to debate, but you know it when you live it. Some experiences seem common, regardless of one's other backgrounds. You learn to expect questions regarding the practical utility of certain subjects, to see the expressions of pride on loved ones' faces even when they don't understand your research, and, in the case of some of us "firsts," to predict your elders' tendency to let everyone know you're Doctor So-and-so. I don't say this in jest or to poke fun even good-naturedly, but because for many families, education remains the crucial path to upward mobility, even when they don't know what that entails or what that requires that we renounce.

However, other experiences are not so widespread, as I and many others have learned. When you're multiply marginalized and working class, you experience problems intersectionally. Like class, disability, race, and gender have each been used to construct the others, giving rise to an inexorable taxonomy of deficiency and normalcy (Davis, 2017, p. 6). If you're working class and disabled, you may be deemed undeserving of services, someone trying to play the system, even a "squeaky wheel" demanding special treatment when you ask your institution for accommodations that are deemed too expensive—accommodations that are legally required, mind you. If you are a working-class woman of color, you're more likely to be tokenized (Sotello Viernes Turner, 2002) and less likely to be regarded as serious a scholar as your white colleagues, whether they are male or female (Niemann, 2012), prejudices compounded by your use of certain dialects or mannerisms. If your research highlights the intersection of these identities, your research may be viewed as limited (Palmer Baxley, 2012, p. 49), and you may be perceived as angry all the time for no reason other than on account of institutional discrimination and microaggressions (Scott, 2013; Olivas, 2009). As a result, we inhabit an odd, precarious position, forced to serve as native informants with specialized knowledges and cultural connections that can help schools serve their ever-more-diverse student bodies. Yet when research shows up our vulnerable positions and those of multiply-marginalized students, or when our methodologies highlight marginalized experiences rather than whitestream ones, we are also more easily regarded as unwelcome strangers with a limited purview.

Attention to these issues tends to be framed as secondary, as an indulgence that detracts from the real substance of learning, but I center them here to make sure that multiply-marginalized students know what they're up against. Not to scare you away from the academy or to discount the strides you've made, but to let you know that your success despite the presence of these problems deserves to be celebrated. At the same time, it's important to draw attention to these issues so that we can work toward real inclusivity. Otherwise, neoliberal notions of diversity will continue to harm us all. Such appeals to diversity function as bait-and-switch schemes. As Ellen Berrey (2015) explains, "Rather than a righteous fight for justice or effective anti-discrimination laws, we get a celebration of cultural difference as a competitive advantage. Diversity, we are told, is an end goal with instrumental pay-offs: good for learning, good for the bottom line, even good for white people." Meanwhile, "[diversity talk] allows us to sidestep persistent, alarming racial inequalities." In recent years, a number of lawsuits involving the denial of tenure to Black women have cited those same tired tropes: their work was seen as less scholarly, less rigorous, too personal, too limited. Alma Jean Billingslea Brown (2012) calls this the "revolving door" of academia because Black women "frequently conduct research and write on issues relevant to their communities and publish in journals that focus on minority issues, their publications are not regarded as scholarly work or as making significant contributions to their fields" (p. 27). Misogynoir, the combination of anti-Black racism and sexism that specifically targets Black women, basically guarantees this view because the typical Subject is middle class, white, and male.

In my own experience, I have had colleagues express their appreciation of my research and teaching from a decolonial perspective while adding that examinations of Indigenous or African American rhetorics are cool but much too focused to be of use to the general student population. More than once I have had a coworker ask why decoloniality even matters to first-year writers, only to be shut down when I try to explain my reasons. Issues of Indigeneity should matter to all students because the United States exists on stolen Native land. Issues of Indigeneity should matter to our students because our school is a Latinx-serving institution, where many of the students are of Indigenous descent. Issues of Indigeneity should matter to our students of color because there are few of us whose histories, languages, and embodied identities have not been affected by colonization. It is reified in our bodies, becomes material reality through its effects on us. As Phil Bratta (2015) argues, political acts become eventful through "embodiment and proprioception," how we exist as bodies, how we sense our body-ness, and how our bodies fit in certain spaces and in relation to other bodies. Bratta explains that the bounds of logocentric interpretations of events "have slippage and can never articulate the exact temporal-spatial dimensions of lived events. The issue also lies in the fact that lived events are ongoing and in constant flux. They are embodied intensities and ephemeral." In other words, so-called "historical" events may be short-lived and yet they can live on in the present, and they do so through the sensoria of our bodies and as our bodies relate to other bodies around us.

Thus, our presence in the academy as working class, multiply-marginalized people transforms into an embodied rhetoric, our way of sending the message that we will not be erased even though institutional norms ignore us or prove harmful and even as we feel their regulation in our very bodies. We all know when we do not fit in or are unwelcome in certain spaces thanks to proprioception; we feel awkward or uncomfortable even if we can't explain why in words, and marginalized peoples come to trust this sense through personal experience. Proprioception helps us to understand whether spaces were made with us in mind or not, and this sense allows us to read conditions that go unnoticed by privileged people whose bodies fit right in. Yet the only response I have ever received from doubtful non-working class, non-BIPOC colleagues is that this knowledge does little to teach students how to read and write properly—as though we don't communicate through our bodies. Notably, though unfamiliar with the racial dimensions of our experiences, my non-BIPOC working class colleagues have tended toward empathy, all too familiar with that sense of self-consciousness and disbelonging.

The denial of our knowledges also enables a double-bind where women of color faculty become simultaneously hyper-visible and unseen. As scholars, our research is often thought to be too concentrated and yet, schools need us to bring this research to bear to corroborate their consideration of diversity. We're told critical distance requires that our everyday existence and our research remain separate domains. Yet all research is constrained by the substance of the world around us. (Currently, materialist methodologies are all the rage in academia though scholars from marginalized communities have been using examples of these for years.) Our personal investments must be expunged, and in our being made to deny them, we are rendered mere surface images that reinforce simplistic notions of diversity. Sofia Samatar (2015) deems this "skin feeling," or what it means to "be encountered as a surface." She writes, "University life demands that academics of color commodify themselves as symbols of diversity—in fact, as diversity itself ..." Told to dislocate ourselves from the concrete reality of life, we take on the ontological status of a rhetorical device, a symbol that allows schools to demonstrate their commitment to diversity and multiculturalism without having to decolonize their foundations or curricula.

It comes down to numbers: "Diversity, unlike, the work of anti-racism, can be represented visually through statistics. How many of X do you have? What percent?" (Samatar, 2015). Not surprisingly, women of color are especially affected by this since we tend to be typecast as nurturers and diversity work is highly emotional labor. Those of us from working-class backgrounds may also take on this additional responsibility, given all-too-familiar gendered expectations regarding work, affect, and authority (see Nixon, 2009).

Furthermore, this process reduces entire identities—and oppressions aimed at those identities—to a few token people rather than omnipresent structures that benefit or hurt all of us. For example, accessibility is a major theme in disability studies but not always in other subjects, even though access should be an invariable concern for all in the academy, whether students, professors, staff, and administrators. After all, "disability is everywhere. Just like we know now that gender is everywhere, even when it doesn't look like gender. Just as Toni Morrison says, Blackness is everywhere, even when we're not talking about African Americans" (Brueggemann, Garland-Thomson, & Kleege, 2005, p. 28). Even and especially when one is non-disabled, not a woman, not raced, not working class, these are axes of identity that organize all of our lives. Hyper-visibility results from labels being placed on some people but not on others, as though the presence of a label indicates an aberration and a lack of one is just "normal." For this reason, visibility can be a fraught aim, too. Grace Hong notes that "visibility can be a kind of violence ... not inclusion, but surveillance" for women of color (FemTechNet Collective, 2018, p. 34). Therefore, we must listen to those most affected by institutional problems to better comprehend our entanglement with/in these categories, to ensure that we do not remain complicit in perpetuating oppressive academic norms. Rather than asking who we want to be in a given situation in order to be heeded, we might ask ourselves who we must be in order to heed. Otherwise, we risk contributing to the "invisibility" of marginalized people, including ourselves.

In closing, I want to repeat why I share these experiences and attendant research with you. As I often tell my own students, the ability to make conscious choices is power; in life and in the academy, we are actors and acted upon, so we must be aware of the rhetorics at play so that we can respond as people with agency. Often, "[we] become who we need to become for the purpose of presenting the best face to the audiences to whom we are playing" (A. Smith, 2013, p. 39). However, we should not have to bear such a burden to be in the academy. Many of us working-class, multiply-marginalized people already bear a more important load—generations' worth of familial and communal dreams.

Notes

1   This essay was composed on Akokisa/Orcoquisa and Karankawa territories.
2   It's important to note that DuBois writes about African Americans in *The Souls of Black Folk*, where he theorized his concept, to ensure that his original purpose in centering Black people is not erased. Given the ubiquity of anti-Blackness even among BIPOC, not surprisingly, much, though not all, of the current scholarship on "triple consciousness" also focuses on Black identity as it intersects with gender, sexuality, and ethnicity (B. Smith, 1978; Patton & Simmons, 2008; Jiménez Román & Flores, 2010), although this framework is also used by other critics and feminists of color (see Moraga & Anzaldúa, 2015).

References

Aguirre Jr., A. (2000). *Women and minority faculty in the academic workplace: Recruitment, retention, and academic culture*. Jossey-Bass.

Ahmed, S., & Swan, E. (2006). Doing diversity. *Policy Futures in Education, 4*(2), 96–100. doi:10.2304/pfie.2006.4.2.96

Beech, J. (2004). Redneck and hillbilly discourse in the writing classroom: Classifying critical pedagogies of whiteness. *College English, 67*(2), 172–186.

Berrey, E. (2015, October 26). Diversity is for white people: The big lie behind a well-intended word. *Salon*. https://www.salon.com/2015/10/26/diversity_is_for_white_people_the_big_lie_behind_a_well_intended_word/

Billingslea Brown, A. J. (2012). Black women faculty in predominantly white space: Negotiating discourses of diversity. In M. Christian (Ed.), *Integrated but unequal: Black faculty in in predominantly white space* (pp. 23–37). Africa World.

Bratta, P. (2015). Rhetoric and event: The embodiment of lived events. *Enculturation: A Journal of Rhetoric, Writing, and Culture*, 19. http://www.enculturation.net/rhetoric-and-event

Brueggemann, B. J., Garland-Thomson, R., & Kleege, G. (2005). What her body taught (or, teaching about and with a disability): A conversation. *Feminist Studies, 31*(1), 13–33.

Chávez, M. S. (2012). Autoethnography, a Chicana's methodological research tool: The role of storytelling for those who have no choice but to do critical race theory. *Equity & Excellence in Education, 45*(2), 334–348.

Davis, L. J. (2017). Introduction: Normality, power, and culture. In L. J. Lennard (Ed.), *The disability studies reader* (5th ed., pp. 1–14). Routledge.

DeGenaro, W. (2007). *Who says? Working-class rhetoric, class consciousness, and community*. The University of Pittsburgh.

FemTechNet Collective. (2018). FemTechNet: A collective statement on teaching and learning race, feminism, and technology. *Frontiers: A Journal of Women Studies, 39*(1), 24–41.

Jiménez Román, M., & Flores, J. (2010). *The AfroLatin@ reader: History and culture in the United States.* Duke UP.

Lindquist, J. (2002). *A place to stand: Politics and persuasion in a working-class bar.* Oxford UP.

Linkon, S. L., Peckham, I., & Lanier-Nabors, B. G. (2004). Struggling with class in English studies. *College English, 67*(2), 149–153.

McKinnon, R. (2017). Allies behaving badly: Gaslighting as epistemic injustice. In I. J. Kidd, J. Medina, & G. Pohlhaus Jr. (Eds.), *The Routledge handbook of epistemic injustice* (pp. 167–174). Routledge.

Moraga, C., & Anzaldúa, G. (2015). *This bridge called my back: Writings by radical women of color.* SUNY P.

Niemann, Y. F. (2012). Lessons from the experiences of women of color working in academia. In G. Gutiérrez, G. Muhs, Y. F. Niemann, C. G. González, & A. P. Harris (Eds.), *Presumed incompetent: The intersections of race and class for women in academia* (pp. 446–499). Utah State UP.

Nixon, D. (2009). 'I can't put a smiley face on': Working-class masculinity, emotional labour and service work in the 'new economy.' *Gender, Work & Organization, 16*(3), 300–322.

Office of the Assistant Secretary for Planning and Evaluation. (2016). *Poverty in the United States: 50-year trends and safety net impacts.* https://aspe.hhs.gov/system/files/pdf/154286/50YearTrends.pdf

Olivas, M. R. (2009). Negotiating identity while scaling the walls of the ivory tower: Too brown to be White and too White to be brown. *International Review of Qualitative Research, 2*(3), 385–406.

Palmer Baxley, T. (2012). Navigating as an African American female scholar: Catalysts and barriers in predominantly White academia. *International Journal of Critical Pedagogy, 4*(4), 47–64.

Parks, S., & Pollard, N. (2010). Emergent strategies for an established field: The role of worker-writer collectives in composition and rhetoric. *College Composition and Communication, 61*(3), 476–509.

Patton, L. D., & Simmons, S. L. (2008). Exploring complexities of multiple identities of lesbians in a Black college environment. *Negro Educational Review, 59*(3–4), 197–215.

Powell, M., & Mukavetz, A. R. (2015, October 30). *Making kitchen tables in academic spaces: Practicing feminist/womanist transformative mentoring* [Conference presentation]. 10th Biennial Feminisms and Rhetorics Conference, Arizona State University, Tempe, AZ.

Royster, J. J. (2000). *Traces of a stream: Literacy and social change among African American women.* U of Pittsburgh P.

Samatar, S. (2015, September 25). Skin feeling. *The New Inquiry.* http://thenewinquiry.com/essays/skin-feeling/

Scott, K. D. (2013). Communication strategies across cultural borders: Dispelling stereotypes, performing competence, and redefining Black womanhood. *Women's Studies in Communication, 36*(3), 312–329.

Smith, A. (2013). *It's not because you're Black: Addressing issues of racism and underrepresentation of African Americans in academia.* UP of America.

Smith, B. (1978). Toward a Black feminist criticism. *The Radical Teacher, 7,* 20–27.

Sotello Viernes Turner, C. (2002). Women of color in academe: Living with multiple marginality. *The Journal of Higher Education, 73*(1), 74–93.

Sweet, P. L. (2019). The sociology of gaslighting. *American Sociological Review, 84*(5), 851–875.

The Cultural Rhetorics Theory Lab. (2014). Our story begins here: Constellating cultural rhetorics practices. *Enculturation: A Journal of Rhetoric, Writing, and Culture,* 18. http://enculturation.net/our-story-begins-here

Welch, N. (2011). 'We're here, and we're not going anywhere': Why working-class rhetorical traditions 'still' matter. *College English, 73*(3), 221–242.

White, G. B. (2017, April 27). Escaping poverty requires almost 20 years with nearly nothing going wrong. *The Atlantic.* https://www.theatlantic.com/business/archive/2017/04/economic-inequality/524610/

Wozolek, B. (2018). Gaslighting queerness: Schooling as a place of violent assemblages. *Journal of LGBT Youth, 15*(4), 319–338.

Zebroski, J. T. (2006). Social class as discourse: Mapping the landscape of class in rhetoric and composition. *JAC, 26*(3–4), 513–583.

CHAPTER 3

Rhetoric

From a Community Yet to Arrive

José Manuel Cortez

"Why did you come to the United States, Dad?"

It's the summer—2006–when my Dad takes me to his hometown for the first time. My tío is with us, too. They're here to settle a land dispute. Some farmers are letting cattle graze on the tract of land our family owns. Dad brought me along to see this mythical place—it's a kind of pilgrimage. We're riding in a Volkswagen Rabbit that is, speaking conservatively, speeding way too fast through a particularly beautiful but precarious stretch of México 23 in the state of Jalisco. We've hired a driver to take us northward from Guadalajara to Dad's hometown, Florencia de Benito Juárez. And we're nearing the Jalisco/Zacatecas state border.

Dad thinks for a minute, but we're both thrown rightward in our seats as the conejo begins to drift around a hairpin turn. We're passengers in a terrifying game of MarioKart. I'll learn later on why we're driving so fast. On one side of the road, an *agave tequilana* farm reaches up the hillside. The agave, planted in neat rows, appears perfectly combed into the land. The succulents will produce the nectar that will later warm in the stomachs of wealthy folks in Los Angeles or Nueva York. The fermented sugars will enjoy a passage north that is protected and documented at every stage. Probably. What would we-Americans do if our beloved tequila never arrived to fuel our Taco Tuesdays and Cinco de Mayos and 21st birthdays and mustachioed campesino costumes?

I think to myself that tequila is probably transported north a bit more carefully. A bit more slowly.

Since we travel in the outside lane of the road, I look out the window and down. On the other side of the road, a sheer drop off into sedimentary rock and *opuntia* cactus. If you've ever seen opuntia grow, you know it doesn't always look like the cute succulent gracing the kitchen window of an Instagram Influencer in Seattle. This space, this other side of tequila discourse that you don't see, and perhaps what none of us ever see, is where Dad and Tío Rafael come from.

This other side of the road—the underside of the transnational network through which bodies and commodities flow north from Jalisco and Zacatecas to the United States—this side is the drop off: of the dropoff from roads and maps. Of the drop-off at coyote checkpoints in Sasabe, Arizona. Of the dropoff at Home Depot parking lots in Southern California. Earlier in the day, Dad tells me a story of being dropped off at a farm outside Florencia when he was a kid. He tells me of working all day without pay. Tío tells me that he and Dad would be dropped off at a farm somewhere near Othello, Washington to pick crops after they arrived in the United States sometime in the 1970s. Tío jokes that Dad could eat a whole carton of huevos for breakfast before that work. I think to myself what a cruel fucking joke it is that Dad and Tío arrived in the United States to a farm town in Central Washington state—really, a migrant farm laborer town—called *Othello*.

My question is deferred as we round a corner and stop abruptly. A log is laying down across the road, and a group of children and adolescents—some older, some younger—are demanding pesos in exchange for our passage north. Our driver seems annoyed. He turns off the engine. I am not familiar with this area, but I guess these children must be at least 50 miles from any town or village. Those from the other side. I have no idea what Dad and Tío pay them, but right now that doesn't matter. What matters is that Mexico has at this point already become a transnational circulatory system for commodities like tequila, and avocados, and cannabis, and human bodies after policies like NAFTA produced a new kind of "free trade." And here, in the temporary clot of this mountainous perforator vein, Dad doesn't answer the question.

When we arrive in Florencia, Dad and Tío take me to the house they grew up in. It has two or three rooms, dirt floors. The roof is caved in. A vine with purple flowers has claimed the structure. They don't say much. I don't know if they can even if they want to.

Do you remember when Donald Trump announced his presidency in 2015? Trump claimed that "The U.S. has become a dumping ground for everybody else's problems." He declared:

> When Mexico sends its people, they're not sending their best. They're not sending you. They're not sending you. They're sending people that have lots of problems, and they're bringing those problems with us. They're bringing drugs. They're bringing crime. They're rapists. And some, I assume, are good people.

You see, Dad never seems to answer the question because the question always seems to be answered for him by the always open mouth. I think about the term working class, a term that, at least as I understand it, signifies those who have nothing at all but their bodies and the labor their bodies sell in return for wages. So why is my Dad so often understood as a problem rather than as a human? At what point, what threshold, did my Dad cease to be read as a human and assume the subjectivity of *problem*? Was it the moment he crossed the threshold of the U.S./Mexico border? And what exactly is it about the movement from one place to another that seems to contribute to this? I'm not sure what my Dad brought—and it shouldn't matter. But it does. And the problem doesn't end there.

Here's the problem I'd like to pose, it's a knowledge problem, a problem baked into the desire for knowledge. When we build community upon the predicate of knowing—say, that we would even need to know why someone is here, in the United States, as the predicate of their belonging to a national community—we seem to subvert the very concept of democracy we pretend to be practicing. Valeria Luiselli's recent book, *Tell Me How it Ends: An Essay in 40 Questions* renders this so awfully clearly. Luiselli writes about her experience as a translator for undocumented, unaccompanied minors who have found themselves in immigration courts facing deportation. Let me remind you that the book is about undocumented *children*. Luiselli's task is to administer the intake questionnaire that will be used to decide their fate. The first question: "Why did you come to the United States?" The problem, she writes, is that, "The children's stories are always shuffled, stuttered, always shattered beyond the repair of a narrative order. The problem with trying to tell their story is that it has no beginning, no middle, and no end" (Luiselli, 2017). How do we begin to practice a new nomos of community that accommodates those who have nothing—those whose stories cannot be rendered within the technology of a narrative order? How to hold something *in common* without the predicate of knowing why someone arrived? How are we to make community with those whose stories may never arrive? We might be able to pursue a different nomos of community—one where putting unaccompanied minors in prison would be unthinkable, where asking someone *why* they arrived would be unnecessary—if we suspend this will to know.

• • •

It is the summer of 2014. And it is very hot in Tucson, Arizona. I have begun to volunteer at a migrant shelter with two colleagues from my graduate program at the University of Arizona. Each afternoon at 4 pm, an Immigration & Customs Enforcement van pulls into the driveway of the safe house and unloads a group of migrants. Sometimes a woman and a baby step out of the van. Sometimes up to four families unload. But each time, the faces of the women and children are marked by kind of exhaustion. On this particular day, I've convinced my friend to come volunteer with me. She's worried she isn't up to the task because she doesn't speak Spanish. I remind her that some of the families don't either. Some speak Chuj, Tojolab'al, or K'iche'.

But unfortunately this is the wrong day for her first day. My partner and I spend the evening with the children from two families while the women rest in the air conditioned house. There are never men older than 16 that arrive in that ICE van. They are taken, instead, to indefinite detention at a facility in Eloy, Arizona. We pick vegetables from the garden in the backyard. I'm always amazed at what will grow in that Arizona heat, given enough care and love. The running joke is that "in Arizona, it's a dry hate." It's not all private prisons, and Joe Arpaios, and ethnic studies bans. Until it is.

Our job that day is to wait until it's dark and then drive the migrants to their next destination. Another drop off. You'll understand why I remain vague here. We load two families into the van that night—two women, four children. Two women who, according to the law, don't even have the right to sell their labor for a wage. Four children who, according to the law, don't qualify for basic social services. According to the law, they have no part and no place. These children are not even those bringing the problems, as Trump puts it. At this point, they do not exist. That is, until I drive the van carrying no one into the driveway of our next destination and I have to slam the brakes because there are ten armed militia men standing in our path, preventing us from driving any further. I stop because they have assault rifles. Bandoliers. Kevlar vests. Ski masks. Bowie knives. Let me remind you that these are women and children. But they're from the other side of the road. The drop off side. I don't really remember what I did next, but I do remember learning that I somehow know how to drive in reverse.

I never ask the children, "Why did you come to the United States?"

•••

I come from a family community that has no pedigree—and for the most part, no recorded genealogy or documentation prior to migration to the United States. I'm always writing to fill that void. I'll never really know the story of my family's migration because its a story that cannot be narrated—it can only narrate the very limits of narrativization. For me,it's a part of the diasporic, working-class experience. When my father arrived in the Yakima Valley as an itinerant migrant farm worker from Mexico, he had no degrees, no papers, and, as he tells the fragments of the story, few memories of the experience of migration. So it's almost unbelievable that my family has moved from the fields to the faculty in one generation. Still, this is why I stopped asking my Dad why he came to the United States.

In *Of Hospitality*, Jacques Derrida (2000) writes of an impossible situation. The question of hospitality, the question of "what arrives at the borders," is a question of how to respond to the stranger who arrives at the doorstep of the dwelling. This is a question of diaspora, and this question encompasses our problem: how to respond to the other at our door? To be hospitable to the stranger, however, requires a host to enter into an impasse: "How can we distinguish between a guest and a parasite? In principle, the difference is straightforward, but for that you need a law; hospitality, reception, the welcome offered, have to be submitted to a basic and limiting jurisdiction" (Derrida, 2000, p. 59). The law of hospitality requires that if a host is to be hospitable, to be welcoming and inclusive, a host must initially be closed off and exclusive. To be welcomed in, a stranger must first be marked as a foreigner—the law of hospitality presupposes and constitutes the stranger as its primary condition of possibility. We might re-mark the stranger, the function of constitutive exteriority, as the primary condition of a community. And yet, "in order to constitute the space of a habitable house and a home, you have to give up a passage to the outside world [*l'etranger*]. There is no house or interior without a door or windows" (p. 61). If the law of hospitality first requires a host to be inhospitable, then it also requires a host to remain impossibly open—open to whomever, whatsoever. There can be no interior (no community) without an opening (a window or a door)—an opening that writes no law about who may enter but merely remains open toward the stranger yet to arrive.

Will it have been possible to think a community grounded not in identification—the most central of rhetorical theories!—but in the preparation of a commons suited for anyone at all that might pass through its doors?

References

Derrida, J. (2000). *Of hospitality*. Stanford UP.
Luiselli, V. (2017). *Tell me how it ends: An essay in 40 questions*. Coffee House Press.

CHAPTER 4

Five Miles and a World Away

A Memoir

Edward J. Whitelock

It was going to be the best year ever.

I walked into Nether Providence Middle School that first day of class in September 1978 excited and ready for change. My new Trapper Keeper was filled with crisp, wide-ruled paper, bought the week before at K-Mart with money my grandmother had given me for mowing the lawn. The school year was beginning with an assembly in the gymnasium; I could hear the manic energy of a thousand murmurs and shouts as I approached the door to enter into my new year, my new school, my new life.

It was going to be the best year ever, and nothing was ever going to be the same.

∴

Just months earlier, in mid-June following my grandfather's death, we'd moved in with my grandmother, giving me two months to explore my "new" neighborhood, one I'd long known in miniature from regular visits but which I could now, as a permanent resident, inhabit more fully. Wallingford was so much more expansive than Upland, the old mill town from which we'd moved. Where Upland was made up of long rectangular plots of row-homes and duplexes, Wallingford's streets meandered amongst single homes. There were no angles here, only soft curves as the streets sauntered by expansive, well-manicured lawns all designed to dissuade anyone from being in a hurry. Long green miniature parks reached up to spatial—to me palatial—homes, all spaced so that there was no bleed over of noise or anything uncomfortably personal from one home to the next. What a difference from the houses on Church Street in Upland, where I'd lived until the age of eleven, and where you could hear every after-dinner argument and crashing plate as the sound passed the short space between kitchen windows, or the stomping feet and slamming doors that bled through the wall of the attached duplex. Privacy, in Upland, was shrouded by walls; here, in Wallingford, it was governed by space.

And driveways, they had driveways. Upland was all curbside parking, which could be deadly or nearly so, as I'd learned five years earlier when bolting between two parked cars and into the path of an oncoming Buick when crossing the street from a birthday party while my dad watched powerless from our front screen door. That week in the hospital amplified my mother's already overprotective streak. After this close call, Upland A.C. football and baseball were out; if I wanted a hobby, I'd have to settle for something safe and non-hazardous. Fortunately, I was a naturally solitary kid with an ability to entertain myself through mild obsessions and I fell into coin collecting. It fit me perfectly, giving something to catalog as I ransacked my father's pocket change for wheat pennies, old silver, and mint oddities.

Often feeling a misfit myself, I fell in love with mint errors and varieties, that is, miss-struck coins and other mistakes. I built myself a little Island of Misfit Coins over which I was, if not a king, then a chief curator. That summer, moving into my grandmother's house, she gave me a coffee tin filled with 1972 pennies that my grandfather, his eyes failing, had set aside. You see, in 1971, the mint made a mistake while preparing the obverse dies for the next year's pennies. A die had to be struck twice in order to receive all of the detail necessary to produce a good coin. This meant that it had to be struck, heated, re-aligned, and struck again. But one 1972 obverse Lincoln cent die was not aligned correctly, so when it was struck the second time it had, all along its outer edge, major doubling of the words "In God We Trust," along with the left side of "Liberty" and the right side of the date. It was a dramatic, beautiful, and valuable error. My grandfather wanted to find one, but his sight was damaged by cataracts. He could just about make out the dates on a penny, so he put every one he found with a 1972 date in the can, hoping that one might just be that magical coin.

I was just the kind of kid who would lay on the floor for hours dutifully sorting through a couple thousand 1972 pennies while truly believing that somewhere among them, the magical coin was hiding. And it turns out, one was. I'd already rolled up over twenty dollars of normal pennies and was down to the last couple hundred in the coffee tin when I found it: bright, sparkling copper in perfect condition, its doubling visible without any magnification whatsoever. It was, valued at $150 according to all the coin books on my shelf, instantly the most valuable and cherished thing I owned. I don't know that I had ever felt such sheer joy, such magic in the world, as I did in that moment, or, even more so, such a connection to my grandfather who, in my memories of him, had always been a sick and bitter man. Yet, the man who would lock me in the laundry room if I got on his nerves while he was supposed to be babysitting me (which happened pretty much every time and usually within about twenty minutes) had left this gift behind, knowing I'd find it.

I shared the news with my new neighborhood friends, whom I'd turned on to the joys of coin collecting. They were immediately jealous and plotting, but I could only identify the jealous part, and I reveled in actually having something of value, something that set me apart from them, because in my eyes they already had so much. I put the coin into a little jewelry box my grandmother gave me, and tucked it away in the drawer of my nightstand, where I could take it out and look at it each evening before I went to sleep. So it went two months through the summer until the evening of our return from our annual week at the shore that August. I ran up to my room and opened the little box to discover, not my bright, shining 1972 doubled die, but a dull, standard 1972 penny in its place. Someone had jimmied the laundry room window, made their way to my room, and replace my magical coin with a dull imposter. I cried and screamed for justice. I knew that my jealous neighborhood friends had conspired to steal the coin—nothing else in the house was disturbed or taken—but my parents would not heed my pleas to call the police. I didn't understand it at the time, but now I wonder if it wasn't because they were already used to having anything special taken from them. They had grown up watching those with everything get more while they spent hours filling out paperwork for government cheese or the most basic healthcare. Maybe this was a lesson for me more valuable that the coin that was lost.

But school would be starting in a week, and with it, my chance to become a whole new person. I'd just have to suck it up and move forward, which is what my grandmother told me to do.

•••

I passed through the doors and onto the gymnasium floor. The sound of a thousand student voices was like the buzz of white noise, but above it all I heard one voice, which turned out to belong to "Nipsey" Johnson (one of the school's very few black kids and the seventh grade class clown, probably out of the personal necessity of himself having to find a place to fit in). He pointed at me and yelled at the top of his lungs "Hey, check out the dude in the bobos!" He was pointing at my Kmart sneakers, which were clearly visible because the pants that my parents had bought at a spring closeout sale were, months later, already too short for my legs. I heard the calls of "Floods!" and I swear that every face in that auditorium was looking at me, every finger pointing at me, all in the joy of communal laughter. That's how it felt in that moment. And so they ended any dreams I'd had of building a new life of new friends and actual connectedness in this new place. I'd always been teased in Upland, and being an overprotected only child I was exceptionally sensitive to it, but that kind of teasing, I would learn, was an affectionate part of fitting in or finding a place within a group. This was different. Everything I experienced from this first day forward was in the service of exclusion. I was instantly identified as a poor kid and an outsider, and that was my identity for the next year.

The thing is: I wasn't a poor kid. My parents were middle class by every measure except the social ones that seemed to matter. My father knew poverty. He was born an undernourished twin on a Maryland farm in 1928; his twin sister was stillborn, and according to family lore he was so small that he slept in a shoebox placed in his father's top drawer until he was three months old. He quit high school to work the family farm and eventually ended up drafted into the military. He got lucky and didn't see combat during the Korean War years of his service, having instead been assigned to a support unit in construction. He learned welding there, and that's the skill he brought back home when his service was done. When he met my mother, he promised her that he was a hard worker whose family would never go hungry, and he kept that promise.

It turned out that my mother had a health condition that doctors told her would prevent her from ever successfully carrying a baby to term. That didn't stop them from trying, though, and eight pregnancies later, I entered the world as frail and frightful as my dad had 37 years earlier. I'd be the only one, but they provided. It's what you did in 1967. They saved money and bought a duplex in a nicer section of Upland away from the 19th century factory row-homes, with a fenced back yard and room for a garden, though the steep slope of our back yard would prevent anything but weeds and zucchini—which my dad had as much regard for as any weed—from growing there. Yes, I grew up with hand-me-downs from a neighbor's older son up the street, but that's what people in the neighborhood did. It wasn't a matter of need; it was shared thrift, helping each other to save for other, better things when something that was still of use became outgrown or was replaced. When the Carrols were able to buy a larger washing machine to handle their four kids, they offered their smaller, still working machine to a neighbor who didn't yet have one. So it was that clothes, furniture, and even appliances moved from house to house until they wore out. Good fortune got shared and people actively avoided waste. We never wanted for the necessities of life, and that was the definition of working class success. Sure, there were bigger, better things that we may have wanted, but we never wanted for anything we needed, and we even got to enjoy some nicer things, like a week's vacation down the shore or a special Christmas gift like the entire World Book Encyclopedia that appeared on my tenth Christmas (any doubt that my parents had college dreams for me?). We left that spirit of community behind when we moved to Wallingford.

The worst accusation you could throw at my father was to say that we were poor. He'd worked too hard to get us where we were to accept any such accusation quietly. He wasn't a prideful man, but there was some shit he wouldn't take. The one time I asked him if we were poor, I saw both anger and hurt in his face, anger at the intimation and hurt that I could believe it. But I was working in comparison and under a constant state of attack. The kids who terrorized me daily saw my ill-fitting clothes and knock-off shoes and decided that they knew the measure of my self-worth.

What I would go on to experience at Nether Providence Middle School was downright mean and systematic in purpose. It was meant to remind those who didn't belong to stay in their place while emphasizing that their place was nowhere. It was soul- and self-crushing in its relentlessness. Not a day passed without humiliating reminders that I was nothing or worse, a buck toothed, pencil-necked geek with bad-fitting clothes and grandpa glasses that, when broken in a bicycle accident, had to be taped down the center bridge and worn that way for weeks because fixing them immediately wasn't budgeted for. Yes, there were some blue-collar kids at NPMS. They came from "the Gardens" section of the county and they'd formed tight bonds going back to elementary school. Many got tagged, or even cynically welcomed the tags, like "gear-heads" or "burn outs," and with my own still obvious grade-striving pretentions, I didn't fit in with them and, even, offered a safe target for their own social placement, someone who could be bullied without a backup clique. It was a bunch of kids from this group who thought it would be fun to encourage one of the "special needs" kids in our class to stand behind me and slam my gym locker shut every time I hit the last number of the combination. When he bored of this after six or seven repetitions, he turned to his own locker and I did it to him. He turned and looked at me with a confused expression, then screamed and punched me in the face. That and the sounds of laughter brought out the gym teacher, who, despite my protestations, sent me to the principal's office where I was given a week's detention and an appointment with the guidance counsellor for a lecture on being more sensitive to those less fortunate. Confused, frustrated, hurt, and alone, I continued on.

Animal House was the popular movie of the year, celebrating the outcasts, and every kid at Nether Providence could recite nearly every line, but they also understood that that movie was not really about the outcasts winning. The true outcasts wouldn't have even made it to fictional Faber College. The heroes of *Animal House* were just the mild oddities that were allowed within the social elite, ultimately proven to be worth redemption because they could party on the black side of town and coopt a sense of cool. And once redeemed, they'd take their proper place in society, as the catalog of allegedly ironic accomplishments that ends the film shows, among their elite social leaders. Like the privileged anti-heroes of the film, my classmates were the corporate raiders of the future, practicing their future craft in miniature, like creeping into a neighbor's house to steal a penny or pitting the weak against each other.

Still, I had one thing going for me: I was smart, straight-A student smart. It was one of the reasons my parents had decided to make the move. Upland and Wallingford, Pennsylvania, are barely five miles apart, yet their school systems are binary opposites. As I write this, the Chester-Upland School District has been operating under state receivership for seven years and is considered a model of administrative incompetence within the state. When I attended elementary school at Hill Street School and early middle school at Main Street Elementary and Middle School, both were considered fine, small town schools with dedicated teachers and, in Mr. Richardson, a top-notch principal. But it was also widely known that the Nether-Providence School District in Wallingford, was superior in just about every way and among the best in the state. The opportunity to send their kid to one of the best schools in the state was something that my parents, with their dreams of college in my future, couldn't pass up.

I'd always been told how smart I was. I had started Kindergarten early, even though my birthday was well past the cut-off date; hence, I was always the youngest in my class. Yet, by fourth grade, there was talk of skipping me up to fifth. I excelled in every course and had an unbroken honor roll streak. My parents pushed college on me as the only viable option to a good life, and this was the 1970s, when jobs were still good in suburban Philadelphia. Everyone in the neighborhood said that there would always be good jobs in the region because "They'll never close the Philly Navy Yard." But my dad never said that. He'd just get even quieter, and I knew what he was thinking, because he'd said it enough on multiple occasions to me or maybe it was to himself when nobody else was near or listening: "Don't believe it. Get out." And that's why I did so well at school; I was doing what he wanted for me. I was proud to be smart. Now, here in this new place, I might be a "poor kid" wearing "bobos" and "floods," but I was ready to show that I belonged in those classrooms, that I was an academic equal.

•••

"Okay, everyone, we need to get started on this year's research project, so please pull out the annotated bibliography cards you completed last year." This was my history teacher on my first day of class. I'd already met Mrs. Schupp because she had helped me figure out how to work the combination on my locker; I'd never had one before: at Main Street we just stored everything in our homeroom desks. Now, my hand was up again, seeking help. I'd never before heard the words "annotated" or "bibliography" and putting them together into some mysterious thing pushed me to near panic. Mrs. Schupp briefly explained that I'd missed the previous years' preparation but that she'd pair me up with someone who would help me get caught up. She meant well, but I would never get caught up.

To the excitement of the class, she then announced that this year's learning game was going to be based upon the Dutch East India Trade Company and would involve teams of traders and shippers re-enacting the seventeenth century Atlantic trade wars. This, too, was foreign to me: learning as a game? The closest to play my educational experience in Upland had been was two years previous when our Social Studies classes competed by decorating our homeroom doors in patriotic themed displays relating to the Bicentennial. That, I realized now, was just arts and crafts. This was real learning. Here was strategy, bargaining, tactics, and communication all being used to face the problems of human enterprise and natural disasters as if we were young, colonial entrepreneurs. But I didn't know how to respond; I had absolutely no preparation for this. Mrs. Schupp assigned me to a group of Gardens kids, who were happy to have someone who actually cared about getting the assigned tasks done. But my cluelessness combined with their cool lack of engagement was not a formula for success. My team members spent most of this active learning exercise as social time while I worked to play the game properly and promptly lost all of our ships and goods in a catastrophic storm. We finished last in the class, but earned a "C" for effort.

I had similar experiences in each of my classes during those first days until I came to a realization: where only two years previous there had been talk of promoting me forward a year at my Upland school, here I was in Wallingford and I was one, maybe two years behind my classmates. Everything they were doing was foreign to me while when I described what I'd been doing at my school the previous year, the standard answer I received was, "We finished that in fifth grade." Or earlier. What I'd been doing before now was memorizing information and giving it back to my teachers, demonstrating basic problem solving skills, and demonstrating myself to be a good citizen. These kids were being encouraged to question their teachers, to challenge themselves and to solve challenging problems, and to develop into good leaders. I realized that all of my honor roll ribbons indicated not that I was smart, but rather, that I was obedient. Even the burn-out kids were more hip to the system than I was; their active disengagement was a more knowing and, probably, emotionally healthy response to it all than was my ceaseless striving to please.

That realization dawned slowly during that first confusing week and it infected me as it grew. These were the kids who were being prepped for college and life among the elite. Not me, and not the kids I'd left behind in Upland. Despite what I'd been told for the first six years of my schooling—all that "Get an education and work hard and you will succeed" shit—I was not, I realized, and had never been considered college material by the larger powers at work.

Even my parents were fooled by this, and my old teachers back in Upland. These kids were learning how to problem solve, how to think critically, how to negotiate, how to speak knowledgeably about the fine arts, and how to appreciate the better things. They were being prepped for an upper class that would never welcome me (like with the weekly evening ballroom dance classes the school hosted and which my mother signed me up for: I went to one where I gamely asked 8 different girls to dance and weathered their laughing refusals, then withstood the spiteful insults of the lead teacher for being a "crybaby wallflower" when I refused to try anymore). I, back in Upland, was being trained in obedience and dutifulness. The true vision of my future success was to take my place on the factory line, to serve as just another cog making the lives of the important people more pleasant.

At the very time I was experiencing this conflict-filled transition in my own personal education, Jean Anyon was collecting data in five New Jersey fifth grade schools that would result in her ground-breaking essays "Social Class and the Hidden Curriculum of Work" (1980) and "Social Class and School Knowledge" (1981). These essays, which I would encounter during my doctoral studies over a decade after their initial publication, clarified the conflict I was experiencing in ways I couldn't fully comprehend at the time. Using Anyon's classifications, in my physical move of five miles from Upland to Wallingford, I had shifted from a "working-class school," where I was being prepared for "future wage labor that is mechanical and routine" to an "affluent professional school," where children acquire "symbolic capital" and the related "skills necessary to become society's successful artists, intellectuals, legal, scientific, and technical experts" (Anyon, 1980, pp. 88–89). Reading Anyon's essays years after my experiences of the 1978–79 school year, I found both reassurance and revulsion: reassurance in knowing that I was not alone and revulsion at my own willing supplication to the system. Up until my experiences that seventh grade year, while at the working-class Main Street Elementary School, I had not been, as Anyon catalogs, "developing the abilities and skills of resistant" (1980, p. 88); rather, I was a devoted people pleaser and grade grubber. I believed in the system and bought every myth. My education into the reality of the situation was all the more psychologically traumatic and violent because of this.

Those honor roll ribbons may as well have been tethers to mediocrity. I could feel smart, but I wasn't allowed to get smart. The curriculum of my old school ensured that, and my inability to catch up to this new curriculum just sealed it. I tried to catch up, to work hard, but I'd never learned the vocabulary. Every step was into a foreign and unfriendly realm. Even the teachers, like Mrs. Schupp, who had been kind to me to at the start, lost their patience with my constant questioning that slowed everything down, and they would pretend not to hear the murmurs of "Shut up, loser" every time I asked for clarity. I saw for the first time just how un-even the playing field really is, and it opened my eyes not only to my own situation, but suddenly all of the prejudice that I'd grown up around began to sound different and more insidious to me. Though I didn't yet have the language to fully grasp it, I began to understand and identify the classist and racist biases that were built into nearly every system of order I'd ever been sold.

This is dangerous stuff for a twelve year-old to realize.

By the Christmas holidays even my parents began to accept grades of "C" or lower without comment. I'd shifted into getting by mode, one that I'd had plenty of opportunity to observe in the adults of my world. I turned to music and would lock myself away in my room each night, listening to weird sounds and conjuring the weird worlds described on albums by Queen, Genesis, and other seeming outcasts (discovering punk rock the next year would change everything all over again for me). I was no longer interested, really, in the present time and place, and if I dreamed of anything, it was only escape.

The relationship between my mom and my grandmother became strained by my own ongoing stress. Nan was someone who had existed by adjusting. Her own life's disappointments were extensive, but she'd endured by adjusting to her circumstances. My grandmother grew up quite well-off before she married my working class grandfather. Her family was wealthy from the business her grandfather had begun and which her father had expanded. But my great-grandfather was of the old world where girls didn't do things like go to college (which my grandmother had pleaded to be able to do) or inherit any of their family's business interests. By the time of my birth, my grandmother's father was dead, her eldest brother had inherited the whole of the family business, and the other siblings were on speaking terms only when plotting combined legal action against any of the others. My Nan couldn't understand the difficulties that I, and in their own way, my parents were experiencing. For their part, they'd not made any friends among their new neighbors, not a single one of whom brought over even a goddamn pound cake when we moved in—that's just what you did back in Upland—but my grandmother would simply sigh that "That's just the way it is here." Again, the implication was to adjust, get used to it, and persevere.

Shortly into the new year, my parents made the decision to move back to Upland and, frankly, it saved my life.

You see, I'd been planning my suicide with an odd efficiency for the three months leading up to their announcement that we'd be moving. I'd been stealing and hoarding assorted among my grandmother's pills, a collection that I figured would be sufficient to kill me. I planned to enjoy the summer then die before the horror of 8th grade begun. But, suddenly, I was back in Upland, and my old friends were actually happy to see me back, and while the few old bullies hadn't changed, they couldn't really hurt me anymore. We were on the same level. So we returned to Upland and everything, my parents thought, would be alright. But it wasn't. For you see, I'd seen behind the curtain. I understood that the game was fixed, and I was on the wrong side. Where my parents thought that the return to Upland would also signal my return to the honor roll and college prep, I had other ideas. I'd developed a new personal philosophy, conveniently supplied by my new love of punk rock: fuck it.

Why bother? Why try? What's the point, if it's all stacked against you and anyone else who doesn't belong to the appropriate country club?

My old teachers were shocked at how I'd changed upon my return, though my classmates actually liked me a little better. I'd given up being the brown-nosing over-achiever and traded it in for the smart aleck who didn't care, trying on assorted shades of the "no future" punk rock attitude to match the rebellious new music I'd discovered. I spent hours poring over the lyrics of records by The Clash, XTC, and Talking Heads. Their messages were consistent: question everything, resist authority, all has been corrupted. When my grandmother asked why I consistently refused her offers to join her at church, I replied "We're all Devo!" I even took a twisted new pride in my hometown, wearing its futility proudly like some subversive banner.

When asked, I'd tell someone that "I'm from Fucked-Upland." Which is when my parents resorted to Catholic High School.

I can't say that the brothers of St. James Catholic High School for Boys didn't knock some sense into me (mostly metaphorically). I maintained my program of stubborn under-achievement throughout my four years of high school, but I did get drawn into some aspects of its social structure (yearbook and TV club) which harnessed my creative side. The school had a track system wherein track one was college prep, track three was for the shop kids, and track two was for the ones who could go either way. Track two became my natural home. Remaining both a voracious reader (just not of what was assigned) and music junkie, I hung equally well with the nerds and the heads, and managed to avoid drugs—despite my next-door locker neighbor running a small pharmaceutical business from his locker—through the truth in my oft-repeated joke that "I couldn't afford both records and drugs, so I picked records because the effects lasted longer." Still, most of my teachers saw me as bright and frustrating; someone who was going to piss away the brains god gave him.

Then an odd thing happened. The SATs were coming up and all of my track one friends were freaking out and taking after-school prep classes where they were given lots of practice tests and advice like "The night before the test, be sure to eat a good meal and get to bed early so that you're well rested at test time." This was not the kind of advice I was prone to follow; instead, the night before the test being a Friday, I did what I did on most Friday nights, which was sneak out of my house around 10 p.m. when my parents went to bed and go to South Street to hang out until the wee hours. Still, I made it to the test on time and ended up with a top ten score within the high school. Despite my stubborn "C" average, I suddenly had a ticket that could get me into a state college. Maybe I was smart, at least, test smart, but that was going to be enough to get my foot in the door. I'd never seen my parents so happy.

I picked my college, Millersville University, because it had a radio station, and I wanted to be a deejay. Much bigger decisions have been made over even more trivial desires. In my case, it all worked out. I fell in love with college and began to actually enjoy doing academic work; I even made the dean's list once on my way to my B.A. in English. About three quarters of the way through, the head of the English Department, Dr. Lilliana Zancu, called me into her office and asked if I'd ever thought about grad school. I told her I hadn't, but she sold me on it, so I hung around two more years for the Masters. After a couple of years trying to make it as a freelance writer, I went back to school to earn a Ph.D. You'd have thought my parents had won the lottery.

During this time, the Philadelphia Navy yard had closed and the repercussions were being felt throughout the region where I'd grown up. Unemployment in the South Philadelphia region reached record levels and the area still hasn't fully recovered. My dad took early retirement, which gave him a few good years to enjoy a little house down the shore before asbestosis and its cancerous cousins left him to drown in the private sea of his lungs. He'd been right all along about college being my only ticket out.

Now, he's twenty years gone and I'm twenty years into teaching at a small state college in rural Georgia. I was drawn to this place because of its high percentage of first-generation college students, of kids who grew up like me, maybe working class, maybe even from a lower economic rung, kids who have maybe one shot and who may be realizing for the first time, just like I did at Nether Providence Middle School in 1978, that they might not have been prepared for what they are being asked to face. I'm here to hear their stories and to help them forward into their next chapters, and, occasionally, I'll tell them a piece of mine, like this.

References

Anyon, J. (1980). Social class and the hidden curriculum of work. *Journal of Education, 162*, 67–92.

Anyon, J. (1981). Social class and school knowledge. *Curriculum Inquiry, 11*, 3–42.

CHAPTER 5

Feeling Like an Imposter at College

Nancy Mack

My high school was one of the smallest and poorest in inner-city Dayton, Ohio. We had no home court or field for athletics, and our uniforms were all from another decade. I lettered in volleyball only because otherwise there would not have been enough players to have a team. Once we were scheduled to play a game at a new suburban school. Upon entering the building, we asked for directions to the gym. The teacher responded by asking us which gym we needed. This district had multiple gyms while our crappy gym wasn't even regulation size. We then passed an Olympic-sized swimming pool on our way to a pristine locker room that was bigger than our whole gym. By that point I was seething with rage at all the amazing things that these kids had that we never did. I suddenly wanted to scratch profanity into the lockers and break all the mirrors. Luckily, my friends talked me out of it. I wasn't really a bad kid; I just became infuriated when I knew that something was unfair. A few times I had ended up in the principal's office because I had protested unreasonable policies like dress code restrictions and the class play being cancelled. During my graduation conference, the principal predicted that I probably would never graduate from college because I would waste all my time causing trouble. It came as no surprise when I was blackballed from joining the Honor Society for my attitude—even though I had the qualifying grade-point average.

I only applied to one state university because of the application fees. My father refused to fill out the financial aid forms because in his words, "Nobody has the right to know how much money we have." Unfortunately, Dad had been laid off during my senior year of high school, and I feared that there might not be enough money for me to go to any college. When my class took a bus trip to a near-by, elite university, I took one look at the matching Georgian architecture and was so intimidated that I skipped out of the tour after the first stop at the bookstore. A friend and I bought an X-rated novel, went back to the bus, and spent our time searching for all the dirty parts. As a first-generation college student, I did not know very many people who graduated from college. Most graduates from my high school never even went to college, let alone finished. I picked the university that I applied to based on the fact that the boy who lived down the street went there. My reasoning was that I might survive there because my neighbor, who was not very smart, had made it all the way to his junior year.

As I waited to hear about my fate, my anxiety about going to college grew. I would lay awake at night, worrying about fitting in at college. I had trouble sleeping and developed a nervous cough that went on for hours. At one point, I morbidly decided that I probably was going to die soon because I could not imagine my future at college. My lack of imagination was somewhat ironic because I could imagine myself adapting to a post-apocalyptic world but not surviving on a college campus. With the family rule of "Use it up, wear it out, make do, or do without," I had learned how to survive a lack of resources but not how to adjust to a world of privilege.

Like most readers of teen magazines, I was obsessed with clothes. Unlike my high school friends, I had lots of clothes because my mother and I were expert bargain hunters. We bought anything that was cheap enough—even if it was the wrong size. My mother sewed, so she would do her best to rob fabric from one part to add to a seam or put in tucks here or there to make a garment smaller. This was the late sixties when college students were expected to dress up for classes. Midwestern campus attire for girls was very conservative. Wearing jeans to class was forbidden by some professors and might even result in being counted as absent. Fall magazines featured plaid kilt skirts and matching solid color sweaters. My problem was that very few of my clothes were purchased together so nothing matched—something that I had been teased about during high school. My solution was to invent an elaborate filing card system; I made a card for each color in a garment's fabric and arranged all of the cards by color. I intended to consult the card file each morning to create beautifully color-coordinated outfits. Needless to say, this great idea never panned out.

On move-in day, I noticed a job ad posted outside of the janitor's room in the basement of my dorm. I was excited to discover that they had jobs for students to clean on weekends. I knocked on the door and requested an application from a nice older woman. I rushed upstairs to share my good news with one of my roommates.

Breathless, I waved the paper in front of my roomie who grew up in the small town of Coldwater, "Hey Donna, look what I found out."

Donna barely looked up from arranging her high school photos above her desk. "Our dorm has cleaning jobs for students." "Really? How could we do that and go to classes?"

I moved in closer to Donna. "It's just on weekends. We start at 6 A.M and we would be back in bed by 10."

"Hmm." Donna paused to consider what I had told her. "We would just be sleeping at that time anyway." Donna decided to get on board with the whole idea.

"We only have to clean the bathrooms. And, the lady said that if we got all of our work done, we could quit early."

Finishing early was a nice pipe dream. We never considered how difficult it would be to jump out of bed and start working while hung over from the previous night's escapades. Our overcrowded dorm had six girls to a room on five floors in four connected buildings. Each hallway had one huge community bathroom containing two long rows of sinks and mirrors, two rows of toilet stalls, and a dozen dark concrete showers. Donna and I wore our junkiest clothes and covered our hair with old scarves. We worked alone, starting on the bottom floor.

The hardest part of the job was mopping the floors. We used a large metal bucket with wheels that had a heavy, mop-wringing device on top. The bucket was kept in a closet at the end of each hallway that had a utility sink where the bucket was filled with hot soapy water and emptied. The gigantic industrial mop added to the weight, making it awkward to move the contraption up and down the hallway.

If I didn't rush through my tasks, the wealthy sorority girls would get in my way while they were getting all gussied up for church. I lived on the top floor, so if I got behind, I would come face to face with the girls who were my neighbors. One Sunday, as I was struggling to get the top-heavy bucket over the lip of the bathroom doorway, the whole thing tipped over and spilled out into the hallway. Just then, a bevy of beauties in their brightly colored wool coats exited from one of the rooms at the other end of the hall.

The first girl announced to the others behind her. "Oh my God, watch out. She spilled the whole thing."

Cursing loudly, I lunged forward on my knees, unsuccessfully trying to scoop the water out of the way with my hands and arms.

"Jesus, it's starting to spread everywhere," the same girl warned.

In response seven wobbly girls moved single file against the wall. I looked up to see the high-heeled prima donnas, nearly toppling over as they grabbed onto each other trying to avoid the rapidly spreading dirty water. All of the girls were so busy avoiding the water flooding the hallway that I foolishly hoped no one had seen my face.

When they reached the elevator, Marlene, who was the ring leader of the popular girls, turned back and angrily said, "Do you have to do that now? Can't you do that after we've gone?"

I kept my distance from Marlene for the rest of the term, not wanting to be reminded of that whole fiasco.

I never felt like I belonged with any of the other college students. I became a loner and usually arrived early for my sociology class held in a gigantic lecture hall that seated 300 students. As I sat in silence waiting for class to begin, I listened to the conversations of the other students around me, sharing their hometowns and backgrounds. I had been a big fish in a little pond in high school: athlete, cheerleader, homecoming queen, and so on. I suddenly realized that the other students had done similar things—only at bigger, better schools where the competition was much more difficult. I nearly had a panic attack before the sociology professor arrived. I resolved to survive by trying harder than my peers. I went to every lecture even though as the term went on many of my classmates blew off attending. I took notes and read every assigned chapter. I found quiet places to study in the evening: empty classrooms and the dorm stairwell.

During a review session that very few students attended, the professor actually gave major clues as to what would be on the exam. I earned an A for the course. By the end of the first year, one of my five roommates had flunked out, one was on probation, another had a weak average, and only two of us had mostly As and Bs.

At the end of spring term, I returned home to attend my high school's Honor Society assembly. The school policy was that any graduate who had made it through the first year of college was an automatic celebrity who had an open invitation to sit on the stage while the new members were tapped. I was determined to take my rightful place on the stage. I showed up that day in the wildest outfit I could put together: a black satin blouse, a micro-mini skirt, fish-net hose, and new four-inch, platform, high-heels, covered in black glitter. I relished the sweet victory of sitting on stage because I had never been asked to join their club. I entered from the back of the auditorium and proudly headed down the center aisle toward the stage while the students were filing in. Seated on the stage were four teachers and the president of the honor society. I recognized Mr. Guthrie, the bald geometry teacher who could never control our constant misbehavior. His face fell when he met my gaze. No doubt he never expected me to survive the first year at college. I filled one of the empty chairs on stage as the lone successful academic model for our whole school, looking more like a bleached blond Dolly Parton than a preppy scholar.

My sense of humor helped to get me through several courses. My first English teacher was an over achiever who had graduated from college before she turned 21. She required us to complete two essays a week and told us frequently how poor our grammar was. One day she typed up a list of all of the titles that we had used on our last essays in order to emphasize how boring we all were. The only title that she praised was the one that I had generated for a personal narrative assignment: "I Am the Happy Victim of a High School Social Climber." This praise gave me the courage to excel in a competitive speech class. I gave entertaining speeches about my childhood gullibility as the neighborhood nerd and our miserable low budget family vacations. In an advanced writing class, I organized my group to write a humorous guide to college life including chapters about discerning which foods were inedible in the cafeteria, passing room inspections by subterfuge, withstanding the required physical education courses, and spotting dangerous predators at the campus bars. I also wrote a monologue for another class about a phone call home explaining how my car had caught on fire by itself while I was attending class.

I graduated in three years with a degree in English education, became a public school teacher, and earned a master's degree by attending classes at night and during the summers. Never dreaming that I could earn a doctorate and become a college professor, I continued taking courses simply because I became interested in theories of language development. After a few months of staying home with a new baby, I got the courage to apply for the doctorate program. Even though I was accepted, I started to doubt myself and procrastinated about requesting to be a teaching assistant. Being a teaching assistant was a necessity because it paid for my tuition. By the time that I finally applied, the only position left was teaching for a degree program in a prison for male offenders. The previous T.A. had quit after she had been attacked, so I wore running shoes the first day of classes in case I had to leave in a hurry. It turned out that my shoes became an issue when I went through the metal detector each day. After setting off the alarm, the guards made me take off my running shoes and go back through again. They claimed that most shoes had some metal in them. I tried wearing all different types of shoes. This delay used up several minutes and often made me late to class, so I decided to solve the problem by purchasing shoes that were completely made out of plastic. When the alarm went off again as I passed through the machine, I knew for sure that the guards were pranking me. I quickly learned that I was in danger from both the inmates and the guards. Growing up in a rough part of town and being a public school teacher for several years gave me the experience to succeed at teaching and keeping myself safe while working in prison.

I also taught writing classes on the main campus where I overheard the other graduate students talking about a three-day, national conference for composition professors. Many of the current scholars that I had been reading were scheduled to be main speakers, and anyone could send in a proposal to be included on a panel. Experts in the field judged each proposal anonymously and selected the best ones to be included for the smaller sessions. I thought about sending in a proposal about several different topics: using graphics to teach writing concepts, qualitative research methods, and the success of an in-house textbook that I had done for the department. Because there was no limit on the number of proposals that could be submitted, I decided to hedge my bets and write up all three ideas. Months later the mail arrived from the national college composition organization, informing me that all of my proposals had been accepted. I prepared three professional presentations and drove to a near-by state for the conference. On the first morning, I saw a small group of the graduate students from my university in the lobby of the gigantic convention center. We chatted, and I inquired about the topics of their presentations. No one spoke, so I awkwardly filled up the silence by telling about my three presentations. I was met with more silence and incredulous stares. None of their proposals had been accepted, and consequently, none of them spoke to me for the rest of the conference.

In the year that followed I continued to struggle to fit in and noticed that all of the participants were wearing dark suits. Men dominated the field, and I did not see a single pregnant woman or any children at the conference. When I returned to the same conference, I was in the second trimester with our third child. I purchased a dark, plus-size suit to disguise my pregnancy rather than choosing to wear maternity clothes. At one point, my advisor asked me if I was planning on continuing to have children or to complete my doctorate. I thought that his criticism was unfair because he had five children of his own.

After passing general exams, I began writing my dissertation. I happened upon a new article by one of the scholars that I respected. After reading the article, I realized that the author had glossed over many of the problems with cultural assumptions about how writing should be taught. As a public school teacher, I was required to assign students to do endless pages of grammar exercises. This experience taught me that drilling the parts of speech and subject verb agreement did not motivate students nor improve their writing— no matter how interesting I tried to make grammar definitions. I had read all the research about language development and knew it was a myth that students needed to learn grammar first in order to be good writers. I tackled several myths about learning to write head on with my college students and assigned them to write about meaningful topics connected to their lives. The students on campus were easier to persuade than the prison inmates. At first the inmates countered that I should write about prison issues because I was a better writer than they were. I finally convinced them that they were the best people to write about life inside of prison. The men wrote about parole board tall tales, the lack of health care, types of guards, prison slang, military veterans, and black market stores. I required students to include visual metaphors into their three dimensional writing projects. The men created elaborate projects with essays about topics such as racial conflicts with guards compared to a chessboard in black and white and a lack of rehabilitation being no better than a warehouse full of broken robots. I began to realize that I could connect my success as a teacher with theories about language biases and the development of critical consciousness. The chapters started pouring out late at night. Meanwhile, I was teaching in prison and on campus, driving over an hour to each job, and dealing with our young children. Near to graduation, my prison teaching experience enabled me to land my first job as an assistant professor at a small college that had two large prison programs.

FIGURE 5.1   News Sun photo, by Scott Kissell

A few years later, I gained an interview for a dream position in an English department at a state university in my hometown. I put on my dark suit and high heels and arrived early for my appointment. I entered the library building and headed down the steps to a tunnel system that connected most of the campus buildings. My nerves got the better of me as I neared the bottom of the steps and I fell down the bottom three steps. Because I didn't fall very far, the only damage was that I ripped a big hole in the leg of my hose. This was not a problem because I came prepared with an extra pair in my purse. I dashed into the nearest bathroom and made a wardrobe change and emerged on time to head confidently to the interview. I got the job and kept my desk stocked with a change of clothes, a sewing kit, band-aids, chocolate, and other emergency items. Other faculty members learned of my stash and often came to my door in need of assistance.

I loved teaching and earned tenure, becoming an associate and then a full professor. I survived by adapting to an elite academic world with a culture that I still find strange. Almost weekly, I commiserated on the phone with a good friend from graduate school who had a similar background. I shared that I often felt out of place in academic meetings, and I was relieved to learn that he also felt intimidated by his aggressive, elite colleagues. Feeling like an outsider, imposter, or a fraud can be overwhelming and even totally debilitating. Early in my career, I heard about the imposter syndrome and decided to learn more about it. Psychologists prefer the name imposter phenomenon (IP) rather than the imposter syndrome because the word "syndrome" implies illness. There are a wide variety of responses to IP that may result in behaviors that are troublesome. The lists below summarizes the problems related to IP.

Fear of Success:
- Doubting one's abilities
- Avoiding exposure through procrastination
- Not working for a promotion
- Dropping out
- Taking a position beneath one's qualifications
- Blaming oneself for failure
- Refusing to share work
- Avoiding risk
- Hiding from the spotlight

Fear of Failure:
- Striving for perfection
- Trying to pass for a member of the privileged group
- Working an unreasonable amount of hours (workaholic)
- Gaining more degrees or credentials
- Changing positions frequently
- Blaming the others for failure
- Being charming or overly friendly
- Innovating and seeking awards
- Showing off to impress others

Just one of these problems can increase stress and lead to major life problems. Psychologists first identified IP in high achieving women. Further research found that many types of people suffer from IP. Some scholars suggest that the more success an individual achieves, the more likely it is that IP can become problematic. Dianne Zorn studies the many factors that influence IP among graduate students. Zorn provides a complex analysis of IP as co-determined and emerging in a competitive, hierarchical environment. This means that the individual is not the victim of a lack of self-confidence or ability. Instead, the individual is interacting in a context where social practices and patterns of communication foster the feelings of IP. Zorn is interested in what universities can do to support students as they advance toward graduation.

Another helpful concept to understand is emotional labor. Emotional labor was first studied in flight attendants who are expected to exhibit pleasantness and helpfulness on the job—even though they may feel frustrated and angry in their interactions with irate customers. Scholar Michael Zembylas analyzes the emotional labor of teachers who feel pressured from administrators, curriculums, state and federal regulations, and the public. Zembylas explains that critical reflection can help individuals to regulate their emotions by making the decision to feel a different way. In other words, people can decide how they want to react emotionally to troublesome situations. It is possible to think about different reactions to a negative experience in order to determine a more helpful response. The drawback is that thinking things through takes time and a great deal of understanding about human psychology, social situations, and the larger forces from culture, history, and the economy.

I have found that my ability to analyze situations is fostered by writing, reading, and sharing experiences with friends and colleagues. Writing journals, emailing friends, and even publishing academic papers have helped me to see situations from a larger perspective. Reading enables me to name and own experiences such as being a first-generation college student, working-class, place-bound female, and care-taker of elderly family members. Sharing with others who are going through similar experiences fosters insights about how people behave.

Reflection isn't just about armchair analysis; reflection is also about taking action that benefits oneself and others in similar circumstances. There are many ways to take action, but most important is to reach out to create a support system of friends, colleagues, and professionals who can help in positive ways. This can just be one person who listens, shares similar frustrations, or has achieved similar goals; or it can be a group of people, an organization, or even an office or center at the university that provides assistance. Not all assistance is helpful, so it is important to continually evaluate whether support networks need to be changed or abandoned. New experiences lead to analyzing those experiences and hopefully to making informed decisions about emotional responses and beneficial actions.

References

Kissell, S. (1988). Writing wrongs: Essays offer LCI inmates an escape from tedium of prison life. *Springfield News Sun, 2*(15), 1.

Zembylas, M. (2005). *Teaching with emotion: A postmodern enactment.* Information Age Pub.

Zorn, D. M. (2011). *Enactive education: Dynamic co-emergence, complexity, experience, and the embodied mind* [Dissertation]. University of Toronto.

CHAPTER 6

(Un)Belonging in Liminality
Garage Stories

Phil Bratta

> Going from experience to theory to reflection and so on will make for a text that cannot be neatly linear.
> VILLANUEVA (1993, p. XVII)

∴

"Never stop working. Keep your body moving. Otherwise, you'll die," my eighty-six year old grandma tells me as she and I sit on a backyard bench at my dad's house in Savanna, Illinois, a small northwestern town of 3,000 people that borders the Mississippi River. I glance at her and nod, and we bask in a brief moment of silence while birds chirp and mosquitoes buzz and smoke lingers in the air on this humid, sunny August afternoon.

It's 2016, and my grandma and I are perched on the bench with cigarettes between our fingers, smoke and humidity in our lungs, and sun on our heads. It's her birthday weekend, and we catch up on family—who's doing what work now, who's not talking to who because of some years old beef, and what yard and house work needs to get done even though today is her birthday. We also talk some surface-level politics, and listen to the dark, basil green oak trees and tall grasslands that back up to the yard. My grandma's advice about working, moving the body, and death comes from me asking her what piece of advice she would offer after all her years on the planet. I should have known that my lawn-mowin, blanket quiltin, Pall Mall smokin grandma would say such a thing. "Time to get back to getting our hands dirty," my grandma says as we take our last drags, meaning she has to get back to pickin weeds out the small garden and I have to get back to organizin the garage. We have to get back to where we belong.

I was raised in an environment of work. Pro-union or anti-union, all my family members believed in that one thing: work, and more specifically the work of manual labor. On both sides of my family, work was never to be forsaken. Going back several generations, my nuclear and extended family has

© KONINKLIJKE BRILL NV, LEIDEN, 2021 | DOI: 10.1163/9789004501508_007 persistently been in blue- and pink-collar jobs: plumbers, carpenters, concrete finishers, landscapers, warehouse workers, grocery store clerks, farmers, nannies, and elementary school secretaries—both skilled and unskilled laborers.

As my grandma and I leave the bench, I arrive upon my dad's garage, noticing the scattering of tools, many of which have a corresponding nail or hook on the pegboards that line most of the walls, except where my toolbox stands and a 2' × 4' semi-grimy, hazy window brings in some sunlight. Under a few of the pegboards are short racks where old Folgers coffee cans store loose bolts and moldering metals. In one corner is a rusted oil drum that houses strips of plywood and 2 × 4s, 2 × 6s, and 2 × 10s pieces of lumber of varying lengths. Next to the drum are smaller scrap pieces of wood, pieces that can't even be used as a door stopper, stacked and saved because my dad believes they will be useful at some point by someone for something.

Everything will have a use, multiple uses. In another corner is the "gardening" wheelbarrow with spots of concrete buildup and dried paint adhered to it and rusted metal handles and undercarriage. I face an overwhelming collection of wood, random screws and bolts, washers and nuts, hand and power tools, buckets and pails, water hoses, tie-down straps, chairs and stools, tables and shelves—an inexhaustible list of items known and yet-unknown uses.

I stand at the edge of the garage, surveying these objects, but thinking about what my grandma said. To live is to work. Movement, labor, and the body; these are concepts emphasized, believed in, and practiced in my family. They mark us. They position us. They give value to us. They orient us.

1   Orientation

About two years prior to sitting with my grandma—early September 2014—I'm a second-year Ph.D. student in a seminar called Embodied Rhetorics. The professor, Trixie, has assigned Sara Ahmed's *Queer Phenomenology* (2006), which I'm excited to read given my interest in queer theory and phenomenology. Our class meets on Thursdays, and for our September 11 meeting, we'll discuss this book. I'm in my Lansing, Michigan apartment, and I sit in a weathered black leather chair that I picked up for $20 from a garage sale and at a cheap black unfolded folding table that my dad bought me ten years ago—a much different writing table than the one depicted on the cover of Ahmed's book with its dark brown crafted wood table and chair that sit upon an open field.

"What does it mean to be orientated?" Ahmed opens her book. I pause for a second, furrowing my eyebrows before I look up from the book and out the window to my left, noticing the light green soon-to-be yellow and orange leaves of the trees blowing in the Michigan wind and thinking about "meaning"— that phrase, that concept, that practice that I had learned so much about in my cultural studies major as an undergraduate at Columbia College Chicago. "Where the fuck am I and how did I get here?" I ask myself, "I'm not working on cars anymore." Instead, I am oriented to this book, to Ahmed's writing. Then, I mull over more questions: "What does it mean for me to be here—in graduate school—and orientated to graduate studies? What does it mean for me—a white working-class man—to be orientated to this queer woman of color's writing and theory? What will her writing and theory offer me and how can I honor her writing and theory?"

From that time of picking up Ahmed book to this writing moment, I think about these questions as a way to work through where I've been, where I'm at, and where I'm going. Where = space and place. Where = embodiment in space and place. "Orientation," Ahmed tells me, "is a matter of how we reside in space" (p. 1). Spaces are sexualized, gendered, and racialized, which also produce the shapes that bodies take and orient the bodies toward and away objects (simultaneously, space relies upon bodily presence). Objects and others direct us to the lines of the world, which give form to matter, shape to bodies. Lines also mark paths. They "depend on the repetition of norms and conventions, of routes and paths taken, but they are also created as an effect of this repetition. To say that lines are performative is to say that we find our way and we know which direction we face only as an effect of work, which is often hidden from view" (p. 16).

There are paths to, within, and made by institutions. Institutions also orient and provide certain comfort for certain bodies. Ahmed remarks, "Institutions ... involve orientation devices that keep things in place. The affect of such placement could be described as a form of comfort. To be orientated, or to be at home in the world, is also to feel a certain comfort we might only notice comfort as an affect when we lose it—when we become uncomfortable" (p. 134). What happens when orientations don't place us in a feeling of home, of a sense of belonging?

Two particular institutions have shaped my orientation: family and academia. Arguably, family primarily shapes our position and directions in life (and of course the family is shaped and directed by larger social forces). The family directs us to permissible objects, allowing our reach to extend (and often extend only so far). "Objects," Ahmed notes, "are not only material: they may be values, capital, aspirations, projects, and styles. Insofar as we inherit that which is near enough to be available at home, we also inherit orientations, that is, we inherit the nearness of certain objects more than others" (p. 86). For years, I found in a set of relations to familial history, work, and the body. I inherit a reach to certain tools for certain work: wrench, hammer, screwdriver, saws, hands. Now, I shift the reach to other tools: books, theories, the page, conversations.

Academia also directs, aligns, and orients bodies, shaping most of the brick-and-mortar for the comfort of white middle- and upper-class men. While the 1970s initiated the noticeable beginnings of working-class students entering higher education, universities continue to make such dominant bodies feel comfortable and at home. As Ahmed remarks, "White bodies are comfortable *as they inhabit spaces that extend their shape* ... whiteness may function as a form of public comfort by *allowing bodies to extend into spaces that have already taken their shape*" (pp. 134–135). Comfort also involves the ease of an arrival. "Diasporic spaces," Ahmed notes, "do not simply begin to take shape with the arrival of migrant bodies; it is more that we only notice the arrival of those who appear 'out of place.' Those who are 'in place' also must arrive; they must get 'here,' but their arrival is more easily forgotten, or is not even noticed" (pp. 9–10). My arrivals to community college, to a small liberal arts college, to two different PWI (predominantly white institutions) R1s as students are welcomed and accepting. In place, of time, belonging. My whiteness does not make my body a migrant body, but my grandma tells me to keep moving. In my arrivals to higher education, I definitely don't *feel* welcomed the way most of the time, and I often notice I am out of place, out of time, unbelonging, disoriented.

2 Of Hands

"Your hands are getting soft," my dad says as we greet each other with a handshake, "you ready to come back and do some real work? You ready to get back to your roots?" I feel the roughness of his hands, as well as the dirt and dust from working in the garage press against my palms and seep between my fingers. It's that August 2016 visit, and while I'm here for my grandma's birthday, there's plenty of time to get some other work done around the house. My dad's greeting pauses me, disorients me. As Ahmed notes, "disorientation is a way of describing the feelings that gather when we lose our sense of who it is that we are" (p. 20). She also writes that "[s]uch losses can be converted into the joy of a future that has been opened up" (p. 20). I chuckle at his comment and question, but this moment of loss doesn't feel joyful, and perhaps I haven't converted the loss. It feels like my hands failed. They have withered, no longer calloused or dexterous. I have uprooted the family tree. I'm out of line; we are not aligned.

(UN)BELONGING IN LIMINALITY

My dad and I walk over to the garage where he tells me some general ideas for how he wants it organized. After he walks off, I pause and a memory emerges.

It's an April Saturday in the early 1990s, and my dad and I are in the garage with the left front section of the family car, 1990 Ford Explorer, jacked up. We have to change the oil, and my dad slides the plastic oil drain pan and three empty gallon milk jugs over to me as I kneel on the concrete floor, ready to make my way under the truck. We'll fill the jugs with the old oil and dispose of it at some point, somewhere. Sometimes we take the oil filled jugs to an auto shop the same day for proper disposal. Other times, the jugs sit in the corner on the garage floor for weeks. In fact, I can see four black jugs out the corner of my eye as I lay on my back ready to slide myself under the truck.

"You gotta master this tool," my dad says as he hands me the 9/16 wrench that I need to unscrew the drain plug. I pause, looking up at his steely eyes and taking the stainless steel tool. I know he doesn't mean I have to learn how to use this tool at this particular moment. I've done this before, so it's not an instruction on how to drain the oil. "You gonna need to pick a trade," he continues. I know what he means. I may choose to be a mechanic, but I don't have to. While this wrench may not be used in every trade, I've got to master as many tools as I can. I could choose to be a carpenter or plumber or welder, which all have their tools. Whatever I pick, it's the tools I need to master. I nod to his comments, turn over on my back, and scootch, moving my back left and right to project myself forward, to position myself comfortably to unscrew the plug and drain the oil. You ain't gonna get far if you all thumbs. Or if you got idle hands.

This experience has always lingered with me. It shaped who I was/am; it informed me on what I (would) do; it directed me on when and where I (could) go. It turned me.

Six years later, I'm a high school senior sitting in my guidance counselor's office in Coal City, Illinois. He and I are trying to figure out what my schedule will be for this final year. "Which trade would you like to do for the afternoons? There's welding, heating and refrigeration, construction, and automotive?" he asks. I've had these kinds of meeting before with counselors. It's how I ended up taking all those masculine, working-class courses: small engine repair, wood fabrication, power mechanics, and so on. I don't remember exactly how I responded to this counselor's question, but I recall a quick decision and registration: automotive. Under their thumb, I get it: Brattas work in blue-collar jobs—ones that require some skills beyond simply flipping burgers, but not ones that require that Bachelor's. Echoing Marx, Ahmed remarks, "If the conditions in which we live are inherited from the past, then they are 'passed down' not only in blood or in genes, *but also through the work or labor of generations*" (p. 125). My hands will wrench.

3   Turnin' the Wrench

Thirteen years prior to sitting with Ahmed's book in my Lansing apartment—early September 2001—I work my fingers to the bone fifty-five hours a week on the clock, a Monday to Saturday job at Goodyear Tire and Automotive Shop in Phoenix, Arizona. The swamp coolers hang on the back wall of the shop garage, working non-stop to calm the scorching desert summer heat that floats in. We mechanics work just as much with nearly every hour booked with jobs. The manager, Carl, also insists on piling more work onto already packed days. Turn those jobs out, gotta move quicker. Get the work done. By this time though, I had somewhat learned the ramifications of always rebelling against most authority. Legal bills and lost jobs cost quite a bit. I had finally accepted what many working-class children come to understand about themselves and the world: listen and do as you're told because that'll be the norm with the boss.

For the first couple of years at Goodyear, I had moments where I longed for something more than the repetitive work orders day in, day out: replace the front brakes, drain and fill the transmission pan, change out the left and right front CV boots, rotate and balance the tires, replace the serpentine belts and radiator hoses, and so forth. I had no elbow room at this job, and I craved for conversations beyond typical shop talk with the other mechanics.

And then, September 11, 2001. Carl's office sits between the garage and waiting room, and through his office windows, I can see smoke from buildings and journalists speculating on the TV. I've got a car in one of the bays, but I'm more interested in what's on the tube. "Get back to work," Carl says as he leaves his office and comes into the garage, "ain't nuttin we can do." I glance at him, nod, and (re)turn to the car while he continues to stand over me, hovering. I guess he's right. I think to myself: "What are we mechanics in Phoenix going to do 2,400 miles away?" But that's a boring question, an apathetic question, and I quickly move on to a more interesting question: "What does this event mean and how and why did it happen?" I ponder in my head: "It must not have happened in a vacuum—an isolated incident with no prior conflicts. It's not some simple cause and effect, but it's got to be more complex, involve more assemblages, working parts." I lean over the car in my bay and do a safety check of its assemblages: belts and hoses, fluids and pulleys, and so on. I jot down my assessment on the work order, and then I pause, thinking about the relationship between mechanical units and hoses, pulleys and belts, sensors and shafts—some seen, others concealed.

I hear Carl walk back into his office to answer the phone, and I look to my right where another mechanic is wrenchin' away. "Why do you think planes were flown into those buildings?" I ask him. "Those Arabs hate our freedoms," he quickly responds. Another mechanic standing nearby chimes in, "hey, you look a little Arab, Phil. You or your cousins coordinate this?" This isn't the first time in my life where someone has said or asked if I was Arab (or Lebanese or Egyptian or Persian or Chaldean or any other other). His comment is in jest, and I uncomfortably chuckle, returning to my safety check and knowing I can't get into a long conversation about 9/11 or these mechanics' comments. "Fuck, I need to get out of here," I think to myself. Besides these co-workers aren't actually interested in discussing politics or culture in any deep way. Simple answers to simply get back to work and get paid. I was out of line, out of place in the garage.

4 To Desire

Such moments reflect some kind of desire rather than identification or social identity. As busy as my hands were, they desired a greater intimacy, proximity with the nameless. I couldn't turn to the back of my hands to find direction. I had to dwell in the inexpressible slippage.

Jacques Lacan would explain to me that desire is desire for the Other—the Law of the Father, the Nation, etc. Desire for recognition from the Other/others. But desire can never be filled; a lack in the fragmentation of the self. Eternally longing as the mirror appeared, fracturing the self, the lack gets the last laugh. Gilles Deleuze and Félix Guattari (1987) would tell me: "you can't reach it, you are forever attaining it, it is a limit" (p. 150). Desire can/will eventually move us to act. After another year or two of working on cars, I came to realize a desire for certain kinds of conversations, as well as work that makes a difference in the world, that contributes to communities. I had been working for the garage, but the garage wasn't working for me. I was always looking *at* rather than *from* the garage. My body never felt comfort, felt at home under a car; it was misaligned. Desire, of course, isn't (about) comfort (although it most certainly can be); it isn't (about) home either, whether we think of home as a place, paradigm, or feeling (although we can desire a place, paradigm, or feeling). Desire is that ineffable tread with ephemeral moments that both pull apart the seams and stitch together the folds of the body. While I couldn't name the kinds of conversations and thinking I longed for, I nevertheless felt that I needed other spaces, other relations, other practices that could extend my mind, reshape my body. My body must move, pass through.

5 Liminality

Liminality indicates a passing through, a transitory and temporary state as one moves into the next phase, step, chapter. Scholars have examined the concept of liminality in various ways. In his research on social movements, Guobin Yang (2000) states that "a liminal situation is characterized by freedom, egalitarianism, communion, and creativity. Freedom results from a rejection of those rules and norms that have structured social action prior to the liminal situation" (p. 383). In his study of the rituals of the Nbembu tribe, Victor Turner (1974) suggests that liminal space is "ambiguous, neither here nor there, betwixt and between all fixed points of classification" (p. 232). And Gloria Anzaldúa (2002) provides a crucial understanding of liminal space, where borders and borderlands—both their geopolitical constructions and their symbolic and social functionality on bodies—construct more permanent, oppressive dwellings for bodies (e.g., the migrant or the queer). Anzaldúa writes, "Bridges span liminal (threshold) spaces between worlds, spaces I call "nepantla," a Nahuatl word meaning "tierra entre medio." Nepantla es tierra desconocida, and living in this liminal zone means being in a constant state of displacement—an uncomfortable, even alarming feeling" (p. 1).

What does it mean for me to *feel* that I consistently, perhaps permanently occupy liminal space—whether under the car, in the classroom, on the page—given my dominant and privileged subjectivity? Part of that feeling grows from an uncertainty. As someone with advanced degrees (the firsts in my family) and a professorship position at an R1, am I now an intellectual? Does my history of labor, my familial narrative of work not matter anymore (when did my class identity disappear? where did it go?)? How did I manage to slip through the cracks into this privileged career? Certainly, in many ways my body is welcomed in academia as a white male subject and identity. But maybe these questions reflect a binary paradigm: intellectual or laborer. I have to choose a side; can't be both. Two separate sides, borders mark their space.

6   Crossing

After I quit working at Goodyear, I go to a community college, hoping that some classes might give me direction in what I could do. They don't, and after two semesters, I drop out and return to Goodyear. Over the next year and a half at Goodyear, I experience the same frustrations and uncomfortability. I decide I really do need to figure something else out, so I quit for a second time, attend a different Maricopa County community college, and take on part-time gigs: car wash attendant, telemarketer, restaurant server and bartender, grocery store clerk, and festival security guard.

It's spring 2006, and I'm at this second community college taking a Humanities Survey class taught by Sandra Desjardins. Over the fifteen weeks, the class discusses various European, Latin American, and African art movements in the nineteenth and twentieth centuries. Throughout the course, Sandra emphasizes the power of art for social causes, the entanglement of art and politics, and the value of the arts in what it means to be human in all these movements. At the end of the semester, I visit Sandra at her office, wanting to thank her for the course, but also to chat more about art, philosophy, and culture. "You've shown quite an interest in the material this semester," she remarks. "You should go get a bachelor's degree." I blush and stumble in head with how to react to such remarks. "In what?," I wonder to myself "and how?"

I simply respond with a "thank you" and shut down because I don't know what else to say. But I think Sandra notices my excitement, insecurity, and ignorance, and she mentions several potential degrees and the process for transferring to a four-year institution. I had already had difficulty in figuring out various academic processes (shit, even registration for courses every semester felt like being on another planet, something that would continue in my undergraduate and graduate studies). Jennifer Beech (2006) notes that "for those of us who are nonmainstream students, school enacts a secondary pedagogy that runs counter to our home worldviews or our primary pedagogies, but for mainstream students, schooling is a continuation of their primary pedagogies" (p. 18). But Sandra guides me over the next three weeks and writes a letter of recommendation for my application to Columbia College Chicago, which I chose because of its open admissions and low tuition (at the time), as well as its student population: artists.

In mid-June, I hear back from Columbia: acceptance. As I read the letter, I'm excited. But I also think to myself: "Is this where I belong?"

7   In (Un)Belonging

Acceptance. Member of. Fitting in. Sense of. Feeling. Unbelonging induces imposter syndrome. In the classroom, in faculty meetings, and at academic conferences, imposter syndrome creeps under my skin, impressing fears. As Nancy Mack (2017) notes, imposter syndrome in academia "can engage a number of contradictory behaviors ... [f]earing exposure from failure can manifest in perfectionism, workaholic tendencies, saying yes to all opportunities, and being overly charming. Fearing exposure through success might lead to self-doubt, procrastination, avoiding risk, and not applying for rewards or advancement" (p. 145). All these fears have gripped me at various times in my undergraduate studies, graduate studies, and faculty life. Syndromes are considered medical indicators of a disorder, disease. Dis-ease: I lack intelligence, intellectual ability, emotional (middle-class) management, proper etiquette. In-between between intellectual and laborer.

Simultaneously, I arguably do not live in an in-between. Edie-Marie Roper and Mike Edwards (2017) remark, "working-class ... sometimes has the curious potential to obscure other identifiers and their positions in relations of domination" (p. 106). Good point. While I have not only advanced degrees now, I am seen as a white man. People of color, women, disabled, and queer people live much more clearly in in-between spaces. So, what does it mean for me to say I live in the in-between? What does it mean for me to *feel* in an in-between space? (Un)Belonging—neither as a mechanic in the garage or as a gopher on the construction site nor as a teacher, researcher, and student in the academy. To take on, to own that feeling of (not) belonging, I write and long to understand and practice the desires. Hands are key(s). "The work of hands," Malcolm McCullough (1998) notes, "intrigues us more than most other forms of action. The hands can lend an interest to full bodily exertion, as in sport, but they can also act as guides or outlets for intellectual endeavor, as in art" (p. 6). Are my hands the location of the in-between? What if my hands work in the both-and rather than an either-or? What desires may open?

8 Walking Memories

It's February 2013, and my friend Jake and I stroll through an industrial park in Gainesville, Florida. We wander along the streets and gravel sidewalks, trying to "construct epiphanies," which Greg Ulmer had assigned us to do. We are both graduate students in Ulmer's graduate seminar Ubiquitous Imaging, and one of the goals of the course is to theorize and explore our everyday experiences. In doing so, we have to be attentive to recurring ideas, affects, and practices, noting patterns that can direct, or redirect, our *einstellung*, a German word roughly meaning the attitude in which one approaches something, psychologically or ethically. Identifying and acknowledging one's *einstellung* is a way of attuning oneself to the moment and "taking it in." Ulmer has added another layer: attunement with one's *einstellung* enables one to understand oneself in the macrocosm and have prudence, or the ability to make flash decisions, in their everyday lives and during moments of political discussions and social tensions.

Jake and I chose the industrial park randomly, but also in convenience as the park is near my Gainesville apartment and within walking distance. We both find value and pleasure in walking and talking, and as we saunter down one street, we notice the numerous machine shops and distribution warehouses

(UN)BELONGING IN LIMINALITY

populating the east and west side of it. We have our phones in hand, taking pictures of sites or scenes or objects that speak to us (as Ulmer had instructed us to do).

We won't think long about what we take pictures of or how and why; that'll come over the next couple of weeks as we search for patterns.

For now, we simply need to find and capture moments that prick us, or the punctum. For Roland Barthes (1982), the *punctum* is allegedly beyond representation as it "break[s] (or punctuate[s]) the *studium*," which is a culturally created and motivated part of a text. The punctum "rises from the scene, shoots out of it like an arrow, and pierces" (p. 26). Barthes suggests that the *punctum* is a "sting, speck, cut, little hole—and also a cast of the dice. A photograph's *punctum* is that accident which pricks me (but also bruises me, is poignant to me)" (p. 27). We are often drawn to images because of their *studium*. But images can also have a deeply personal affective meaning on the viewer—found in the details, piercing us in a way that rationalization of the moment, if it ever happens, cannot be communicated, articulated.

After reaching the end of the street, Jake and I turn left and stroll over to the next street, which includes some auto shops—more abandoned ones than operating ones. "That's interesting, but unsurprising," I think to myself. We walk for about fifty feet, chatting and looking around at the buildings, fences, vehicles, etc. "I'm going to go check out that yard," I say to Jake as I point at the backyard of an out of business auto shop. Coming around the corner of the shop's building, I pause. I slowly glance over the whole yard. Seven stacked used tires. The bed of a pickup truck—faded maroon with powdered white and daffodil yellow bondo fiberglass strips and spots along the sides and edges—sits vertical to the ground, as if the truck's cab is six feet under and I'm really just looking at the tombstone. Two small 1980s motorcycles sit with a pile of rusted brake rotors resting upon the wheels. Next to them is an engine block half-rusted, half-torn apart, resting on its end. My hands feel pricked, shoulders feel heavy. A memory of a philosophy, a belief, a desire emerges: At Goodyear, I often thought how the work I was doing wasn't really contributing to others and community. I longed to have complex conversations with co-workers and friends. I desired to engage with others about complex issues and contribute to the well-being of communities.

Another memory emerges. It's in the early 2000s, and I'm on the phone with my dad.

"I think I'm going to quit Goodyear and stop working on cars altogether," I say.

"Well, what's your plan?" he responses, "what are you gonna do?"

"I'm not sure."

"Maybe you should stay working on cars."

"Maybe I'll go to college."

"For what? What are you gonna do there that you can't already do now?"

Patterns. Threads. Traces. Out of service, abandoned auto shops. Such sites feel comforting as I roam the yard. At Goodyear, I knew my place in the garage, even if I didn't feel in my place in the garage. There's a difference between knowing and feeling. Nostalgia. Writing about this difference solidifies a conflicting nostalgia. bell hooks (2009) is right: "Writing about the past often places one at risk for evoking a nostalgia that simply looks back with longing and idealizes. Locating a space of genuineness, of integrity as I recall the past and endeavor to connect it to the ideals and yearnings of the present has been crucial to my [creativity, aesthetic, and imaginative] process" (pp. 4–5). What happens when a nostalgia confirms a decision to unreturn to the past despite some sense of familiarity, of belongingness?

9   Moving

In my dad's garage on that August 2016 day, I put tools back up on the pegboard and organize the space for my dad and his work. After ten minutes, I pause and look through the semi-grimy, hazy window *at* my grandma *from* the garage. My grandma steadily works at the soil in pulling weeds, the flora that doesn't belong. Bending down, gripping a few weeds, standing upright, and stepping a foot forward, only to bend back down and repeat, she completes the task at hand. Her body has slowed down in the last couple of years, but for being eighty-six years old today, she moves at an admirable pace. Determined, invested, passionate. She moves with a rhythm of a life, a desire to work. To work is a life worth living, a life of meaning. For now though, I think to myself that I should probably go see if she wants to take a break and have another cigarette. I want to chat more about working and moving.

Acknowledgment

I would like to thank Rachel Jackson for her time and labor with feedback on an early version of this chapter.

References

Ahmed, S. (2006). *Queer phenomenology: Orientations, objects, others.* Duke UP.

Anzaldúa, G. E. (2002). Preface: (Un)natural bridges, (Un)safe spaces. In G. E. Anzaldúa & A. Keating (Eds.), *This bridge we call home: Radical visions for transformation* (pp. 1–5). Routledge.

Barthes, R. (1982). *Camera Lucida: Reflections on photography* (R. Howard, Trans.) (2nd ed.). Hill and Wang.

Beech, J. (2006). Happy accidents: The unofficial story of how i became an academic. In S. L. Muzzatti & C. V. Samarco (Eds.), *Reflections from the wrong side of the tracks: Class, identity, and the working class experience in academe* (pp. 9–21). Rowman & Littlefield Publishers, Inc.

Deleuze, G., & Guattari, F. (1987). *A thousand plateaus: Capitalism and schizophrenia* (B. Massumi, Trans.). U of Minnesota P.

hooks, b. (2009). *Belonging: A culture of place.* Routledge.

Mack, N. (2017). Emotional labor as imposters: Working-class literacy narratives and academic identities. In G. M. Carter & W. H. Thelin (Eds.), *Class in the composition classroom* (pp. 140–160). Utah State UP.

McCullough, M. (1998). *Abstracting craft: The practiced digital hand.* The MIT Press.

Roper, E. M., & Edwards, M. (2017). Changing definitions of work and class in the information economy. In G. M. Carter & W. H. Thelin (Eds.), *Class in the composition classroom* (pp. 104–123). Utah State UP.

Turner, V. (1974). *Dramas, fields, and metaphors: Symbolic action in human society.* Cornell UP.

Villanueva, V. (1993). *Bootstraps: From an American academic of color.* National Council of Teachers of English.

Yang, G. (2000). The liminal effects of social movements: Red guards and the transformation of identity. *Sociological Forum, 15*(3), 379–406.

CHAPTER 7

Book Smart AND Street Smart

Valerie Murrenus Pilmaier

When people find out about my background, they often remark, "Your family must be so proud of you!" I honestly have no idea how to respond. Yes, on a cursory level, sure, they are very proud of me, as a Ph.D. is a huge achievement and having tenure is phenomenal. But this remark belies something much darker, something that I have been trying to figure out for many years myself: I am not certain that they really are proud of me because I think they feel that I have betrayed them. For many years, I felt like I lived in the Upside-Down. No, I don't have a demi-gorgon chasing me through a dank netherworld, but I do have to navigate economic class identities within my own family, and that can be equally exhausting. As a first-generation working-class woman who "made it" (definition to follow), I often feel like I inhabit two worlds but never fully belong to either. By "made-it," I mean that I have a terminal degree and tenure, and I, therefore, work at a job where my labor is mental rather than physical. Unlike most of my relatives, I am not required to scrub oil off of my hands at the end of the day, I can take off when my kids are sick or I need to ferret them to doctor's appointments without risking getting written up, and I have the luxury of teaching either at night or online during the summer, so I am a "stay-at-home" mom during that time. I genuinely enjoy my job and live the "life of the mind." However, in order to have this, I had to leave my extended family behind.

Objectively, you could look at my life and say that I am living The American Dream. It's true; I am. What enabled this for me were the sacrifices of my parents. I was not the one who grew up without heat and electricity and had to go to work at age 11 to provide money for the family—that was my mother. I was not the one beaten repeatedly for the smallest real or imagined infraction by an alcoholic father who held a steady job infrequently—that was my father. Their stories became a part of my story in a way that they can never become a part of my own children's stories. My parent's gift to me of social mobility enabled me to live a life I cherish, but it has exacted a personal toll of familial estrangement and class liminality, which are things that my own children will never understand. Indeed, my children are the children of a lawyer and a professor, and they are rooted solidly in the middle to upper-middle class. They will never know the pride—and guilt—of "making it." They will never worry that their dialect, whether around colleagues or around their own family, betrays them. They will never wonder if they are following the correct rules or understand all of the social mores of the class they now inhabit or the one they left behind. They know how to do it correctly because they do not have to code-switch to survive.

My own story begins with that of my parents. You could consider this a prime example of bootstrap theory, except I think it was rooted as much in dumb luck and circumstance as in hard work. At age 19, my father was drafted into the Army where he flew and fixed helicopters. When he returned home, he resumed the job that was saved for him (luck), a solid factory job in the inner-city that he had acquired only three months prior to leaving for Vietnam. This job changed my father's life. For the first time, he was at a place where he made good money doing an honest day's work, he had benefits from being in the union and he had paid vacation. Realizing that this factory had the potential to bring them all out of poverty into the middle class, he proceeded to recommend all of his family for jobs at Master Lock, and one by one, they were hired on the line and started to climb the ladder out of poverty. Recognizing my father's quick mind, the management invited my father to enter the apprentice program and over many years, he became a journeyman machinist and, later, even a Union representative. My father occupied the most prestigious positions that could be held by a laborer at Master Lock, and he was very proud of his job and his place of employment.

My mother, who once aspired to be a concert musician and had to turn down a college scholarship because she became pregnant prior to *Roe v. Wade*, spent forty years on the line assembling lock bodies, which exacted a toll on her body that crippled her hands, gave her carpal-tunnel and blew out her knees. Because she considered her friends on the line her family, she never applied for transfer to a job that was less demanding on her body. However, this physical labor translated into an ability to pay off the house in the suburbs in 20 years instead of 30, put one child through college and then provide a dream wedding for that child, and help raise her other child's son. This factory job bought the middle-class life for her children that she had always wanted to have for herself.

For our family, Master Lock was the goose that laid the golden egg. At one time, going to the Master Lock picnics was like going to a family reunion because my aunts, my uncles (on both sides), my mother and even my brother were all employed there. The factory system moved my entire family from working-class to middle-class, thus enabling me to achieve what my grandparents never even dreamed possible for working-class kids from the slums.

Before we moved to the suburbs, our entire family (both my mother's and father's) lived within a four-block radius in Riverwest in Milwaukee, which is where they all grew up. Perhaps due to the bonding that comes of poverty and childhood trauma, all of my aunts and uncles were extremely tight-knit. Friday night was cribbage night, and all of the relatives would gather at one house with games that would last to the wee hours of the night. I remember a haze of cigarette smoke and the sound of laughter, sitting on my mom's lap while she was playing her hand or bringing my dad a beer before running out of the door with my cousins to play ghost in the graveyard. While I had friends at school, I considered my cousins my "real" friends because I spent the most time with them. As the youngest girl, I received a lot of attention from my family and always felt loved and visible. They knew everything about me and I belonged.

Therefore, moving to the suburbs caused me to miss them terribly. My family believed in upward mobility, so as soon as they were able, they sold their tiny house in the city and moved us to the suburbs. Because it now took half an hour to get to my relatives' houses in Milwaukee, weekly parties turned to bimonthly, then monthly, then sporadic or limited to holidays.

As a city kid who loved the noise and excitement of the city and who was used to houses almost touching and being able to walk to see any member of my family, the suburbs were daunting. The houses were all so big and spread apart. No one seemed to talk to one another in our subdivision. The other kids went to public school and did not want to associate with us "city kids" who went to Catholic school. At our school, no one else's parents worked at Master Lock or even in factories, it seemed. Most kids had a mom that didn't work and if she did, she didn't have dirty hands when she came home. Most kids had a dad who wore a white button-down shirt and a tie. Most kids had parents who talked like tv announcers, unlike my parents whose vocabulary included phrases (such as "shoot the shit" or any such liberal peppering of all conversation with swear words), distinctly linked to working-class Milwaukee and factory life.

With more time at my disposal because we weren't always with our relatives anymore and since I had no friends in our subdivision and didn't understand how play dates with kids from school worked quite yet, I became a really bookish kid. I had always been precocious and gravitated toward books, but the isolation of the suburbs, the othering I experienced as the new "city" "working-class" kid at school, and my newfound social anxiety caused me to tumble down the rabbit hole of reading. I read everything I could get my hands on: Little Golden Books, Disney Books, library books, and even romance novels. I couldn't wait to get home from school to pick up my book because I felt that was where my real life existed. There I didn't have to worry about wearing the wrong clothes, saying the wrong thing or having no friends. There all of the stress melted away and everything just made sense. I was home. As my reading increased, so did my aptitude in school. All of the subjects, especially reading and math, became exciting to me and I found myself gravitating toward other students who enjoyed them as well. I began spending time with the children of learned people and having conversations with their parents about these subjects in ways that I couldn't with my own parents. It wasn't their fault, but I couldn't see that at the time. Since the house they bought was more expensive than they could actually afford, my dad spent all of his spare time fixing up cars to sell for extra money. I only saw him at dinner and right before I went to bed. My mother was forever doing chores or making dinner, with any extra time spent watching mindless television as an escape from her day of toil at the factory. I was allowed to talk to her when I was doing my homework while she was making dinner, but I learned not to bother her with my incessant questions or insights when she was relaxing. I went from being the center of attention of everyone in my family in Milwaukee to feeling invisible in Menomonee Falls. The only place that felt welcoming was inside the world of books. My parents encouraged this in me as much as possible as they felt that this was a building block to a new life. I was the one who would do what they were unable to do and go to college. I would have a different life. I would be successful.

This also translated into my relationships with my extended family. When we lived close to them, they knew every aspect of my life because they lived it with me, but now, they only knew what my parents or I would choose to tell them. Since my parents didn't have the energy and I didn't have the words, my existence became equated with how well I was doing in school. I became the "book-smart" kid, which was both a cause of pride (Valerie was smart; Valerie would go to college) as well as a place of scorn. As all working-class kids know, "book smart" means that you might know a lot of information or have a great deal of knowledge, but you have no common sense. My mother explained this to me thousands of times and always punctuated it with, "You are book smart. Your brother is street-smart. We worry more about you." I tried to suggest that a person could be both, but that answer was never acceptable: "You are either book smart or street smart. You cannot be both." Since I was this thing that was special but different from everyone else, I started to feel uncomfortable talking about myself and my interests. I wanted to hide all of that so that I could just belong and be like them again. However, the longer we lived in the suburbs and the better I did in school, the deeper the divide. What started out as distancing from adults then trickled down to my cousins, and I got the reputation of being boring, bookish and square.

My parents underscored me as being different, as college-bound and not meant for menial labor, whenever possible. While kindly meant, it translated into shame for me. They came from a background where you undervalue your merits and over-emphasize your faults, so the stories that they told about me started with the good things but always ended with the ridiculous: "she had the highest math score in the class but she sprained her ankle because she was walking and didn't notice the curb; later that day, instead of turning off the stove when she was done making her lunch, she left it on and could have burned the whole house down: book-smart. She has to go to college because she can't make it in the real world." Looking back, I think they were trying to prepare my family (and reinforce to me) that I would not follow their path but would choose a different one. However, at that time, it only meant stinging humiliation and proof that I didn't belong in my family, unlike my brother.

My brother and I followed very different paths in life. I believe that he has an undiagnosed reading disability, and, as such, he never excelled in school. For him, school meant humiliation and shame. Being incredibly bright, he excelled at manual tasks and verbal puzzles, but this doesn't count in school. He spent more time outside of school than in it, so he was constantly in detention or in trouble. While this upset my parents, it didn't bother them nearly as much as it should have. Therefore, the stories that they told about my brother were met very differently. For him, the narrative was always flipped. His stories started out with not doing well in school but ended with what extracurricular activities (sports, mechanics, fishing) he did do well, proving that he could "make-it" in the "real world" because he was "street smart." This made sense to my family as none of them finished high school (save a few cousins and my mother). Further, they enjoyed all of the things that he enjoyed, so it was further proof that he belonged with them. They had a common language that I was not privy to, and it emphasized that I belonged in a different world.

When I would talk, my family members would talk about how "rich" I sounded and how "fancy" I was now that I lived in the suburbs. I now think that they were proud of me, but I only heard mockery. I was encouraged to talk about the grades I received or the awards that I won, but I realized that no one could relate to what I was talking about and I found it easier to change the subject when their eyes would glaze over when I was describing the latest academic achievement. I learned to be very quiet and melt into the background. I no longer rushed to hug my aunts and uncles when they came, and instead tried to hide. Instead of talking with my cousins, I would hide in my room, bury my head in a book or watch tv. I was both othered and othering myself.

Since I had been in the suburbs since the second grade, I felt able to navigate the rules of life there. This did not translate to my parents, who were friendly with other parents and people but never made any real friends there. They lived in the suburbs, but their hearts were still in the same enclave of Milwaukee that they came from, so all of our interactions were either with family members or friends of theirs from the factory.

I, of course, made friends with the kids at school, which was encouraged by my parents, who wanted us to fully embrace the suburban lifestyle, so my brother and I were able to engage in any activity that struck us: swimming, softball, baseball, football, volleyball, etc. We had the typical suburban upbringing: huge yard, lots of extracurricular activities, after school jobs to make pin money for ourselves. Even though our family had very little disposable income, they made sure to work overtime so that we could wear the latest fashions (but it had to be on sale and we couldn't go overboard) and take advantage of all of the special things at school that they could never dream of attending (or being offered to attend) at their own schools (a canoe trip to the Boundary Waters, a school trip to Germany).

Because my brother was two years ahead of me at the same high school, going there seemed more comfortable than frightening. He was not a good student, so I was considered a "wunderkind": I remained in the top 5% of my student class of 281 each year, even making number 10 out of 281 my first semester in school. I did just about everything and won just about every academic award. It was proof to me that I was good at school and should go to college. My parents dutifully paid for a weekend of SAT prep for me and I sat the exam. We attended panel discussions on different colleges and had lengthy arguments about where I should apply: I wanted to go to a either Marquette University or St. Norbert's College because I felt they were more prestigious and I had won scholarships to attend both, while they wanted me to go to UW Oshkosh because they could afford it. The state school won out.

College was daunting. I felt like I had "nailed" it with high school, but college was so different. I purposefully picked a school that none of my high school friends would attend because I wanted a new adventure, but I had no idea how marginalizing that would prove. By a twist of fate, the roommate assigned to me chose not to attend at the last minute, so I had no "buddy" to commiserate with at night during those first lonely months at college. I was completely out of my comfort zone and had no idea how to make it more comfortable. I had huge pit classes (for all but my English classes) and it was a sea of faces alien to me. It felt like everyone else understood exactly how everything worked, except for me and I, again, was that scared kid who wanted to hide because I didn't have the words to even ask the questions if I did find the right person to ask. I wasn't supposed to see my advisor until much later in the semester to sign up for classes, so that wasn't an option. The friends I amassed were equally clueless, and we all felt like inhabitants of the Island of Misfit Toys, but our sense of otherness cemented us together.

I also couldn't quite figure out the social scene. I briefly entertained the idea of pledging a sorority, but then decided that wasn't for me. I tried a variety of clubs but either never felt a connection with the other students or the clubs eventually went defunct. I was not a drinker (bad experience in high school), so attending parties was agonizing. To make matters worse, the school I attended had a "party school" reputation, so the culture revolved around drinking starting Thursday and extending to Saturday night with Sunday and Monday for recovery. Juxtapose this with me: the super nerd who traipsed to the library each Thursday to find the book to "date" for the weekend. My only vice was smoking, and this started as an act of rebellion in high school, it but proved beneficial to me at college because it led me to the Smoking Lounge, where I found some kindred spirits, all of whom ended up being slightly or manically depressed. It was here that we bonded over our differences. Linda, a Navy brat, just moved back to the States after living in Scotland for four years and then three in Germany, loved to shock unsuspecting Americans with her dark, European sense of humor, which drew me to her immediately. Michelle, in her ever-present bunny slippers, was the poster-child for depression and quickly realized college was not for her. Jessica disclosed that she had just been diagnosed with schizophrenia and forever put herself into dangerous situations with guys she dated. Sean w as 24 and a transplant from Oregon, brilliant and funny but awkward and out of place. They became my crew, but they all seemed to disappear at night and on the weekends.

I had plenty of acquaintances, but that wasn't enough for me. As a social person, I was used to having scads of different kinds of friends, but my once easy ability to make friends seemed to work only with the smoking kids. Looking back, I realize that I kept all of my non-smoking res hall friends at arm's length because they seemed to fit in too effortlessly, always happy, always smiling, only offering pleasantries. I felt like the Grim Reaper in comparison.

I think I could have weathered this if my grades had been solid, but for the first time in my life, school did not come easy. I studied and studied but couldn't figure out the right things to study, and ended earning bs, cs, and ds on my math and bio tests. Of course, I didn't ask for help because I didn't want to look stupid to the teacher. I hated my World Religions class because the professor droned on the entire hour, never once asking a question or coming up for air, so I found myself zoning out or doodling the entire class rather than paying attention. To my great shock, college German was infinitely more difficult than high school German, but at least the grandfatherly professor was funny and kind. The only class I excelled in was English Composition for Teachers, but that didn't count because English was in my wheelhouse. If I couldn't do well in that class, I didn't feel like there was any point to me even being in college. I had no idea who I was any longer and felt devastated by this change in identity: I started college as University Scholar but was kicked out of the program because I ended my first semester with a "C" average. Just months earlier, I was considered one of the smartest people in my high school class, and now I was praying that I would pass some of my classes. The sense of shame was stultifying.

I could not discuss any of this with my parents. They had sacrificed everything to get me there and were so proud that I was doing what they had only dreamed of. Furthermore, my grandfather was in hospice and they were shouldering that. He died over Thanksgiving break, which meant that I spent time with my whole family and felt like a fraud when they would ask how things were going in school. What could I say? I told stories about the gross food or my weird World Religions teacher or the huge pit classes, but I couldn't say that I was drowning. I had always been "book smart," so this was supposed to be my thing.

When I had sought help from an advisor, he told me to read the catalogue, and he did not think to ask how I was doing or what questions I had about college, so that was useless. I eventually found my footing, but that was through my own perseverance. I scoured the course catalogue and planned out my schedule for each semester myself, realizing that I did better with a packed schedule. I took courses that I needed as well as ones that sounded fascinating to me, which meant that I had a plethora of history and English classes, but I never intended on majoring in English because I did not want to be an elementary or high school teacher, and everybody knew that you could not get a job with an English or History degree. The English advisor turned out to be equally clueless, as he knew nothing about me, as I was just another name on the stack of hundreds of students he was assigned to advise. I knew that I had to go at this alone.

It wasn't until my actual English professors starting mentoring me during my Junior year, the year of the many English classes, that I began to see a degree in English as a possibility. Prior to this, English was going to be the conduit to law, but I started to realize that I didn't want to be a lawyer. I had no idea what I did want to be, but I knew that I wanted to gobble up as many English lit courses as I possibly could before I had to graduate and get a "real" job. Therefore, each semester, I plodded through my gen eds but gave myself a literature course as a reward. World literature lead to Medieval and then Renaissance to Shakespeare. One Winterim, I took Shakespeare II and blissfully plodded through blizzards and record windchills to make it to the three-hour class each day to delve deeper and deeper into the Bard' words. I could not believe that we were graded for reading, discussing and writing about literature. It seemed too good to be true. I literally took every British literature course that I could (even the Bible as Literature) because I was hooked.

As a result of my overwhelming enthusiasm, my English professors began to take a personal interest in me and seemed to be inviting me into a scholarly world that I had always so desperately wanted to be a part of: from the prodding of Dr. Roberts, I joined English Club and quickly became the VP. Because of Dr. Lopresti's class, I became a reviewer for the school's literary journal. With the finagling of Dr. Roberts and Dr. Lauter, I attended MLA in Chicago (for free!) and they also provided my transportation. I was personally invited by my professors to the English Department poetry readings and they asked my opinion about books to include in course curriculum. Because of Dr. Herzing's Romantics class, I felt confident enough to submit an essay I wrote for that class or a prestigious English Department scholarship and it won. I finally felt like I had found a home.

One by one, my English professors started asking me if I was going to take the GRE. GRE? What is that? What does that even mean? Go to grad school? For what? With what money? I shrugged off their belief in me because I felt it was a pipe dream for someone who could never come up with the cash that would be required to attend another two (or more) years of school. However, I never said that to my professors because I was too ashamed to admit it and too proud that they assumed that I was like those rich kids who could afford graduate school. It was during the spring of my Junior year that fate intervened in the form of one of my Brit Lit professors, Dr. Herzing, who looked at me and said, "so where are you applying to grad school?" and I looked at him blankly. "Dr. Herzing, I have no money. My parents sacrificed everything they had to get me through school, and I have to get a "real" job. I can't be a grade school or high school teacher because I think I would be bored to death. My parents are factory workers.

There is no way that I can go to grad school." With that, I assumed the conversation was over.

"I was you and you can do this. I promise." With those words, a whole new world opened up to me. I was dumbstruck to find that he had been just like me: the brainy kid of factory workers who fell in love with books but had no money for graduate school. Then he told me the thing that absolutely blew my mind: you do not pay for grad school in English. You get a TA or RA and they pay you. Shut the Front Door. I thought he was joking. I think he had to repeat it to me at least ten times. I still didn't believe it when I left, so I researched it and found that, yes, this was a thing. Not only that: this was a thing that could happen for me. And it did.

The rift with my family only intensified when I went to graduate school. At family gatherings during high school, I had learned to talk only of the ridiculous parts of school and emphasized stories of my life in "the real world"—waitressing or working as a maid, as these would be met with enthusiasm. When I decided to go to graduate school and no longer worked those jobs to get by, the equalizing stories disappeared. I was now teaching and taking classes. Complaining about grading or how much reading I was doing seemed privileged and, frankly, disgusting, compared with the physical realities of their day-to-day jobs. The first semester of graduate school seemed a repeat of my first semester in college: a very bumpy ride. While I sailed through my Restoration Literature course, I had major adjustment issues and ended up with a B in my History of the English Language class because I would talk myself into believing that every multiple choice answer on the scantron test was feasible. My professor, bewildered by how poorly I did on those tests when it was obvious from class discussion that I knew the material backwards and forwards, actually changed the final exam to an essay so that I could demonstrate my knowledge and not fail. I had no idea how to teach, so I "put on" an authoritative teaching persona for my first comp class and decided to be myself for the second. The first class was an absolute nightmare, ending with a student writing "Hey, teacher! Leave them kids alone!" in red pen at the bottom of his final essay. It was the worst experience of my teaching career and a reminder that I had to always my authentic self into the classroom.

 I had no idea how to process any of this. My first support system had been my parents, but it really was beyond them. At the beginning of the semester, my parents called me nightly to check up and I could translate teaching mishaps and triumphs easily enough, but I found that I didn't have the language to explain what I was learning in my courses or the difficulties I was facing in that world, nor did they have the capacity to understand the extent of my angst. It was ok to tell a funny story from teaching or vent about a student issue, but it was not ok to complain about the school part of grad school. The first time I complained about how hard my classes were and that I was feeling overwhelmed, my dad very quietly said, "I'd give anything to be in your shoes" and my heart broke. He had sacrificed so much so that I could do this, how could I possibly complain? I also had no idea how time is marked differently once you become a teacher: the never-ending stack of papers consumes every spare minute until you learn how to adjust. Ungraded assignments that demand quick comments, rough drafts, final drafts, revisions ... Student work was all-consuming and ever-present. The new demands of graduate school meant that I had less time to devote to family functions (even to my nuclear family) and this created a great deal of bitterness and resentment. When I decided not to attend my cousin's housewarming party because I had papers to grade and a paper to write, my mother and aunts tag-team called me, continuously, for two hours from the party and drunkenly yelled at me to come over. I did not relent and my mother promptly uninvited me from Easter. I was devastated.

I had no idea that I would be forced to choose between school and my family. When I couldn't come, I was told that I should not expect our family to come to my events if I couldn't be bothered to come to theirs, that I was acting like I was too good for everyone else and that I was now a big snob. I didn't only hear this from aunts, uncles, and cousins; I also heard it from my own mother. When I did come, I was met with "I can't believe that you actually decided to show" or "Hmmm, I guess you could find time in your busy calendar for your family, finally" or "Well, shouldn't we feel privileged that you bothered to actually come this time." When I didn't come, I was a cold bitch and when I did come, I was mocked.

I was invited to fewer and fewer family events, and after my father died, all communication from my family members ceased. I was now a tenured professor and working at a Two-Year University whose mission of access resonated strongly with me. I was not at a ritzy school. I did not make a lot of money. In fact, my teenaged son made more delivering pizzas than my take-home pay as a tenured professor in the UW system. I chose to teach those kids, like me, who needed reassurance that college was the right place for them, and I loved it.

Therefore, when my uncle died and I decided to attend the funeral, I wondered how I would be treated. Would I be welcomed? What would happen? I bet you will assume that everything was different and I was welcomed with open arms and it was a happily ever after, right? Wrong. I attended the mass and was in a pew by myself, and then made it a point to sit at a table with my family during the funeral dinner. During those two hours, my aunts said all of the biting things that they had always said to me, I swallowed it, politely hugged them, and left. After analyzing that interaction, I have come to recognize that I exist in a liminal state with my family that I will never be able to relinquish; I am a part of the family but by default. I can't blame them for how they feel because they are right: I wasn't there for a lot of their lives, just as they were not there for mine. There is a sadness in that. They do love me, but they will never know me because I will always be an example and not a real person to them. I am the one who got a Ph.D. and abandoned my family. They will never understand the emotional weight of the personal choices that I had to make to privilege my education. They will never understand the loneliness that I felt due to their rejection of me. They will never understand that I didn't know how to maintain ties while navigating a whole new world of higher education (where I felt like an imposter every day) and when I could finally go back to them because I had achieved my goal, the door to them was closed.

The shock of that struck me at my uncle's funeral—the door was closed and it was now too late. I had moved beyond them and they would never need me because they learned to live without me.

Given all this, I still do not regret my choice. What I do regret is that because I was the first, it was always only an either/or but never a both/and. Even with my parents, I often felt that I was betraying my family by choosing school even though they wanted me to choose school. I became the site of all of their fear of abandonment and class rejection and issues of self-worth. As the first, I had no idea how to ameliorate that and probably unintentionally exacerbated it. For me, they became the site of misunderstanding, being othered, and emotional rejection. I don't know how to fix that. Honestly, I don't know that it can be fixed.

I utilize all of this angst when I am working with my students. On the first day of class, I talk about being First-Generation and the daughter of factory workers. I talk about feeling like I didn't know how anything worked in college and I was too afraid to ask questions because I didn't know who to ask and then when I did, I didn't want them to think that I was stupid because I had to ask. At midterms and finals, I talk about how tough it is when your family pressures you to go to family functions and you can't because you have to study or finish an essay. I talk about how proud I am of them for making this investment in themselves and that they need to be proud of themselves, too, because sometimes support doesn't come from your family. I remind them that they do belong here, but if they feel like they don't to please come and talk to me because I know exactly what they have been through and I can help them see to the other side. I hope that my experience shows my students that this is possible for them, even if they don't have family support, and that it is worth it. Because all of it, all of it, WAS worth it. I love what I do and cannot think of a better career or one that would bring me more joy.

However, this has come at a cost: I am The American Dream my family worked for, but they no longer know how to see themselves in me and I refuse to apologize for what I have achieved. I can only hope that my story, and the stories of other First-Generation and Working-Class professors will enable our students' fulfillment of their own dreams to encompass both/and rather than either/or. For me, was it ever a choice? No; my family chose for me. Yet, this is not how it has to be for those coming after us. Our stories can be the bridge that we didn't have when we were on the journey and can serve as a source of support when it feels like no one is there holding them up. We are there and we made it. They will, too.

CHAPTER 8

"Remember the Spartans"

William Thelin

My dad would use these words as a rallying cry for us three boys—my brothers Rick and Dave and I—when difficulties confronted us, and he did not want to hear us whine, to use his term. As a professor of English now, winding down my career, it strikes me how odd the expression was for a family living in northwest Glendale in southern California. We lived in an exclusive neighborhood, bordering the hills. Homes of millionaires and those close to it surrounded us. The current value of our home, built in 1963, is 1.5 million. A sturdy colonial style house, it now looks better on the outside than on the inside, which is saying something because the exterior features a crumbling retaining wall, an ugly chain link fence my mom erected to separate our property line from the neighbors, and a sunroom added in the 1990's that is not up to code and shows it. But at one time, it was the most prominent house on the block, the only two-story structure allowed due to zoning regulations, set nicely away from the street and with a view out into the city below.

The house represents all of the contradictions of my upbringing. It suggested wealth and refinement, yet the upkeep was lacking. As all houses do, it needed painting after a few years, but my parents let that go to the point that chips were noticeable everywhere, especially on the garage door and shutters. Inside, the house was worse. The living room furniture, mismatched to begin with, had tears in them with stuffing coming out. If something broke, it remained that way, be it an electrical outlet or a television. I remember one summer where my brother Rick and I would go across the street once a week—it might have been on Wednesdays—to watch the cartoon, "Where's Huddles?" Our neighbors Mr. and Mrs. Roberts were very nice about it, but they would ask occasionally, "So when is your mom going to have someone over to look at the tv?" But that wasn't going to happen. My mom had obsessive-compulsive disorder (undiagnosed until years later), so she would not throw out toys or clothes that we had outgrown. Boxes of old clothes lined the walls of her bedroom, and my dad always thought he would be suffocated if an earthquake hit and the clothes tumbled down on him. Baskets of toys and stuffed animals were stacked against the hallway walls and in our closets. She could not find the time to cook, so we ate Swanson's TV Dinners every night. She did not trust us to throw out the foil containers they were cooked in, and she never did it herself, so she had us push the containers into the middle of the table to make room for the next dinner. Our dining room table looked like someone had poured a trash can over it.

From this upbringing, I emerged. From an early age, I wanted to escape the system, to not devote my labor to making someone else wealthy. Maybe this came from my dad's muttered complaints about the "old money" in the neighborhood or some subconscious conflation of the conflicts in my house as the norm, but I was skeptical of wealth accumulation. I desired to escape it all, to write novels and leap out of the system, so I studied English, as it seemed less constrained than other areas of study. I went to state schools, first for my BA, and then for my MA. I worked full-time, doing unskilled, often arduous labor during the day at Kaiser Medical Center and attending classes three nights a week until my first degree was completed. It turns out writing requires time, and when a person works and goes to school as much as I did, those spare hours for writing the great American novel do not exist. I continued working at the medical center on the weekends while I had a teaching assistantship during my MA, staying at it almost until I left for my PhD in Pennsylvania. I figured I could enter academia and start a career that would give me the time to write. There, though, I married, and having to support a baby that came quicker than we expected, took a teaching position at the University of Cincinnati, where I eventually got tenure. But the position paid very little money, so I sought out and accepted another position at the University of Akron, where I currently work.

I still have no novel to my credit. Instead, I wrote articles about composition studies, where I noticed that so much of the theory and research seemed to have a certain stereotype of a middle-class student as its model. I puzzled over this, as I saw it as my duty as a professor to make education accessible to all. But academia, I discovered, was far removed from this mission, and it unveiled itself as just the type of system I had always wanted to escape. In fact, it reflected the class system in America. Part-time adjunct labor did the real work in the classroom for undergraduates, while privileged professors taught less labor-intensive classes. Programs designed to accommodate open-admissions students received little financial support from the university, lacking funds for resources. Faculty consigned to them taught more classes than other faculty across the university and did not receive released time for research or professional development, as administrators assumed no connection between the quality of teaching and additional knowledge in one's field, much less the need to study the type of students who populated such programs. Prestigious universities and the experiences that go with them flood the media as the representation of college life, but they mask the tension between what I believe are working-class sensibilities and middle-class, elite ambitions. Like my family's house, academia looks good on the outside but is highly dysfunctional and abusive on the inside. In many ways, this tension reflects my life.

•••

"Remember the Spartans!"

Much went wrong in my upbringing that can be traced to my mother's OCD. Many people think those with OCD are obsessively organized or perhaps tidy to a fault. That wasn't the case with my mother. She desired to have everything perfect, as one might expect, but this made the smallest of household duties and even personal hygiene a chore. She did not like to do chores, so she avoided them. If one of our shirts lost a button, she would take it to sew a new one on, but could never get to anything right away, so she'd put it in a pile with the other clothes that required patches or some form of sewing and never do it. After a while, we boys knew giving her an item of clothing was tantamount to never seeing it again, so we stopped giving them to her. She had to inspect every dish to make sure no food particles remained on them.

She would count as she turned a bowl over in her hand: "1, 2, 3, 1, 2, 3" and then finish with, "Okay, okay. Fine, fine" before putting the dish away. This process was grueling for her so her solution was not to do the dishes. When that didn't work, she turned to paper plates and Styrofoam cups. She rarely showered because of the ordeal she made of it. She'd always take the phone off the hook so she would not be interrupted and then soap and scrub her body endlessly. We'd hear her say, "Body, body, body. Arms, arms, arms. Legs, legs, legs" over and over again. She was simply a wreck and was incapable of raising three boys.

When the three of us got of age where we realized the way we lived was not normal, we would occasionally talk about it to friends. While most would just say, "That's weird," and move on, word would trickle back to their parents. There would be some whispers about how the Thelin boys lived, some blaming us for keeping our mother so occupied with sports teams, trouble at school, or whatever else that she couldn't do. The truth is that my dad handled most everything that concerned us. He'd drive us to school, bathe us, and keep track of all of the recreational activities. I played baseball, basketball, and football throughout my childhood. My mother never attended one game. We sure as hell were not keeping her too preoccupied to take care of the household. When more observant parents noticed that she was never around, we would say she was sick. She did, in fact, have multiple physical problems, but it was her obsession over them, not the conditions themselves, that kept her away. Things had to be perfect so if she wasn't regular or had nasal drainage or experienced pain of any sort, she sought out all remedies, driving many doctors crazy to the point some wrote her off as a hypochondriac. Far too many, though, wrote out prescriptions quite liberally that later led to her addiction to pain medication that haunted her for the rest of her life. Our friends' parents knew nothing about this. They believed my mother was debilitated to the point she could not take care of us.

"Why doesn't your father hire a maid and a cook?" Mrs. Taylor once asked me.

Unspoken in her question was where we lived. Surely people living in the hills—the rich folk—could afford to get some help in the house. Your dad needs to loosen the purse strings. I could only shrug. I knew the answer. We could not afford any type of help. Unlike our neighbors, my dad made ends meet paycheck to paycheck. We did not have any savings or assets. There was no money left over at the end of the month. But my dad would never admit this to anyone, not to his family or friends or well-intentioned teachers wondering if everything was all right at home. My dad had come too far to be thought financially in ruins.

•••

"Remember the Spartans!"

My dad was raised in near poverty by immigrant parents. Four of his siblings did not survive childhood, one dying as an infant. I never met my grandfather, and my dad did not mention him much. I could not figure out if he was a hard worker who sacrificed but just could not bring enough money home to support his family or if he was a drifter of sorts, a guy who had no profession and couldn't hold down a job. To this day, I do not know what he did for a living. My dad would dodge those questions, never disparaging his father but never really talking about him. What he would speak of were the many evenings he had to go to bed hungry because food was scarce. His mother actually worked outside the home, at least for a little while, running a café and baking pies. But whatever my grandparents tried, they did not make enough to pay the rent. They were evicted or otherwise forced to move at least seven times during my dad's childhood. Of the children that did survive, my dad was the youngest. His oldest brother became an Episcopal priest. His sister married a post office worker many years older than her. His other brother ran a little wild, having some brushes with the law, until being drafted for World War II. He worked in a gas station or something like that afterwards. Like with my grandfather, I could not say what he did for a living. Amidst all of this, as my aunt would tell me more than once, my dad vowed one day to live in northern Glendale. He did not want to settle for one of the working-class neighborhoods he had known his whole life. He wanted better.

If one listened to my dad's tales, one would think he deprived himself of all joy as a child. He played some sports, but I don't believe he ever played in organized leagues. He never mentioned any neighborhood girls he had a crush on or of playing pranks or of running around with friends. He instead would tell us of the afternoons he spent after school, washing dishes in the café for money, and then reading alone in his room at home. He did well in school and earned a scholarship to UCLA. When Japan bombed Pearl Harbor, my dad told me he headed right to the nearest Army recruitment center to volunteer. His eyesight was determined to be too poor, however, so he continued his schooling. His vision must have miraculously improved because in 1942 he was drafted.

He served for three years, seeing combat, and being discharged when Japan surrendered, physically unscathed and mentally ready to go home. My dad would never take us camping or go on hikes. He would wave it off with a shake of a hand. "I had enough of roughing it in the war," he would say. "It's not my idea of fun." He moved in with his mother in southern Glendale, his father having died while he was away, and took advantage of the GI Bill to get a law degree at USC. I never understood why he didn't join one of the firms emerging in the post-war years, as he would have earned a better salary that way, but he opened up an office in downtown Glendale, perhaps as a way of serving the citizenry. He never had financial success being a lawyer.

Yet, it led him to politics. Glendale was not the large, bustling city then that it became in the last decade of the 20th century. It was a small town. My dad attended political meetings, met people, ran for office, and eventually in 1955 was elected to the California Assembly for his district. His life took a drastic turn. He had to refine himself to be more than the working-class kid from Glendale. He approached this with gusto. He studied etiquette. He found a tailor to not just make him suits but to teach him fashion. He learned elocutionary skills for the speeches he would give. He, in essence, learned how to fit into this new element he was entering. And fit in, he did. He enjoyed the legislative process during the day and the night life that came with it afterwards. He was rubbing elbows with the class of people he had always wanted to, still, however, returning to the room in the house his mother rented when the Assembly was not in session.

Back in those days, most politicians at my dad's level had to continue working at their careers, as the pay was not great. So my dad was still seeking out clients and going to court on their behalf. He was able to save a little, and he was on a first name basis with most of the bankers in the city. In 1958, my dad was

38 years old when he met the 21 year-old daughter of a Hollywood art director. It's hard to know if they fell in love or if things just seemed right, but after their third date, Vivien Odell called up my father.

"Howard, is it okay if I tell everyone?" she asked. My dad was hungover, still in bed.

"Tell them what?" he asked.

"About our engagement, silly," she said.

I guess my dad thought things over quickly. Vivien was a beautiful, young woman. A churchgoer. She had been the valedictorian of her high school and was an accomplished tennis player. On top of that, if he were going to have a family, he would have to start soon, as he was approaching 40. I'd hate to think that her father's wealth had much to do with it. Whatever the case, my dad had apparently proposed to her in front of a group of people at some fundraiser, and she had accepted. So in the light of sobriety, he muttered, "Sure, go ahead."

They were married in November of that year. My mother became pregnant shortly after. My dad felt he had it all. He won re-elections and was hobnobbing with major players on the political scene. He had rented a house, but it was too small for the family he wanted. He wanted more and made his feelings known when he socialized, which was frequently. In 1961 or so, some bigwigs in Glendale approached him about the possibility of moving into a new street being developed. They liked the idea of the assemblyman having a house on the block and picked out a prime spot for him. They found architects to offer up designs. All of this overwhelmed my dad, but he really wanted it. The problem, he knew, was affording it. The value of the property far exceeded his means. He spent time doing calculations to see how he could make it work, and he could not figure how any bank would give him the type of loan it would take. Ashamed of himself, feeling the poverty of his youth yet again gnawing at him, he had to call them and decline the deal. "But why?" the bigwigs wanted to know. Apparently, after some hemming and hawing, he finally mentioned the price. Well, why didn't you say so? We can take care of that.

Yes, my dad had made some friends, and they worked together to find a way to give him the loan at a rate of interest a man of his means would not usually get. The house was built. Our family of then four moved in and welcomed my youngest brother Rick a few months later. The Glendale bigwigs were right, as well. Houses went up quickly and very wealthy families, both young and old, started moving in. My dad had finally made it to upper Glendale.

• • •

"Remember the Spartans!"

My dad could afford his monthly mortgage payments. He never failed to make them. But the money left over got gobbled up by utility bills and the raising of three children, not to mention my mom's increasing medical expenses. My dad ran for state senate but was defeated. The prospects of living in the neighborhood on his meager earnings from his law practice must have frightened him terribly, but his connections came through again. The governor appointed him to the state municipal court as a judge. The salary assured him of a solid middle-class life—except for the house. I remember overhearing conversations between my mom and dad where they would argue about the need to move. Ultimately, though, my dad wouldn't budge.

Many of my dad's working-class habits from childhood leaked into our upbringing. Nothing could be wasted. We had to do with what we had. Outings had to cost little or no money, so we would go to city parks sometimes. During the summer, we would knock on the doors of our neighbors who had pools, asking if we could swim. During the school year, my mom would leave us at the library for hours, using it as a babysitter of sorts, and my dad would take us down there on weekends if we complained of boredom around him. We visited the observatory in Griffith Park. We really could not have gone to any place other middle-class children would go, however. My brothers and I wore clothes with holes in them. As my mom's mental illness became more pronounced, our shirts and pants simply did not fit us. My dad would growl at my mom that we looked like "ragamuffins," but she did little about it. Occasionally, she would pick up clothes that looked durable to her, like Sears' Toughskins, and buy them in a size too big so that although they would be large on us now, they would last longer, as we would grow into them.

We grew distant from the children of our wealthier neighbors. Some of that had to do with my mom's increasingly strange behavior, but we also just did not know how to behave around them. My dad—not so much my mom—stressed the importance of education and modeled the behavior of a cultured citizen—reading, listening to classical music, and eschewing any popular movies in favor of films deemed of high quality by the critics. I sometimes tried to emulate this behavior, becoming an avid reader, for example, but as I moved into my teen years, the contrast between his culture and the way we actually lived confused me. The manners and the communication skills my dad stressed seemed impractical, even effeminate, to us, a pretense of politeness. When my brother Dave was a teenager, he became interested in cars and got into the drug scene at his high school. The friends he would bring around all came from southern Glendale. My dad would lament, "Why don't you give Curtis Baker a call and go out with him?" Curtis was the son of Sheldon Baker, a wealthy contact of my dad's, and Curtis engaged in all sorts of meaningful activities, whether it was taking lessons in Russian or winning science fairs. "He's a nice guy," Dave would say. Sometimes he would claim that my dad didn't know the real Curtis Baker, that Curtis did naughty, mean-spirited things alongside all the other activities, but the truth was that Curtis would have nothing to do with Dave. Curtis dressed immaculately. Unlike all of us, he had gone to a dermatologist and did not have an acne-laden face. Curtis washed his hair every day and got haircuts every two weeks. Dave did not belong with Curtis.

In fact, all of us subconsciously drifted toward the less affluent cliques during junior high and high school. Their parents were less involved with the lives of their kids. We didn't endure judgment as much. It felt much more comfortable. While I liked to write and I still read quite a bit, the friends I started to hang out with did not do that much. The sons of construction workers or mechanics, we talked and played sports. We obsessed over girls and talked about a lot of things we really knew nothing about. We sought adventures in any way we could find them. I still wanted to do well in school, but knowledge-seeking no longer fascinated me. In the meantime, I would bemoan what was happening in the house. The further we got into our teenage years, the worse it got. My dad would get frustrated, believing we were not tough enough. "Quit your bitching," he would bark, in a voice very different from the eloquent one he used publicly.

• • •

"Remember the Spartans!"

I actually never saw the movie, *The 300 Spartans*, that my dad was referencing until I was an adult. It involved the Battle of Thermopylae and the 300 Spartans who would fight until the last of them was dead. They were outnumbered, out-supplied, and surrounded, but they never gave up. I suppose my dad invoked the expression as a way of telling us to fight against the odds, to not complain about hardships, to remember that many people have it worse off. The phrase stuck with me throughout my life. I left home when I was 17 to go to college. I never came back to live. My friends could not understand my living in one-room apartments in southern Glendale, spending money on rent and utilities, when my parents lived so close. One woman visitor to my apartment once commented, ironically enough, that I lived a very Spartanesque lifestyle. I did not decorate with pictures of posters. I kept my various places clean, but just about every apartment I lived in came furnished, as working in unskilled positions while I went through college, I could never afford furniture. I wouldn't buy any new clothes until what I had could no longer be worn. I had enough spare money to go out with the guys once a week or have them over for beer, but I spent most weekend nights alone, watching ball games or reading for class. Working out at the gym became my main passion. My friends—some of them going to college while living with their parents, others working for a living but still staying at home—dressed sharper, drove better cars, and did not have to worry about buying groceries. I remember feeling how spoiled they all were, all the while longing for those luxuries.

Something very revealing happened to me during this time. I was at Santa Monica beach with three of my friends, relaxing in the sunshine as waves crashed in front of us. A woman approached us and said she worked for a studio. A premiere had been scheduled for the film, *Children of a Lesser God*, and she had free invitations. All we had to do was give our thoughts about the film after the fact. We all looked at her, wondering why Hollywood would want our opinion, but nodded in agreement.

"Super," she said. "I just need to get a little information about you." She started with Benny, asking his age, occupation, and address. My turn came next.

"I'm a hospital employee," I said. "It's kind of hard to explain what I do. I lift and move things around mostly. I transport medical charts across the medical center throughout the day."

"So you're a manual laborer, then?" she asked.

I didn't hesitate. "Yes," I replied and then gave her the rest of my information.

Carl's turn came next. "I'm a student," he said. "I'm studying architecture." He did not mention that he broke concrete at his dad's construction site when not in school, which is how he spent most days that particular summer. The woman accepted his answer, told us the tickets would be waiting for us at the box office, and took off.

But as I sat there in the sand, it dawned on me I had identified myself as a member of the working class. Among my friends, I was often called "the judge's son," and I would get teased for using larger words than I had to, not knowing much about cars, and reading in my spare time. They perceived me as solidly middle class, despite my living conditions. Yet, when it came down to it, I did not feel like a student who was working his way through school. I felt like a worker who masqueraded as a student at night. Maybe college would prove to be a way out of living paycheck to paycheck, but that life was not who I was.

My dad kept wondering when I would find a career path. Even as I started my M.A., trying to build on what I had learned about writing fiction, he had already dismissed the possibility of my becoming a writer.

"Bill," he said in a typical conversation. "All professional writers I have read about have one thing in common. They write every day. They practice. You don't do that." This was true. Working all day and going to school at night left me little time to write on my own. I wrote only when the mood struck me or I had a story due for class. He mentioned one novelist in particular whose name

I have forgotten. "Why, in this interview, he said he gets up every morning and does at least two hours of original writing. Then after breakfast, his secretary has typed up what he wrote the day before, so he goes through that and edits and adds to it or sometimes decides it's no good so he starts all over again. That's what writers do!"

While I nodded in agreement as I usually did in our conversations, I thought to myself, "How can I do that?" I got up every morning at 5:30 or 6:00 and headed for work. I often was physically exhausted, sometimes skipping my workout. I had schoolwork to do. I had to cook dinner for myself and keep the apartment clean.

"Turn your attention elsewhere," he would advise other times. At first, he encouraged me to be a lawyer, but when I started my master's and he saw that my grades were still strong, he thought of something else. "What about becoming a professor?" he started suggesting. "You'd have lots of time to write and make a decent living." I'd laugh, as the image of a professor in my mind was of someone much more erudite and refined than I was. Yet, even as some of the professors who taught me literature and writing struck me as a little too arrogant and book-smart, they were also nice to me. They sparked my interest in literature. They could make me laugh.

After a year of teaching experience under my belt from my assistantship, I thought that maybe, just maybe, I could do the same as a professor. The only problem? While my working-class friends did not think of me as one of them, I exuded "working-class" to most everyone around me on campus. The women in the TA office would gossip in unflattering ways about my muscular appearance and my lack of refinement. In the lunch room near the writing center, I overheard a conversation about my supposed interest in a fellow TA.

"He's too rough for her," a woman named Ida said. "He's more suited for a construction site."

"She needs someone with more class," Susan agreed. "I mean, he walks around like this." They laughed at what I assumed was Susan's impression of me.

"Oh, you're being mean," Mary said. "Bill's nice. He just doesn't get it."

"Janeen could do better, a lot better," Ida said. Janeen was the TA who, I admit, had caught my eye.

"He's smart enough," Mary said.

"Maybe about lifting weights," Susan said, again to laughter.

"He's just very basic," Mary said. I think her comments were meant as a defense of me.

"Not the type you'd take to a French restaurant," Ida said. "Janeen needs a man who can help her grow. Bill would keep her where she is. He's all wrong for her."

I should point out that I had never been in a class with any of these fellow TAs and I had barely spent any time in the office with them. They had made assumptions based on my appearance and whatever limited chatter I had been a part of in the office. I wondered if it was how I talked. I do not think that I have or had at the time any type of stereotypical working-class accent, but I did tend to talk very quickly. At the university, I avoided the cussing and busting of chops that was a regular part of discourse in my social circle. Perhaps some things slipped out here and there. Sean, a fellow TA, one time told me that I needed to increase my vocabulary after I did not know what he meant by "paradigm." Once in a Shakespeare class, I pronounced the character's name "Mortimer" as "more timer," as I had never seen the play performed before so did not know how the name should sound. At an outing one time, a fellow TA named Rebecca playfully told me that my lack of culture was "endearing." I'm not sure what inspired her to say that, other than I told her I did not like opera and was not a vegetarian. If we had taken a poll, then, about which of the graduate students was most likely to move on in the profession, I would have come in dead last.

But the field of composition studies had been gaining some steam and my research into the job market told me that most of the openings in English departments across the nation would require work in that field. It seemed to be different than the traditional course of study in literature. It did not seem that far from who I was. So I decided to do a doctorate and try it out.

• • •

"Remember the Spartans!"

I did my Ph.D. out of state and dove into my course work with a fury. I read beyond what I had to and built a decent reputation, especially in social justice pedagogy. I again had no money, accepting a very low assistantship offer to move across country, but I gritted my teeth, budgeted, and made ends meet. Since no one knew where I came from or what my dad did or what my background was, I could pretend to be something I was not. I tried to embrace that lifestyle, but again, it just wasn't meant for me. The friends I made tended to have working-class or mixed-class backgrounds. Some listened to country music. One had been a boxer earlier in his life. Another was a Mr. Fixit who would go on to own a bar, never really using his degree. I was shunned a bit because I could come across as aggressive when, from my perspective, I was being direct. I had not learned academic niceties.

Even my mentors and supporters noted the way I was rough around the edges. As part of my TA-ship, I was assigned to study and then find a method of evaluating the effectiveness of the Writing Across the Curriculum program. My mentor, Dr. Williamson, arranged a meeting with the associate provost about the project and invited me. I felt nervous but dressed up as well as I could, even shining my shoes, and I rehearsed what I would say when asked certain questions.

We met in the vice-provost's office, and he seemed very welcoming. I let Dr. Williamson do most of the talking, but when it came down to the actual plan, my suggestion about an ethnographic approach was greeted with skepticism. The vice-provost instead wanted a survey of those teaching in courses designated as "writing intensive" to see their impressions of the Writing Across the Curriculum program.

"So you just want me to interview these professors to see what they think?" I said.

"Yes."

"So I should just go through the catalogue and see who's teaching it and go talk to them?"

"No, no," he said. "I'll have my secretary give you a list of instructors who have been the most active in it."

Dr. Williamson said something at this point, but I interjected quickly. "If these instructors are the ones most active in it, aren't they going to have the most positive things to say about it?" The vice-provost raised his eyebrows and Dr. Williamson turned to give me a stare. "I'm just thinking that a study should contain some voice from those who didn't like it so we can figure out why."

The vice-provost looked at Dr. Williamson.

"I'll also arrange for a list of some who did not come back to the program."

"I just want to make sure we're doing this right," I said, sensing their displeasure. "I mean, I don't even know how we're going to find out how effective the program is if we don't talk to students and find a way to measure their learning."

"We'll start here," the vice-provost stated.

I asked a few more questions, making sure I understood my responsibility, and we left cordially. But Dr. Williamson called me into his office the next day. "You need to dial it back a bit," he said. "You were perceived as suspicious." I must have looked surprised because he waved his hand. "I know you think you're just asking questions, but you're a little different than others around here. You're plain spoken, like you're arguing with your boss at a machine shop. You come across as aggressive, like you want to brawl. You have to find a softer side to yourself if you're going to succeed at this level."

I'm not sure if I ever succeeded in finding that softer side, as I eventually clashed with too many professors and fellow students. I felt we argued over issues of honesty and integrity, as I felt it was with the vice-provost. Others believed it all boiled down to an issue of decorum.

Despite this, I did well in my doctorate, but I left the university before finishing my dissertation in order to support my newborn daughter, obtaining a job in what was then called University College at the University of Cincinnati—their open admission program. It would take me three years to finish up my dissertation and graduate, but I was finally both a doctor and a professor. I felt like I was teaching the type of students I should be, those in need of extra help and attention, those whose backgrounds, though drastically different than my own, shared many features. I entered the professional side of the field, publishing a few articles, working on an edited collection, and making presentations at conventions. I started meeting a few of the major figures in the field and I learned to network. Yet, nothing changed. I was still me. I was rough around the edges, more comfortable playing pool in the bar than listening to a panel presentation at a professional conference. I embraced many of the –isms that were introduced to me—feminism, Marxism, multiculturalism, antiracism—but sometimes I knew them more than I felt them. To this day, I probably bristle more than most when academics complain about the white, male oppressor. Was that supposed to be me? But whatever the case, I never felt comfortable. I remember once a colleague telling me that students related to my teaching style because I was "at their level." It sounded like a compliment wrapped up in an insult.

At several junctures, I tried—perhaps like my dad—to broaden my cultural understandings. I used to listen to the classical music station, for example, trying to learn the differences in symphonies. I started watching art films. I made lists of books I should know and spent many summers pounding through them. I tried to learn more about geography, and I made a point of travelling to different parts of the country to see landmarks and such of supposed importance. I attempted to find academic friends and to engage in the types of discussions and activities they seemed to like. Yet, things would slip out. Maybe a joke would not go over well. Maybe a coarse expression. Maybe I talked of my enjoyment of James Bond movies. But there were more subtle matters. A colleague asked one time whether I knew the location of a certain store. I gave general directions and then said, "It's right next to the Burger King. You can't miss it." My colleague sniffed. "I wouldn't know where the Burger King is," he said.

For the next 20 years, I would bounce back and forth between wanting to embrace the academic, middle-class life that I sometimes could genuinely find enjoyment in and a more working-class, physical life that also seemed to suit me in some respects. So on one hand, I would write a textbook and appear at functions my publisher put together to support it. On the other, I would join a boxing gym and get excited at the prospect of sparring. My retreats from academia eventually seemed to come more often, but I did enough to earn a promotion to full professor. I was even appointed to the chair position at the University of Akron's English department, where I had settled after my initial appointment at the University of Cincinnati.

As a full professor, I had an epiphany at a conference. I was doing my usual conference duties—networking, checking out new scholarship, and attending sessions. But I was bored. I had a couple beers with two guys I had met—both finishing up dissertations, one on the market, the other hoping to go on it the following year—but they didn't want to stay, so I went back to the convention center with them. I looked over the program and found a panel to attend. One of the two guys was going to the same panel, so we sat down by each other just as the first speaker was being introduced. I listened at first, nodding in agreement, but my mind started wandering. Suddenly, I was being tapped on the shoulder by my new friend. "You started snoring!" he hissed. I had drifted off to sleep. I saw heads turn back toward the presenter, and I heard a few chuckles. I muttered some apology toward the stage and got out of there.

I ran into my new friend later at the hotel bar, where I had gone. He apologized for waking me but laughed. "It was a boring panel," he admitted.

"You know something," I told him. "You're new to the field. You're going to be coming to these things for years. So I'm going to tell you something. They're all boring." The words came out of my mouth before I knew what I had said, before I realized that I was supposed to be Dr. Thelin, an academic who had given over 100 presentations and had a reputation in the field. What would this newcomer to the field think?

But he again laughed. "Is any of this supposed to be interesting?"

I drank another beer with him, but I soon found myself alone. I looked around and saw people from the conference gathering together, asking questions about studies, swapping teaching stories, discussing antiracism efforts, giving advice to each other, laughing, but it all seemed so alien to me. I did not want to join any conversations, although I recognized a couple in the corner with whom I had collaborated previously. I wondered if I had ever enjoyed this scene or if I had always been trying to figure it out. Had there ever been a panel that truly interested me or had I just been pretending? I asked myself, "What would you rather be doing than this?" The answer was to be anywhere but there. My retreat from academia was complete.

I still teach, but it's to make a living. I do not attend conferences anymore. I write articles sparingly. I fulfill my professional obligations by reviewing manuscripts and books, but I have little desire to contribute. I do not socialize with any of my colleagues and only keep in touch with friends in the field through Facebook. I prefer watching the Browns play on Sundays during the fall, reading what I want to rather than what I feel I have to, bowling, and hanging with my friends. Maybe I could have been more. Maybe I was more. But I just could not live with the constant balancing act.

• • •

"Remember the Spartans!"

My grandfather died in 1983, and the wealth he accumulated fell to my mother and her sister. It was a considerable sum, one I never knew the extent of. I had moved out of the house long before, so the changes that money brought did not affect me directly, but I know my dad felt more secure than he ever had in his life. He would mention, jokingly, that he could never divorce Vivien because she was now an heiress, but her behavior, exacerbated by her prescription drug addiction, plagued his life and caused him tremendous depression. I could not understand why he did not divorce her, as she became more and more of a social embarrassment, but, perhaps, I never completely grasped him. You did not walk away from problems. You endured them to the bitter end. And it was bitter.

The house in northwest Glendale became a disaster. Early in the 21st century, I had heard enough about the way they were living and traveled back. My mother never let me stay at the house when I visited. Truth to be told, there was no place I could have slept. She had packed the house with garbage to the point that the mattress she slept on had a slew of empty pill bottles on it. My dad slept in a separate room, also surrounded by garbage. I cleaned the house. My mother kicked and beat on me and then called the police to have me arrested—unsuccessfully, thankfully—but I filled three dumpsters with garbage and gave them back some semblance of a home. Once a month, I would travel back on long weekends to wash their dishes and clean whatever else I could. My dad did not eat regularly and his health suffered. I would buy groceries when I went back but it was not enough.

Eventually, my dad hired a maid and a cook. Along with my grandfather's estate, he had made a killing after retirement by entering into private judging and arbitration. He could afford so much more than he ever had. Yet, aside from buying a luxury car and getting season seats for the Dodgers, he did not live a life of great comfort. The house continued to be a disaster. They had a landscaper who kept back the brush and mowed the lawn, but the house looked beaten, like it had endured a hurricane and kept standing, nothing glamorous but still there.

In 2011, my dad suffered a fall due to chronic dehydration, kidney dysfunction, and heart disease. He spent the rest of his life in a convalescent hospital. On his 90th birthday, some of the old big wigs left in Glendale—maybe their sons, as most of the originals were gone—gathered in his room. Through some political process, they had that date declared "Howard Thelin Day" and had a party, celebrating my dad's accomplishments. Six weeks later, he was dead. He had always exhorted us to let him die in his home, to not confine him to an old folks' home, but he never would abandon my mom. On my last visit to him, I told him I could get him home with the caveat that he had to have 24/7 care, on the doctor's orders. My mom wouldn't allow it, not wanting to have some caregiver bathing him or changing his clothes. No matter what I said, he would not override her and allow me to arrange for the needed care.

Shortly after my dad died, my mom's drug addiction shut down her kidneys. She lived the rest of her life in bed, with a 24/7 caregiver, Alzheimer's disease taking over. She actually was more pleasant to visit, as she no longer exhibited obsessive-compulsive tendencies. But it pained me the first time she didn't know who I was. It was a relief when she passed away in 2015.

I have visited the old home once since she passed away. Although we three sons jointly own it now, my brother Dave inhabits it, so I was basically his guest. Dave had developed into a serious alcoholic, having in his late 20's spent some time in county jail after too many DUIs but continuing to drink from morning until night. Somehow, though, he became a successful Beverly Hills accountant. Most would say his appearance belies his personal wealth, as he refuses to take care of his teeth and wears clothes for convenience rather than any sense of style. He chain smokes. We argue, especially about his smoking and drinking, but I have a true fondness for him. On the last day of my visit, we had to take care of some business with the family lawyer, so he had taken the day off work. Afterwards, I rambled out to the balcony, which had a particularly nice view that day. Dave joined me, giving me a beer.

We looked out at the mountains in one direction and the city sprawled out in front of us in the other. He mentioned a few things about the property and told an old story about Glendale that I had not heard before. My mind was elsewhere, though. "Do you ever think of us as working class?" I finally asked.

"Working class?" he snorted. "Bill, we're among the elite."

"But we never had much as kids," I countered. "And look at this house." I pointed at the retaining wall that had collapsed.

"Social class is what you make it," he said. "It's who you are, not who you were. You know, Bill, your father struggled to give you a better life than he had. Do you know what his finances were like before Grandad died?" Dave had taken over the family bookkeeping years ago and had done quite well by my mom and dad, making smart investments and growing their portfolio. "He sometimes would be down to his last $10 in his checking account before he got paid. Don't you remember how mom used to rush to the bank to deposit his check so nothing bounced?"

"That's what I'm talking about," I said.

"But you would have never known he was penniless," Dave countered. "And he persevered and rose above all of that. He worked for years after retirement to secure our futures." Everything he said was punctuated with coughs. He has developed COPD after a lifetime of smoking, but still smokes, even when he appears to be choking.

"I don't know," I responded. "I mean, look at us."

"You're a professor. I'm an accountant. Go on."

"Ok, we inhabit middle-class positions. But that's not who we are. Underneath it all, we struggle. I know you like the same things I like. I know we have the same kind of friends. We did not suddenly shift habits when we got money. I mean, think about it. We don't go to the ballet. We don't belong to any social organizations. No one is inviting us to fundraisers or formal parties. We don't get pedicures."

"You got it all wrong," Dave said, waving away smoke that had drifted in my direction. "It's the money that matters. If I wanted to go to the ballet, I could go. Dad started getting pedicures after he retired for good. If I wanted to, I could."

"But you don't want to," I said. "That's the point. It's not what you can do. I've had to go to functions at the university that I hate. I didn't want to be there. I didn't like it. There's someone out there somewhere who wants to do those type of things. But it's not us."

"I guess the bars I go to are all pretty much dumps," Dave said. "You know, Bill, Dad could never figure out why I didn't go to higher end places. I guess I didn't like them. Maybe there's something to being multi-classed. Just don't go calling us working class. That's insulting." He lit another cigarette. "Because you know, Bill, if I wanted to go to upper-scale places, I could afford to."

We talked for a little longer, mostly shooting the shit. He wants me to eventually retire and to move in there with him, and he made that pretty clear then, talking about my legacy and my father's wishes. I doubt, though, that I'll move there any time soon.

CHAPTER 9

Honest Work

Katherine Highfill

This is an essay that almost got scrapped on the absolute edge of the deadline after the proposal was accepted. Because I was ashamed of how angry it made me, trying to write it. Every word is accompanied by churning, grinding heat from teeth to toes. Roiling my brain around adjunct labor and institutionalized racism and prestige-hungry peacocks masquerading as tenured professors. I'm also angry that I'm ashamed to be angry. Nothing quite says gaslighting like an institution convincing you you're wrong to feel the way you do.

Deciding which of your two 'nice' dresses to re-wear to a department function at which you will be judged on not only the fact that you've re-worn something but also whether or not that was the right thing to re-wear and if your performance as a graduate student has been such that you can be excused for this faux pas.[1]

Knowing that the obstacles your peers of color, non-cis gender and/or non-traditional sexualities, and neuroqueer face are far, far more difficult.[2]

Understanding that speaking to support them risks your own precarious position even as it rests upon their backs.

While academia certainly isn't the only profession to fall completely in love with its own importance, it somehow seems that it ought to be the least likely. Especially the humanities. If we are truly concerned with the work of knowledge in the human condition, how have we allowed our institutions and our programs to become sites for the accrual of capital? The answer, of course, is that they were never anything else.

Being on first name terms with the person of color who cleans the department building.

Honest: 1. Marked by or displaying integrity; upright.[3]

Being off balance and on guard continuously is what it means to be working class in academia. Because you don't know the moves or have the skills to interpret what's going on around you—spoken and unspoken—that tells you who has power, who to avoid, and how to sell yourself most convincingly.

Watching your more socially savvy peer's work the professors for the capital you so desperately need to accrue but can't seem to untie your tongue to cultivate.

Listening to more economically stable peers bemoan the quality of the food and wine at the department function you came to mostly for a free meal.

This is also an essay about mental illness. Major Depressive Disorder is part of my working-class identity. If I had more resources, perhaps I'd be able to get more effective treatment. If I could get better treatment, perhaps I could accumulate more resources.

Begrudging every cent you pay (because you're technically part time so the university doesn't cover it all) toward the expensive health care that is making it possible for you to stay in your program because you are literally allergic to every plant in the state.

Learning in a fluke conversation with a friend right before graduation that your health insurance includes a dental plan (that you've so desperately needed) but have never heard your institution or department mention before. Ever.

Manners and social graces are just the trappings of class. Understanding the necessity of AP courses and ACT/SAT prep was beyond my parents. Despite college degrees, they chose to remain working class. My father started a concrete construction business in small town Wyoming to pour footings, sidewalks, and driveways while building the occasional garage or shed. He supported a family of 5 on less than 40k a year when he could have stayed on as a supervisor for a road construction firm and climbed their ladder. My mother stayed at home after marrying my father largely to escape the poverty of single parenthood created when the ex doesn't pay child support and you can't substitute teach in the summer. She took care of the garden and chickens while baking bread, sewing my clothes, and serving on the local school board. Her work for our family didn't offer her a retirement account the way a permanent teaching position would—but in a small Midwestern town, those positions are few, far between, and not necessarily given to those who deserve them so much as those whose favor should be curried for one reason or another.

Knowing you need to publish. Having no idea how to do so. Being afraid to ask for help because your professors always seem so busy and you're not sure you deserve their time.

Consulting your advisor on how to get published and being given a few vague references you can "easily Google" ... none of which show up when "Googled."

>**Honest:** 2. Not deceptive or fraudulent; genuine
>**Work:** 1. a. Physical or mental effort or activity directed toward the production or accomplishment of something
>b. Such effort or activity by which one makes a living; employment
>c. A trade, profession, or other means of livelihood

At 12 my parents divorced. I have no doubt they once cared for each other, but their divorce was a relief from years of crackling silence. I'm still amazed at how the arguing was somehow better because at least then they were trying. After an unpleasant custody battle and a couple years of saltines and hot dogs while cleaning the school full time and commuting for a MA, my Mother moved us so she could find a job rather than marry for security yet again.

Holding strong opinions about the best roach eradication methods and strategies.

Foucault explains that rebellion can only exist within systems of power. It is a product of the system as surely as the ideology supporting that system. But only tolerated as long as it produces just a sphere for likeminded rebels who stay within their disloyalty allotment.

All of my wanting to 'be' something else has never really been about me. It's about my discomfort with the outcomes available within systems of power. Class, obviously, and all the other systems predicated on gender and race that power upholds and in which its wielders feel safe. And most people are comfortable with the status quo. I do not mean to suggest that class stratification or racial and gender discrimination are acceptable—merely to point out that if we all stay in our 'place,' we are more secure. Which is what academia teaches us how to do.

Figuring out that your program only has 1 plan for your PhD: for you to get an academic job that reflects well on it. Or else you were always a failure and they're not sure how you got through but your lack of success is obviously a personal character flaw and had absolutely nothing to do with the quality of advising or complete lack of preparation you received (especially for any job outside academia).

I feel myself being sifted down to the level I belong.

> **Honest:** 3. Equitable; fair
> **Work:** 4. a. Something that has been produced or accomplished through the effort, activity, or agency of a person or thing
> b. An act; a deed
> c. An artistic creation, such as a painting, sculpture, or literary or musical composition, or a creative result of other human activity.

It is understood that a working-class person will never be a star in academia. They aren't allowed to break the careful social order that ensures the continuation of the institutional system everyone loves to hate. It may be unfair, of course, and that's so unfortunate but standards must be adhered to.

Realizing that your state school degree (and it's even R1) isn't a 'top' program: so not only are you not getting jobs at a SLAC or good state schools (those go to the ivys) but you're also not getting a job at the second tier state schools because those will go to top program graduates and you have no choice but to accept whatever job you can get—especially adjuncting—because you need to eat a little at least but have also been fed the horror story of 'don't let your time in the profession lapse!' Of course none of your so-called advisors explained how this works at any point up to and including preparation (this varies horrifically by institution) for the job market.

I say *fuck* a lot. And while I'm not completely sure I've figured out how to use it as a preposition, the other parts of speech are covered. I'd like to think that particularly ill-mannered habit keeps me from being fully accepted as an academic but it's really my low brow sophistication: I'm not ashamed of what I am. Working class. Self-sufficient. Mentally ill.

Cuttingly intelligent. Terribly insecure. Capable of celebrating these simultaneously while also asking for reassurance that I'm allowed to be proud of myself.

Seeing the same more socially savvy peers win awards and special positions you are qualified for ... but you don't already have prestigious awards to show this and aren't on a first name basis with the selection committee.

Liking those socially savvy peer's Facebook status celebrating their latest prize/ fellowship/publication (that you could've won if you'd already been able to show you deserve it) because your social capital could use any boost it can get.

But class is more than security too. I didn't understand how to work the school system any better than my parents. Didn't actually understand there was a system to work. I spent high school mired in depression with no direction and no idea about how to find one. Doctors medicated me, my mother thought I was just a 'teenager,' and my father and I eviscerated each other through the mail (good rhetorical training) since his idea of proper conduct for me was far, far different than mine. I liked boys and booze. I did not wish to get married and live two streets west after graduation. I passed my classes by showing up. Until I quit doing that. Nobody knew quite what to do with me. Nobody could control me. I brazenly flouted all attendance and homework requirements. I still passed. I was unfailingly obstinate and pleasant. I just wouldn't be good.

Going without a good hair cut because it costs more than your weekly food budget. Spending that food budget on utilities so you can keep up with your classes.

> **Honest:** 4. a. Characterized by truth; not false
> b. Sincere; frank
> **Work:** 10. The manner, style, or quality of working or treatment; workmanship

I've seldom been so pleased as when I received a miniature wheelbarrow and shovel on my fourth birthday. My greatest life aspiration was to shovel and haul "fines" like my father. That same father who replied, "No, she couldn't" when a close family friend suggested maybe I should have stayed in the Midwest all along since I ended up back here anyway. I couldn't explain to a man that watched me grow up, and had to watch my father suffer when I left, that I had to get out to be able to come back. That I can only be here on my terms. Which are that I will be who and what I choose, not what the systems of power I inhabit chose for me. But those are just a less popular set of terms. For which I pay in prestige and missed opportunity.

Having your intellectual work (for which you receive little support) valued more highly than your teaching (for which you receive slightly more support) even as the department insists that teaching is how you pay your way via a stipend and tuition waiver.

Hearing your business major undergrad student brag he's only applying for positions where he'd make 50k while you're on the job market hoping to at least get a part-time adjuncting position so you can stay in your career field.

The first glimmer that I was maybe something other than weird because I was mentally ill came from the director of my alternative high school. She said she'd "kill for [my] intelligence." The military recruiters came calling after I took the ASVAB. Too bad my eyes weren't good enough to fly. But I couldn't chain myself to them any more than I could to a husband or a baby or meth. So I went to college and promptly failed out. It didn't mean anything. Knowing what I do now, I'm not sure it ever will. College doesn't overcome your roots. It lets you know you can leave them. But then what? Perhaps I'll start doing workshops on how to write pleasant rejection letters. At this point I've seen enough to have a clear grasp of the genre moves.

Sharing a glance of mutual shame with other graduate students at the campus mental health clinic.

Tossing your attendance policy mid-semester for the student whose boss now requires her to work Fridays—No. Matter. What.—because she helps support her younger siblings and parents who need to eat more than she needs to come to an hour of class.

Unlike many of my students and somewhat fewer of my peers, I am second-generation college. My Father holds a Bachelors in Civil Engineering and my Mother a Bachelors in English Ed. and Masters in Curriculum Design. Their achievements showed them that there were ways of being in the world predicated on social and cultural skills they didn't grow up learning. So I took 10 years of piano lessons. Learned place settings and butter knife etiquette.

Plucked chickens, pulled weeds, skinned deer. At 12, the lowest legal age limit, after years of target practice, varmint control, and passing Hunter's Safety, I couldn't hunt for the table. I knew death too intimately already. Had the seeds of suicide in my mind. How far from taking another life to taking my own? But I'm a hypocrite; I still eat meat.

Surprising the seminar group by having a pocket knife. No one else can open the vegetable crisps, but somehow it just isn't 'nice.'

I came to academia by accident having had a couple of teachers at my state school undergrad suggest I would do well in a graduate program. I didn't quite believe them. I also had no idea what I was going to do with a B.A. in English after having seen the local technical writing opportunities. I knew from my work as a mechanic that the university graduates of my program who were so proud of their positions as technical writers couldn't read an electrical diagram correctly. That faulty manual brought me here.

Wondering if you should have gone after that Mrs. after all.

But where *here* is and whether I want to be there aren't settled yet. I'm supposed to be writing my diss and I'm on the market and it's April and I can't get through the first round of cuts because I don't have single author published articles and I'm probably fucking up my job letters even after I paid Karen Kelsky (money well spent) to look at my materials and I don't come from an Ivy or top tier R1 program.

Wondering how much the secretary (who arrives late every morning and spends the first hour of her day online shopping) gets paid.

Knowing your jealously towards the secretary is a reflection of your own precarity and not being able to rise above it.

> **Honest:** 5. a. Sincere; frank
> b. Without affectation; plain
> **Work:** 12. Works Moral or righteous acts or deeds

Even now, at 36, my mother unwaveringly supports me financially, emotionally, mentally. She knows what my other options are. I'm terrified of what will happen to me when she's gone.

Because I just don't quite trust myself to survive—I'm supposed to be a huge success with a degree of every kind and I can't even get a job in my chosen field.

Going without dental care so you can get your pets a treat because they seem to be the only ones who don't seek to leverage your relationship.

I've never used drugs or slept around (because that was still a 'thing' when I was a teenager). I did drink to excess with regularity, but at 16 that isn't the daunting prospect it poses now. I wish so many things in hindsight. Someone/

thing to show me there was another way to make a life for myself beyond being pretty. I had "Genie in a Bottle" and "Baby One More Time" role models.

Sitting in interminable meetings where you've been included as window dressing disguised as graduate student opportunity while everyone spouts their opinion on everything except actually doing something. You play jargon bingo and allow yourself to check Facebook each time you fill the card ... 6 times in an hour.

Also creating an elaborate jargon scoring system whereby the professor who uses the most jargon well is declared the MIMA (Most Important Meeting Attendee). Double points for anyone who can use "diversity" and "inclusion" separate from each other.

Knowing that someone reading this is pissed because they think I'm making light of diversity and inclusion.

Hoping they'll understand that reaction is actually about them and their positionality.

To be working class in academia is to be faced, every—damn—day, with people who refuse to join the bucket line because they don't want to muss their clothes. They're content to hang out in the tower spouting ableist, ageist critiques of my rigor because I didn't use the right jargon to tell them the building is burning.

Freezing your facial muscles while listening to the recently hired assistant professor from *insert Ivy League Institution* joking about how bougie they are.

All our pretty thoughts and stories about education as a social leveler and the humanities as teaching foundational critical thinking and writing skills have always been an ideology deployed to allow us to deny our own complicity in the larger social order of class and race hierarchy predicated on oppression and greed while we engage in teaching and grading practices to reify that order. Our hypocrisy is, indeed, breathtaking.

Listening to your professors who came from the working class wax poetic about their Marxist credentials in between updates on their children's private school tuition and family's latest home acquisition.

> **Honest:** 6. Virtuous; chaste
> **Work:** 13. Works a. Informal The full range of possibilities; everything
> b. Slang A thorough beating or other severe treatment

And what do the academics do? Publish in corporate journals about how horrible it all is so they can get tenure and collect a bigger paycheck.

Missing out on informal mentoring and relationship building opportunities because you can't afford to live in the trendy part of town with the professors.

Feeling that critique is unfair? Myopic? Of course education has done some good. Few things are ever wholly bad (except climate change—that shit is seriously going to fuck the human race in the foreseeable future). But look at our society. Our society is paralyzed because corporations control everything and the will/desire of the people cannot be expressed through existing systems—those same systems that our education system touts.

Calculating that you will pay an additional 50% over the total of your student loans in interest on the fastest (10 year flat) repayment plan that you can't afford.

Being working class is recognizing that the only way to save the academy is by letting it burn, fire has great cleansing and tempering properties, then rebuilding with people from the only class who really know how to construct something meaningful that lasts. These are the people who can build the academy we say we want because they know what it needs to be *and they can't afford for it to screw them any longer.*

They've poured themselves into the existing system for so long—believing the lies of meritocracy and outcomes and just not the 'right' degree—that they're ready to pour the gas and toss the match. To let whoever can promise them a better life lead the way. Academics unafraid of work can be quite useful here. We're already living the alternative, so perhaps it's time to buck up.

Because education is not just art and craft. It needs a solid foundation of sweat. Of hands permanently clawed to the handle of a tool. Perpetual farmer's tan and pearl snap shirts. Did you know those clichés represent something other than backwards hicks in MAGA hats? People who understand that each piece—the rock in the foundation, lumber in the studs, and screws in the tin—all matter equally if the job is to be well done. So far academics have been content to contribute curtains to hide that the window is out of square—and we let the corporations pick the print. We need the careful, common work of construction done by people who understand the value of dirt if we're to have an institution that makes meaning instead of funneling capital.

Learning how your friend correlated public bus routes to spend 4 hours of her day in transit for herself and her children to three different schools because she can't afford a car payment.

Purchasing a blazer to attend a professional conference, tucking in the tags, wearing it only for your panel, and returning it afterwards because you couldn't actually afford it in the first place.

> **Work:** v.tr. 1. To cause or effect; bring about
> To cause to operate or function; actuate, use, or manage
> To shape or forge
> 8. To make, achieve, or pay for by work or effort

Honest work is studiously avoided by those who wish to be stars. Because it hurts. It screws your soul out through your words to say what is real. It's steel toed boots and store brand coffee and being held accountable to who said you'd be.

Taking apparently subpar leftovers from the department function to your friend who couldn't come because of family responsibilities, but they still need to eat and feed their children on a GTA stipend.

This is not, finally, more rage quit lit. So why write this nastiness? Because I finally get it. It's not me. Imperfect and uncouth as I am, I am no less intelligent or capable than my better rewarded peers. I do have something worth hearing to say, even if I don't know how to find an audience who believes that. How many more of me are there? How many people who don't go to college because they don't think in ways that lend themselves to standardized testing? Whose aptitudes can't be gleaned from their K-12 grades? How many students who would like to pursue a graduate degree but don't quite know how to do it or how to ask for help? How many graduate students pushed aside because they don't know how to navigate the system? Or who don't fall for the lie that they should value the system more than their health and family? How much knowledge is wasted because of a system we can change? These are the people deemed unworthy by fiat. Because they don't quite 'fit.' Who have more to offer than they've been allowed to demonstrate. All they need is an academy that returns what they've already given: honest work.

Possessing the theoretical background and training to understand exactly how and why you're in the position you're in as part of a system that is happy to have your knowledge and ability until it renders you no longer able to serve.

Notes

1. These snapshots of working class life in academia are not all my own; they are used with permission.
2. While I do identify as mentally ill, I am still working to understand the theories of neuroqueerness and disability so do not wish to appropriate an incorrect identity.
3. Definitions from the American Heritage Dictionary.

PART 2

Critical Essays

∴

CHAPTER 10

Bodies in the World of Labor

Class, Affect, and Rhetoric in IWW's "What Is What in the World of Labor?" Poster

Phil Bratta

With a cream beige background, midnight black serif typefaces, and two crimson red and two solid midnight black playing card symbols, "What is What in the World of Labor?" (Figure 10. 1) (Industrial Workers of the World) demonstrates complex and creative "embodied language" (Knoblauch, 2012). For over one hundred years, the creators of the poster, Industrial Workers of the World (IWW), have made and circulated posters to convince the public, and more specifically laborers, to join their cause: to expose the exploitation and injustices by capitalists and organize collectively with the goal of better working conditions. As noted by Thomas Benson (2015): "Posters, as they exist in our vernacular cultural experience, are fundamentally rhetorical" (p. 5). They also function as effective cultural texts to engage publics because, as Jeffrey T. Schnapp (2005) asserts, posters "provide a literal, material bridge between the new public sphere constituted by mass communications and the public spaces that become the sites of modern politics as street theater" (p. 20). Unlike other material presentations of public knowledge, such as books, which, according to Johanna Drucker (1998), can be "closed tightly to preserve [their] power" (p. 172), posters resist closure. Their intent is to be open, exposed, and readily available for the public, serving as swift texts that grab viewers' attention without much effort. Posters are also greatly capable of mobility, distribution, and circulation, which make them desirable texts to produce for political causes and calls to action. We find such purposes in "What is What in the World of Labor?" with its titular question that immediately sets the scene for the unfolding of a narrative. As with all worlds, the world of labor includes various bodies and relationships that situate practices, beliefs, and values. And as this poster illuminates, IWW desires to deliver a narrative that unveils such a world.

In 1905, U.S. labor activists and organizers created IWW, which attempted to unite all labor industries in a fight against capitalism and capitalist exploitations and oppressions. From its inception, IWW also looked to bring together the labor class across social registers—ethnicity, race, gender, creed, and nationality—which was a much different approach than other late nineteenth and early twentieth century unions, many of which had racist, xenophobic, and

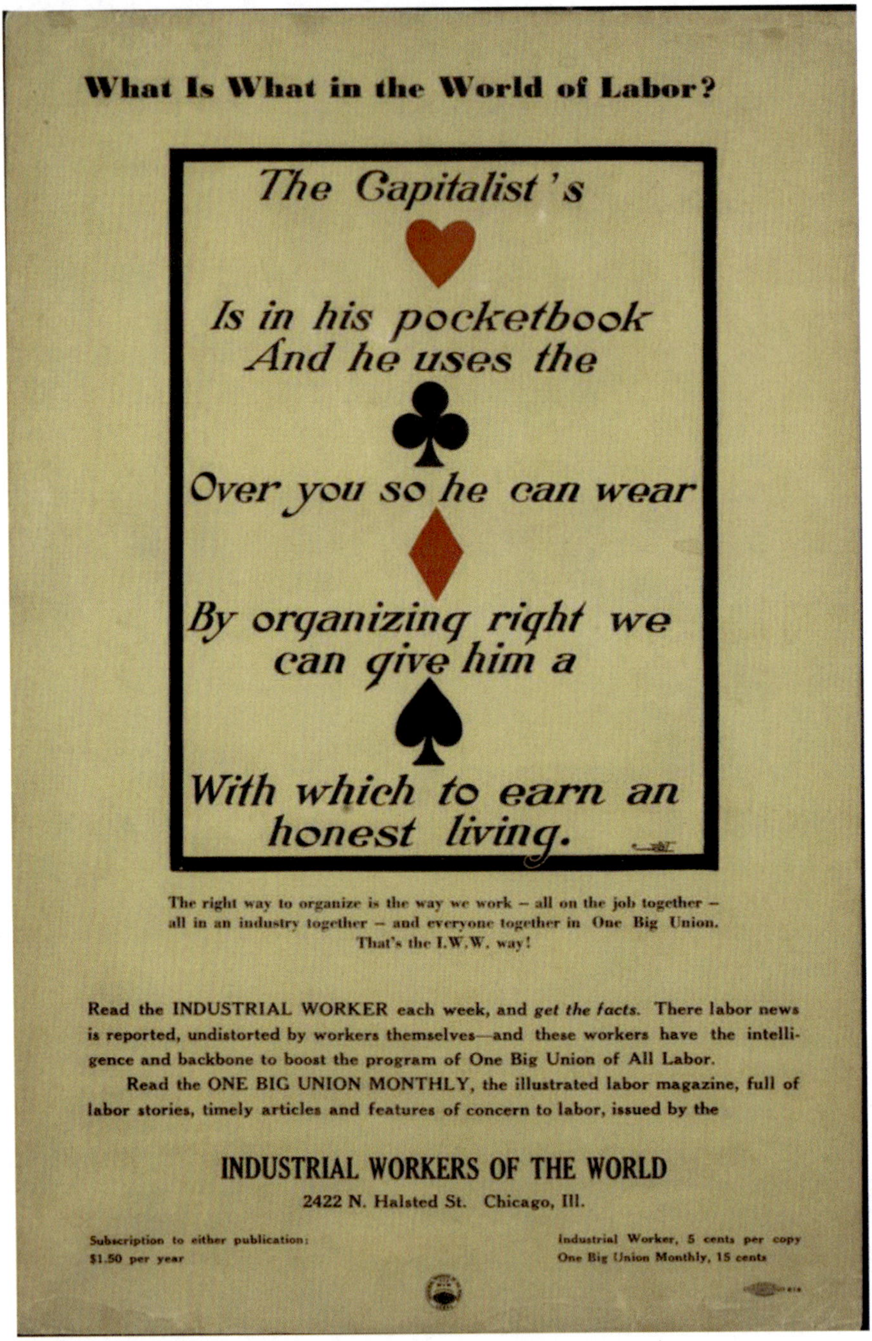

FIGURE 10.1 "What Is What in the World of Labor?" (Jospeh A. Labadie Collection, University of Michigan)

sexist paradigms and approaches. While pursuing solidarity across social identities, IWW's foundation was grounded and focused on exposing the exploitative economic system and capitalist-laborer relations through a number of texts, such as newsletters, pamphlets, and posters, that reflected the organization's philosophy and beliefs. In many of these texts, Wobblies (IWW members) worked with language and rhetoric in creative ways that called particular attention to bodies and the laboring of bodies without explicitly representing them as visual renditions in photographs or drawings or paintings. They used what A. Abby Knoblauch (2012) remarks as "embodied language," which is the "use of terms, metaphors, and analogies that reference, intentionally or not, the body itself" (p. 52). As we will see later in this chapter, IWW uses a complex layering of metaphors and analogies that demonstrates a rhetoric undergirded with a particular ideology and affect. Such a rhetorical approach and production allows the organization to build a narrative of economic exploitations and necessary solidarity.

In what follows, I first discuss visual rhetoric and activism to show the non-discursive, non-linear textual value of images and bodies in activist moments. Then, I briefly review affect theory, providing a tentative definition and its relationship to working-class rhetoric. Next, I delineate some background on IWW in order to understand the historical context of Wobbly activism. Finally, I analyze the poster "What is What in the World of Labor?"—a rhetorical image that presents embodied language and working-class affect. By unpacking the poster's visual rhetoric, we can see how Wobblies used working-class affective language strategies to try to connect with working-class folks in the hopes of identification, unveil the exploitative relations between bodies and labor, and call for necessary unity and solidarity.

1 Visual Rhetoric and Activism

Classic Western rhetoric emphasizes the study and use of discourse; that is, written and spoken communication. Beginning in the 1970s, however, rhetoricians took more seriously and frequently the study of visual rhetoric, which is somewhat surprising given Western culture's emphasis on sight as the dominant mode for epistemological and social formations. This turn to extend rhetoric beyond discourse was met, according to Sonja Foss (2005), with "vociferous objections. Such objections included the concern that rhetoricians lack knowledge about visual images" (p. 142). But rhetoricians pushed on, and in the last twenty years or so, visual rhetoric scholarship has gained momentum, encompassing the study of design, visual content, and materiality. Typically, visual rhetoric scholarship includes "a study of the process of looking, of 'the gaze,' with all of the psychological and cultural implications" (Hill and Helmers, 2004), but scholars have also tied visual rhetoric to literacy and embodiment (Fleckenstein, 2003), the construction of subjectivity and reality (Fleckenstein, Hum, & Calendrillo, 2007), materiality and technology (Propen, 2012), and typography and design (Wyatt & DeVoss, 2018), to name a few. The study of visual rhetoric also connects to rhetorics of display, which includes, Lawrence Prelli notes, rhetorics "enunciated through speech, inscribed in linguistic texts, depicted visually, circulated and viewed electronically, embodied in material structures or materialized in bodily form, or enacted through exhibitions, demonstrations, or other performances" (p. 11). Other visual rhetoric scholars have argued for the importance of the role of affect within digital-visual rhetoric, such as Joddy Murray (2009) discussing "image and the affective domain as critical to the way writers invent and compose text ... to achieve consensus, form communities, make connections, build knowledge and/or persuade" (p. 9), and Laurie Gries (2015) connecting agential power to digital-visual images and their circulations.

Visual modes for argumentation have been crucial in activist moments and movements, and several scholars have examined the work of visual rhetoric in various causes, as for example with anti-war activism during the Vietnam war (Benson, 2015) and environmental activism (Delicath & DeLuca, 2003). Recently, Dana Cloud (2018) examined the visual efforts of activists to challenge hegemony in politics and culture in regards to women's rights. Cloud connects the body, particularly women's bodies in public discourse, to visual resistance in the case of the 2013 Texas legislation for antiabortion bills. Protestors, Cloud notes, wore "hats and garments made of tampons and us[ed] labels to coordinate action on Twitter around the hashtags #unrulymob and #feministarmy" as a way to appropriate "the discourse of unruliness and the symbols of bodily leakage" that was proclaimed by Texas Republicans (p. 28). Ultimately, visual rhetorical thinking and practices carry immense value and impact for activist causes and efforts, particularly in terms of drawing our attention to bodies—whether the representation of bodies or actual, material bodies—in image making and circulation in public space.

2   Working-Class Affect

Coinciding with the rise in visual rhetoric scholarship in the last twenty years, scholarship in rhetoric, composition, and writing studies has also examined the subject of affect as a way to think through the relationship between bodies, sensation, and rhetoric. The task of summarizing and synthesizing all this scholarship, as well as offering a fully comprehensive theory of affect, is beyond the scope of this chapter, although a number of books and edited collections provide overviews and proposed theories within and outside the field; for example, see Jacobs and Micciche (2003); Ahmed *Cultural Politics* (2014); Massumi (2002); Brennan (2004); Gregg and Seigworth (2010); and Clough and Halley (2007). According to Melissa Gregg and Gregory J. Seigworth (2010), a "single, generalizable theory of affect" does not exist; at least "not yet, and (thankfully) there never will be" since affect very much is about the "not yets" (p. 3); and Jenny Edbauer Rice (2008) notes that affect studies is "hardly unified in its rhetorical scope, methodology, or even a shared bibliography" (p. 202). Nevertheless, for this chapter, we can consider effect as intensities and fluxes, whether represented in texts or experienced in events, that facilitate the orientation of material embodiments.

This definition of affect is influenced by Sara Ahmed's (2006) theory of orientation, which will help us also better elucidate working-class affects. In her study of sexuality, gender, and race in relation to phenomenology, Ahmed suggests that "orientations involve different ways of registering the proximity of objects and others. Orientations shape not only how we inhabit space, but how we apprehend this world of shared inhabitance, as well as "who" or "what" we direct our energy and attention toward" (p. 3). In our daily lives, we encounter material objects and language that continually direct and orient us to ideas, paradigms, and practices. Those directions and orientations take shape through the impact and circulation of affects, positioning our bodies in relation to larger social systems, institutions, and other bodies. One aspect of working-class affect, specifically, is that it positions and makes value for bodies in relation to labor. Working-class affect involves cultural significations of class that are felt experiences and ideas about work and labor, potentially illuminating exploitative practices on laboring bodies and calling for changes to working conditions and relations. These laboring bodies, as well as the objects used (such as tools) and made (such as commodities), have a history; that is, they do not simply exist in vacuum in a given moment. Ahmed reminds us of a fundamental component of Marxism: "Marxism provides a philosophy for rethinking the object as not only in history, but as an effect of history" (p. 40).

Such effects of history upon bodies, objects, and labor also involve the formation of affect, which is different from emotions. Emotions tend to invariably be internalized states of the individual. In Aristotelian rhetorical terms, emotion ties to pathos. The concept of affect, however, calls our attention to the larger system or organism of bodies. Michael Hardt and Antonio Negri (2004) remark, "Unlike emotions, which are mental phenomena, affects refer equally to body and mind. In fact, affects, such as joy and sadness, reveal the present state of life in the entire organism, expressing a certain state of the body along with a certain mode of thinking" (p. 108). The concept of affect allows us not to fall into an individualized, isolated sense of feeling that neglects the social materialities, institutions, systems, and contexts, as well as the implications of living our lives with emotions in our minds and bodies. For many in the working class, affect is ideologically felt in a different way than those in the middle and upper class because of their relationship to labor and capital. Such felt and ideological experiences work rhetorically upon working-class bodies to orient them in various ways. For example, the dominant class (capitalists, politicians, those with capital and who can decide political and economic agendas, petite bourgeoisie, and so on) circulates the ideology that hard work allows anyone to move up in society—one way to understand "the American Dream." If you work hard enough, you can achieve anything—regardless of your social identity or material conditions.

This ideology masks actual social inequalities and complexities, such as access to education, technology, capital, and so on. As such, it can maintain the status quo, even pacifying those who are oppressed to accept the conditions and continue working hard(er). When working-class folks feel and believe this ideology, they are oriented, and they orient themselves, to investing more time and energy in their work and perhaps remaining silent (or being silenced) with unjust conditions and relationships.

When we talk about, study, and make working-class rhetorics, we must always pay particular attention to laboring bodies and the affects they produce, represent, consume, and circulate that orient themselves and others in the world. In doing so, we can better understand how working-class affects are intricately tied with ideology and hegemony. Such is the case in not only in IWW's philosophy and mission, but also its cultural productions: songs and music, posters, pamphlets, newspapers, and rallies. IWW's rhetoric directs those in the working-class to acknowledge their identity in contrast to capitalists and put forth energy and attention or join IWW's mission that may undo the capitalist system and its exploitative practices. I now turn to a brief history of the labor organization, followed by a visual rhetorical analysis of the "What is What in the World of Labor?" poster to show the representation of working-class affect.

3   Industrial Workers of the World

One of the reasons for the creation of IWW was to counter craft unionism.[1] In 1883, craft unionism developed out of the American Federation of Labor (AFL), which, as Dylan Miner (2005) notes, primarily "sought to organize skilled workers (almost entirely white and male) only" (p. 9) and based its organization on "negotiations [that] were entirely separate for each type of job, and workers in one part of a business had no reason to strike with workers in another part of the business" (p. 11). By the turn of the century, the AFL became outdated and the "conservative alternative to working-class radicalism," having, along with other craft unions, "assembled a working-class elite" that sustained the status quo as "long as wages rose[,] ... hours decreased[,] ... [and] security increased" (Dubofsky, 1969, p. 12). While the AFL in various regions and time periods made some efforts to reach out to African-Americans, women, and immigrants, it often dismissed and neglected workers whose racial, national, and religious identities did not fit within a white Protestant male subjectivity, usually seeing these others as only part of and offering unskilled labor. Crucial to the formation of IWW was to bring these neglected workers together, and IWW's approach was centered on a sense of solidarity.

On June 27, 1905, organizers and laborers gathered for an open convention where William D. Haywood—"Big Bill," a miner since he was nine years old and who was blind in one eye from a mining accident—declared to over two-hundred delegates and spectators: "Fellow workers, this is the Continental Congress of the Working Class." As Joyce L. Kornbluh (1988b) states, "From the start of the convention Haywood expressed his interest in organizing the forgotten unskilled workers, those without votes and without unions" (p. 2). While Big Bill may have been an initial voice to the attendees during the conference and a force to be reckoned with, the crafting of the IWW philosophy, the speakers' platform at this convention, and in various other ways included women and persons of color and their labor. African-American/Mexican-Indian[2] revolutionary Lucy Parsons, the courageous, witty, and "the greatest woman agitator" year old Mother Mary Jones, and Daniel de Leon, to name a few, "along with countless other people of color, women, and foreign-born workers, would play an instrumental role in creating IWW philosophy" (Miner, 2007, pp. 57–58). IWW's newspaper, Industrial Worker, and the numerous other cultural productions (oral histories, songs, posters, and others) also involved a heterogeneous racial and gender collection of artists, laborers, and activists. Miner continues: "In traditional Wobbly folklore, many of the oral histories, stories, and songs revolve around heroic women and people of color, so often excluded from mainstream labor discourse" (p. 58). In sum, the convention, participation, and organizing of these bodies served as a foundation to unite workers, regardless of political party or industry and across differences of race, ethnicity, gender, creed, and nationality.

Since the convention, Wobblies have engaged in a number of tactics for their activism. Many of these tactics even continue to this day, such as the wearing of union pins and distribution of union literature, workplace specific direct action, informational picket lines, and marches on the boss (Keenan, 2015, pp. 218–219). For these actions to have the most impact both in an immediate activist moment and in the larger labor movement, IWW historically needed (and continues to need) to develop "a common understanding of solidarity" (p. 219). This emphasis on solidarity amongst laborers appears in the IWW political poster "What is What in the World of Labor?"

4   What Is What in the World of Labor?

In returning to the poster (Figure 10.1), we can first examine the poster's materiality and paratext to draw some conclusions about its history and production. Based on the deteriorated condition, the poster was likely created and appeared in Chicago in the first half of the twentieth century. Although no production date is available or any information on exactly who created it, we can surmise the poster was created between April 1933 and February 1970 because of the address at the bottom (2422 N. Halstead, Chicago, IL), where IWW had its longest location for its general headquarters. "What is What" is not a large poster—standing at only about 15" × 10"—and has some sturdiness to it, resembling cardstock paper. It has no staple or thumbtack holes, but the corners are faded and worn with some tape remnants, which are also on the back of the poster. We could surmise that this poster was taped upon a wall and/or it simply sat upon a shelf for display. The original poster is housed in the University of Michigan (UM) Joseph Labadie Special Collections archive, which I visited a couple years ago to examine several IWW posters, but it can be accessed digitally via the recent digitization project carried out by Labadie Collection Curator Julie Herrada and other UM librarians.[3]

Next, we can begin to examine the content and design of the image-text, which shows an embodied language for the purposes of identification rather than deliberation. According to Kenneth Burke (1969), "nothing is more rhetorical in nature than a deliberation as to what is too much or too little, too early or too late" and "in such controversies, rhetoricians are forever 'proving opposites'" (p. 45). In moments of deliberation, rhetors try to persuade their audience. But Burke argues that identification is crucial to—and even more important than persuasion in—the core functioning of rhetoric. He remarks that "a speaker persuades an audience by the use of stylistic identifications; [one's] act of persuasion may be for the purpose of causing the audience to identify itself with the speaker's interests; and the speaker draws on identification of interests to establish rapport between [oneself] and [one's] audience"

(p. 46). That is, a rhetor's audience needs to see themselves—whether in self, principles, values, and/or associations with other people—in the rhetoric in order to get onboard with the argument. With the IWW poster, identification begins with the initial framing question, or what we would colloquially say is a "rhetorical question": What is what in the world of labor? This question not only evokes viewers to consider who labors, what relationships are formed with labor, what is produced by labor, and what is the larger world (system) of labor, but where they identify themselves in such a world. This identification directs viewers to reflect on their own laboring bodies, and the opening question lays a foundation for a working-class affect to be solidified and accentuated through rhetorical symbols and text in the rest of the poster.

The question may not be the first noticeable element of the poster—arguably, below the question is a vertical rectangle frame that more prominently draws the eye toward more alphabetic text and four well-known playing card symbols: heart, club, diamond, and spade. The symbols and alphabetic text respond to the opening question and communicate, as I detail below, to viewers *how* labor is valued, *which* bodies are valued, and *why* those values and relationships are formed. These explanations operate through the form of a social narrative about bodies. The creator of this poster uses embodied language as a way to form a social narrative about the working class and employing class and the bodies in these classes: the capitalist's desire for profits, the laborer's (violent) embodied experience in economic production, the capitalist's material benefits from such production, and the need for laborers to organize and teach the capitalist a lesson in ethical labor practices.

The narrative begins with one body: "the capitalist." The narrative then moves to a specific body part of the capitalist—the heart—with the enjambment of a crimson red heart symbol, dislocating it from his chest to "his pocketbook" with the words "Is in his pocketbook." This construct of subject-verb-direct object presents capitalists as having a heart, and indeed feelings—specifically a desire for money. Those feelings, however, are displaced, even concealed. They could be pulled from the pocketbook as items typically in one's pocketbook can be presented in public, visible space. Yet, they remain hidden. Valuing money, the capitalist dehumanizes labor through intention: profitability. The poster presents an abstraction with the nuanced tone of dehumanization: profit over humans.

The creator of the poster continues with an explanation of how money and profit filled the pocketbook, evoking affect along the way through allusions of physical activities. Following the heart are the words "And he uses the" and a second playing card symbol: black club. The club becomes a weapon used by capitalists with intention upon a laboring body ("over you"). These rhetorical moves shed light on the violent background of the politics of economic production: "he [the capitalist] uses the [club] over you." The club is the trump card, and viewers of "What is What" might have understood a narrative about the affective context of bodies and objects—one based on violence, exploitation, and injustice. This poster's expression of this rhetorical narrative was/is indicative of the exploitative practices in late industrial capitalism. IWW activists create not only a narrative about labor relations, but also present intensities of workers' lived, embodied experiences. Workers' bodies may metaphorically (or literally) feel the intensities of the capitalist's club—a narrative laden with affect, a particular working-class affect. As workers extract resources or physically make commodities, the capitalist brings the commodity to the public. In doing so, the capitalist and the market create and circulate an affective commodity; producers (re: laborers) exchange their labor for wages and consumers typically do not have any connection to workers' affective experiences of laboring. In the end, capitalists profit from and enact this affect and signification: they use the profits to don diamond jewelry.

The poster continues with the next line: "Over you so he can wear." To develop coherence among the symbols, the thought/sentence is completed with a red diamond. Both the diction of "wear" and the symbol of a diamond allude to the presence of a body: bodies wear jewelry. And the bodies that can afford jewelry, particularly diamonds, are typically of, or aspire to be, the middle and upper classes. We might also take note that the IWW activist(s) may have been working with irony and satire in delivering their message because many of the union workers in the IWW were miners, extracting resources from the western United States. This poster, arguably, called particular attention to these miners through a working-class affective rhetoric. In doing so, the idea that the capitalist abused workers to don diamonds—a resource obtained through mining—was connected even more tightly to the labor and bodies of workers.

Thus far, we have seen no literal representation of the body (photograph, silhouette, etc.); yet, the full sentence—"The Capitalist's [heart] is in his Pocketbook And he uses the [club] Over you so he can wear [diamond]"—implies bodies and evokes the affective relations of bodies within labor actions. There is a hierarchy here, and workers are affected by it; their bodies used and alienated for the production of material goods (soon-to-be commodities). Viewers can infer that workers are being beaten—whether literally or symbolically—to produce commodities that would enter the market for profit acquisition. The heart and club function to create not only an emotional appeal, but also an affective appeal: bodies were affected by the hierarchical relation between capitalist and laborer. This hierarchy facilitates greed, as emphasized with the diamond that the capitalist dons. IWW tells us the appropriate response to such a narrative: organizing.

The creator of the poster changes the active subject of the narrative and inverts the last suit: "By organizing right we can give him a [spade]." The combination of the alphabetic text and the black spade was a peculiar choice. Of course, the IWW activist(s) needed to use the fourth playing card symbol to complete the suits; and, of course, in IWW fashion, they needed to end their message with a call to organizing and becoming a union member. After giving the capitalist a spade, IWW suggests the purpose of the tool: "With which to earn an honest living." Ahmed (2006) notes that tools are not merely instruments, but useful in their "capacities that are open to the future. The capacity is not so much 'in' the tool but depends on how the tool is taken up or 'put to use'" (Queer, p. 46). Tools "bring forth" the shape of bodies and perceptions. This poster does not necessarily present the idea that the capitalist and worker should change places. It also may seem that IWW simply blamed those in power and with privileges, which can easily "reinforce class boundaries" (Hoover, 2007, p. 45). Such a claim might appear valid. However, if we return to Burke's identification rhetoric, the desire to undo this hierarchy is not to simply flip the hierarchy, but allow the capitalist to understand the tool-labor that makes up his beloved commodities from which he profits. That is, the idea might have been that the capitalist's embodiment needs to experience the labor of the work and be affected by the working-class tools rather than the adornment of the commodity produced by those tools. In doing so, the capitalist might gain a better understanding of the physical investment and exertion, working conditions, and employee-employer and labor-capital relationships.

Still, such a situation would not necessarily change capitalism's hierarchical system. It would not initiate a revolution of social relations. But perhaps the poster does not need to show a path to revolution. Indeed, if we remember Gregg and Seigworth's (2010) comment about affect as being about "not yets," the revolution as unique event is perhaps *the* example of something to come. Perhaps this poster simply functions as a creative delineation of the world of labor and recruitment for the union and a call to join their cause. The affectively charged symbols mark laboring practices and the material circulation of bodies, tools, and commodities: manual labor was honest work whereas the labor of the capitalist was not. By underscoring the fact that the capitalist lived on the backs of workers, IWW remarks on the affects of labor that provide its targeted audience (laborers, the working-class) with a clear depiction of the structure of labor life and the necessary actions to take in developing a different set of (ethical) relations.

Below the vertical rectangle frame, IWW expressed the overall philosophy of the organization: "The right way to organize is the way we work—all on the job together—all in an industry together—and everyone together in One Big Union. That's the IWW way!" As Nigel Anthony Sellars (1998) notes, "the Wobblies rejected that most sacred of political icons—the ballot box—as virtually useless. They fully recognized that the American system gave labor the right to vote but in it saw almost no room to maneuver for its own benefit. Only through direct confrontation with business could workers gain their rights" (pp. 5–6). The only way a revolution in labor will happen is through organizing, unionizing, and confronting, not by voting. This will require building a coalition regardless of skilled or unskilled labor or social identity differences (race, ethnicity, gender, creed, nationality). It will require some sense of unity and solidarity, a collection of recruited bodies, hopefully in turn creating more social power and justice in the world. Following its creative narrative about bodies and their affects, IWW wraps up the poster by calling viewers to subscribe to the *Industrial Worker*—arguably a gesture to the importance of both individual and collective action, education and organization. While the poster contains neither representation of a human body in its entirety nor a crowd or collection of bodies, its displacement of organs through the metaphor of a card game gives us a visceral sense of the different parts and pieces of the body and bodies in the world of labor.

5 Conclusion

In the last hundred years, activists have used posters in various contexts and for myriad purposes. Wobblies exemplify such practice in their goal of building a solidarity labor movement. Across many of their hundreds of posters, Wobblies have creatively used embodied language to call attention to workers' bodies and laboring conditions, striving to expose the exploited system of capitalism. Such messages are evident in "What is What in the World of Labor?," where IWW combines symbols and words to present a social narrative that distinguishes the configuration of bodies, labor, and work. The narrative, and indeed the whole poster, functions to recruit workers, but it does so with an emphasis on working-class affect: the (re)orienting of bodies to capital and labor. Although IWW uses working-class affect to recruit workers, anyone who views the poster comes to it from a particular orientation that, especially in the case of scholars interpreting it in the present, can yield even more meaning and affective charge than IWW's goals. Ahmed (2006) reminds us, "We are turned toward things. Such things make an impression upon us. We perceive them as things insofar as they are near to us, insofar as we share a residence with them. Perception hence involves orientation; what is perceived depends on where we are located, which gives us a certain take on things" (Queer, p. 27).

Undergirding the poster's narrative is working-class affect, which creates identification for laborers upon their encounter with the poster. IWW and this poster provide us with one example in studying and making working-class rhetoric: a particular attention to affect and activism. The poster orients viewers, but more specifically the poster attempts to (re)orient workers to labor and the world of labor. These IWW activists rhetorically used alphabetic text, symbols, and design to create an interaction between poster and audience that required viewers to reflect and feel their substitutions and circulations, which does three things: (1) unveil the capitalists' affect: to profit by affecting exploitatively other bodies and labor; (2) emphasize the relations of bodies within labor actions: workers exchanged their bodies for wages and sustain the economic system while also being affected by the hierarchical class structure; and (3) affectively call for unity to change the system and current relations between laborers and capitalists.

Acknowledgments

I would like to thank Jake Riley, Sam Hamilton, the reviewers, and Matthew Guy and Jennifer Beech for their time and labor with feedback during revisions.

Notes

1. For more details of IWW history, check out Paul Buhle and Nicole Schulman's *Wobblies!: A graphic history of the industrial workers of the world*, Fred W. Thompson and Jon Bekken's *The Industrial Workers of the World: Its First 100 Years*, Stewart Bird, Dan Georgakas, and Deborah Shaffer's *Solidarity Forever: An Oral History of the IWW*, Len De Caux's *The Living Spirit of the Wobblies*, Donald E. Winters, Jr.'s *The Soul of the Wobblies: The I.W.W., Religion and American Culture in the Progressive Era, 1905–1917*, and Joyce L. Kornbluh's *Rebel Voices: An IWW Anthology*.
2. Different sources label her subjectivity differently: some identify her as African-American; others as Mexican-Indian. One thing all sources do agree upon is that she was a woman of color.
3. See https://www.lib.umich.edu/labadie-collection/labadie-collection-digital-collections

References

Ahmed, S. (2006). *Queer phenomenology: Orientations, objects, others*. Duke UP.
Ahmed, S. (2014). *The cultural politics of emotion* (2nd ed.). Edinburgh UP.

Benson, T. W. (2015). *Posters for peace: Visual rhetoric & civic action.* Pennsylvania UP.

Bird, S., Georgakas, D., & Shaffer, D. (1985). *Solidarity forever: An oral history of the IWW.* Lakeview Press.

Brennan, T. (2004). *The transmission of affect.* Cornell UP.

Buhle, P., & Schulman, N. (Eds.). (2005). *Wobblies! A graphic history of the industrial workers of the world.* Verso.

Burke, K. (1969). *A rhetoric of motives* (California ed.). U of California P.

Cloud, D. L. (2018). Feminist body rhetoric in the #Unrulymob. In J. Alexander, S. C. Jarrett, & N. Welch (Eds.), *Unruly rhetorics: Protest, persuasion, and publics* (pp. 27–44). U of Pittsburgh P.

Clough, P. T., & Halley, J. (Eds.). (2007). *The affective turn: Theorizing the social.* Duke UP.

De Caux, L. (1978). *The living spirit of the wobblies.* International Publishers.

Delicath, J., & DeLuca, K. M. (2003). Image events, the public sphere, and argumentative practice: The case of radical environmental groups. *Argumentation, 17*(3), 315–333.

Drucker, J. (1998). Critical metalanguage for the artist's book. In *Figuring the word* (pp. 171–174). Granary Books, Inc.

Dubofsky, M. (1969). *We shall be all: A history of the IWW.* Quadrangle Books.

Edbauer Rice, J. (2008). The new "new": Making a case for critical affect studies. *Quarterly Journal of Speech, 94*(2), 200–212.

Fleckenstein, K. S. (2003). *Embodied literacies: Imageword and a poetics of teaching.* Southern Illinois UP.

Fleckenstein, K. S., Hum, S., & Calendrillo, L.T. (Eds.). (2007). *Ways of seeing, ways of speaking: The integration of rhetoric and vision in constructing the real.* Parlor Press.

Foss, S. K. (2005). Theory of visual rhetoric. In K. L. Smith, S. Moriarty, K. Kenney, & G. Barbatsis (Eds.), *Handbook of visual communication: Theory, methods, and media* (pp. 141–152). Lawrence Erlbaum Associates.

Gregg, M., & Seigworth, G. J. (Eds.). (2010). *The affect theory reader.* Duke UP.

Gregg, M., & Seigworth, G. J. (2010). An inventory of shimmers. In M. Gregg & G. J. Siegworth (Eds.), *The affect theory reader* (pp. 1–25). Duke UP.

Gries, L. (2015). *Still life with rhetoric: A new materialist approach for visual rhetorics.* Utah State UP.

Hardt, M., & Negri, A. (2004). *Multitude: War and democracy in the age of empire.* The Penguin Press.

Hill, C. A., & Helmers, M. (2004). Preface. In C. A. Hill & M. Helmers (Eds.), *Defining visual rhetorics* (pp. ix–xi). Routledge.

Hoover, J. D. (2007). 'Miners starve, idle or working': Working-class rhetoric of the early twentieth century. In W. DeGenaro (Ed.), *Who says? Working-class rhetoric, class consciousness, and community* (pp. 32–46). U of Pittsburgh P.

Industrial Workers of the World. (n.d.). *What is what in the world of labor?* [Photograph]. Joseph A. Labadie Collection, University of Michigan. http://quod.lib.umich.edu/l/lbc2ic/x-sclp0534/sclp_0534_la

Jacobs, D., & Micciche, L. R. (Eds.). (2003). *A way to move: Rhetorics of emotion and composition studies*. Boynton.

Keenan, D. (2015). Is another unionism possible? Solidarity unionism in the industrial workers of the world in the U.S. and Canada. *Working USA: The Journal of Labor and Society, 18*(2), 211–229.

Kornbluh, J. L. (Ed.). (1988a). *Rebel voices: An IWW anthology*. Charles H. Kerr Publishing Company.

Kornbluh, J. L. (1988b). One big union: The philosophy of industrial unionism. In J. L. Kornbluh (Ed.), *Rebel voices: An IWW anthology* (pp. 1–7). Charles H. Kerr Publishing Company.

Knoblauch, A. (2012). Bodies of knowledge: Definitions, delineations, and implications of embodied writing in the academy. *Composition Studies, 40*(2), 50–65.

Massumi, B. (2002) *Parables for the virtual*. Duke UP.

Miner, D. (2005). El Grito del Diseño: The radical visual language in Chicana/o newspapers. In P. Buhle & N. Schulman (Eds.), *Wobblies! A graphic history of the industrial workers of the world*. Verso.

Miner, D. (2007). El Grito del Diseño: The Radical Visual Language in Chicana/o Newspapers. In J. MacPhee & E. Rueland (Eds.), *Realizing the impossible: Art against authority* (pp. 55–67). AK Press.

Murray, J. (2009). *Non-discursive rhetoric: Image and affect in multimodal composition*. SUNY Press.

Propen, A. D. (2012). *Locating visual-material rhetorics: The map, the mill, & the GPS*. Parlor Press.

Schnapp, J. T. (2005). *Revolutionary tides: The art of the political poster, 1914–1989*. Skira.

Sellars, N. A. (1998). *Oil, Wheat, & Wobblies: The industrial workers of the world in Oklahoma, 1905–1930*. U of Oklahoma P.

Thompson, F. W., & Bekken, J. (2006). *The industrial workers of the world: Its first 100 years*. Red Sun Press.

Winters, D. E. (1985). *The soul of the Wobblies: The I.W.W., religion and American culture in the progressive era, 1905–1917*. Greenwood Press.

Wyatt, C. S., & DeVoss, D. N. (Eds.). (2018). *Type matters: The rhetoricity of letterforms*. Parlor Press.

CHAPTER 11

Mind on Heaven

Working-Class Rhetorics in Serpent-Handling Rituals of Southern Appalachia

Heather Palmer

> The church becomes a refuge in places where life is hard.
> Brown and McDonald (*The Serpent Handlers: Three Families and Their Faith*, 2000, p. 233)

∴

> And these signs shall follow them that believe: In my name shall they cast out devils; they shall speak with new tongues. They shall take up serpents; and if they drink any deadly thing, it shall not hurt them; they shall lay hands on the sick, and they shall recover.
> MARK 16:17–18

∴

> Behold, I give unto you power to tread on serpents and scorpions, and over all the power of the enemy: and nothing shall by any means hurt you.
> LUKE 10:19

∴

Notable in the stories of both the older generation of serpent handlers and the new is the enmeshment of the cultural identity of these communities with what can be considered the working-class. Although the economies of the regions are dying or dead, the art is not. A full overview of the history of the practice of serpent-handling sects or the economic and labor history of the US South exceeds the scope of this chapter; however, it will mark out several aspects of these rituals that emerge from the Appalachian South's working-class experience of job scarcity and economic hardship. This paper argues that these rituals often function as epideictic rhetorical strategies that ultimately acknowledge a way of life under threat and assert shared cultural identity. The rhetorical purpose of such services aligns it with the epideictic, in at least two ways: one, to confirm communal identity under duress and, two, as a way for adherents to become consubstantial with community and religious values based on labor as physical and spiritual, their mind on heaven.

The obvious question is precisely how does one define the working-class? Often, the pop culture trope of the working-class subject is that of the uniformed, dirty, often urban blue-collar industrial worker, as in On the Waterfront, not the Southern Appalachian preacher, typically in ill-fitting dress clothes, dancing, singing, and handling snakes.[1] There is a clear gap between such popular representations of the various forms of the working-class and their lived experience that a term such as "cultural identity" can bridge. For this study, I will follow Julie Lindquist's sense of the term "cultural identity," rather than insisting in any categorical way that to consider our subjects properly "working-class," they must occupy specific jobs that meet specific criteria. As with Lindquist's subjects, bar patrons engaging in political argumentation, my subjects may not currently be employed at blue collar or service-oriented jobs but nevertheless they value and identify with this work as part of their cultural heritage. As Lindquist explains, for her subjects, class identity "came as much through an ideological orientation to the value of labor as a productive character and community-building activity is it did through the mean fact of participation in a certain kind of labor" (271). This orientation to labor will remain key to my argument that epideictic forms of religious rhetoric in serpent-handling sects confirm a working-class cultural identity; thus, attending to the practices of the working-class through the lens of class culture is useful in that it points to the place where, "social structures and material conditions meet the particulars of local practice, in the politics of the everyday" (Lindquist "Class Identity" 2). Also for the purposes of this study, I'll rely Nancy Welch's conception of the working-class drawn from Michael Zweig's findings,[2] as those who must sell their labor, physical or mental, in exchange for a wage or salary and who as individuals have little say in the content and pace of their work or their rate of compensation. This definition is key to this analysis because it highlights the links between social class and social power and between rhetorical means and authority in these epideictic ceremonies (p. 225). Also along with Welch, I'd like also to emphasize the concept of "working-class" as an expressive rather than descriptive model.

According to recent reports, U.S. economic growth has not been broadly shared; even with high corporate profits, the working-class has experienced stagnant pay and for millions of workers, specifically those without four-year college degrees, there is a downward pressure on employment, wage growth, job quality and opportunity in specific communities ("Blueprint for the 21st Century," 5/14/2018, americanprogress.org). Prospect.org gives a compelling account of how the US South drives a low wage economy, a trend that has spread northward with the rise in "right to work" states and anti-union and minimum wage standards. For many global manufacturers, the South has become the low-wage alternative to China.[3] As a result of such policies, for example, even as auto factories open all across the South autoworkers' earnings have been falling.[4] Despite the influx of jobs, wages continue to fall throughout the South precisely because of political and economic interests leveraging against legislation and institutions that protect workers' interests. As recently as June 14, 2019, workers at the Volkswagen plant in Chattanooga, Tennessee, voted against the UAW's efforts to unionize the plant. As the *New York Times* points out, this loss highlights the difficulty of organizing private-sector workers in a political environment that is overtly hostile to labor unions. Tennessee's Republican governor, Bill Lee, a former contractor, opposes the U.A.W. campaign because the presence of a union would make it harder for the state to attract other businesses (NYT, June 14, 2019). Further, states that have no minimum-wage laws are Mississippi, Alabama, Louisiana, Tennessee, and South Carolina. Georgia is one of the two states (the other is Wyoming) that have set minimum wages below the level of the federal standard.

Astoundingly, some reactions to these circumstances in the media have been to blame the white working-class directly—for Donald Trump, their addiction to opioids, and their economic crisis. As conservative National Review's Kevin Williamson explains, "Donald Trump's speeches make them feel good. So does OxyContin." In typical polemic fashion he pointedly tells readers:

> Nothing happened to them. There wasn't some awful disaster, there wasn't a war or a famine or a plague or a foreign occupation. ... The truth about these dysfunctional, downscale communities is that they deserve to die. Economically, they are negative assets. Morally, they are indefensible. (Williamson, 2016)

Seen by the popular press as mired in ignorance, squalor, and now moral degradation, it is understandable why typically those from the Appalachian South would shun outsiders[5] from all ideological and political sides, particularly in the media. However, Julia Duin points to a new generation of serpent-handlers who do not necessarily shun outsiders—for example, Mack Wolford or Andrew Hamblin, who actually widely circulates his practices in social media, filling his Facebook page with photos of his handling of copperheads, cottonmouths, and rattlesnakes, in spite of Tennessee's ban on their possession and transport (p. 30). Mack Wolford has since passed away due to a snake bite and Andrew Hamblin, after quite the rocky relationship with social media and press coverage, took a brief hiatus from both, and founded a new church on the condition that no snakes were allowed, perhaps due to sensationalist and negative press.[6] Despite its diversity, signifiers of Appalachia remain monolithic in their significations of the "hazily defined conceptual category of the white working class" (p. 4) embodied in the white cole miner from depressed towns rampant with opiod addictions. As the introduction to Appalachian Reckoning (2019) points out, contemporary scholars of Appalachia are increasingly emphasizing the need to "challenge distorting and debilitating stereotypes" (p. 4) of the region, a challenge this essay hopes to partially take up.

What follows doesn't parse out the specifics of such economic systems via labor studies, rather, using direct oral histories and video recordings of services, it seeks to trace how the lived experience of those who consider themselves working-class at the fringes of mainstream culture interanimates their religious practice. For example, the historic Church of the Lord Jesus in Jolo, West Virginia, was founded in 1956 by Bob (Joe Robert) and Barbara Elkins, a coal mining family. Barbara's daughter, Columbia, died of snakebite at 23. Speaking of his employment to his interviewers Fred Brown and Jeanne McDonald, Bob explains:

> I was a coal miner. I worked in deep mines, mostly. I bossed about all my life, but I [also] worked operating machinery. I operated miners, scoops, tractors. The last ten years, I was superintendent for No. 10 coal mine. I was down in the mines for about forty-two years. While you are superintendent, you don't stay outside all the time. You got to make your rounds to make sure you know what's going on inside. I also worked in Virginia. (p. 259)

Although we are told it is quite beautiful, Jolo is marred by strip mining scars, and its natural beauty punctuated with "cinder block houses, trailers, makeshift structures covered with insulation, sheets, rusty skeletons of abandoned automobiles, and random piles of litter" (Brown & McDonald, 2000, p. 234). I raise the material circumstances of this founding family because, although I have written about these practices as forms of the epideictic species of religious rhetoric previously (Palmer, 2021), what is new about this piece is tracing how they emerge from specific material conditions brought on by global economic and political systems. Also unique to this study is the digital archive upon which I rely for access to access to working-class voices and perspectives.

UTC's digital collection, The Ralph W. Hood and W. Paul Williamson Holiness Churches of Appalachia,[7] features a small sample of more than 400 hours of church services and interviews documenting contemporary serpent handlers of Southern Appalachia from which I draw my examples. Ranging from 1975 to 2004, this collection focuses on the major Pentecostal congregations that practice speaking in tongues, imbibing poisons, and serpent handling in the southeastern United States.

I take seriously Russo and Linkhon's call in New Working-Class Studies to collect and study representations in oral histories, songs, personal narratives and, in this specific analysis, video documentation of intimate religious rituals (p. 11). What follows is my effort to make working-class voices a primary source for the study of one of the more misunderstood aspects of life for a certain faction of rural Southern Appalachia. The archive is vast so the scope here is limited a sampling of the oral histories and services from the pastor Jaime Coots of the Full Gospel Tabernacle in Middlesboro, TN and Bob Elkins and Carl Porter of the Church of the Lord Jesus in Jolo, West Virginia. In the next sections I offer a working definition of the epideictic as it is commonly understood and try to show that the services of the serpent-handlers are constituted by some its key rhetorical components as a way to draw them closer to heaven and away from the harsh realities of the life they experience as working-class Appalachian subjects. I hope to offer a more performative[8] understanding of such ceremonies to show the deeply imbricated linkages among subjects, environments, and discourses or the personal, cultural, and discursive.

> When I Lay my Heavy Burdens Down I'll go Home to Be with Jesus. (Jaime Coots, Church of the Lord Jesus, Jolo, W VA, 9/3/96)

In 2014, Jaime Coots, a Kentucky pastor who starred in National Geographic's "Snake Salvation," a reality show about serpent-handling, died of a snakebite after refusing to be treated. Coots was a third-generation "serpent handler" and aspired to one day pass the practice and his Appalachian church, Full Gospel Tabernacle in Jesus Name, on to his adult son, Little Cody. Jamie Coots, pastor of the Full Gospel Tabernacle in Jesus Name in Middlesboro, was a coal miner before being put on full disability. He was part of the "Jesus name" churches who believed you could only be baptized in the names of Jesus, whereas the Trinitarian churches are baptized in the name of the Father, Son, and Holy Spirit (Duin, 2017, p. 45). The National Geographic show, which has since been cancelled, featured Coots and cast handling poisonous snakes, such as copperheads, rattlers, and cottonmouths. According to the show's website, the Pentecostal pastors Jaime Coots and Andrew Hamblin struggle to keep an over-100-year-old tradition alive: the practice of handling deadly snakes in church. Coots and Hamblin believe in Bible passages from Mark and Luke that suggest a poisonous snakebite will not harm them as long as they are anointed by God's power. National Geographic tells us that pastors must frequently battle the law, a disapproving society, economic hardship, and even at times their own families to keep their way of life alive.[9]

A way of keeping one's courage, as Coots often calls it, is through rejoicing in the glory of God in church ceremonies. These ceremonies at which serpent-handling takes place can be considered epideictic as that species of rhetoric which establishes, reconfirms, or revisions general values and beliefs. Although folks are most intrigued by the mechanics of the actual serpent-handling, this study doesn't isolate the serpent-handling act from the entirety of the ritual itself. Traditionally associated often with ritual, ceremony, and performance, the epideictic, in Aristotle's conception, is different from the two other branches, or species (eidē) of rhetoric, the deliberative and forensic. In its incipient conceptions, the epideictic was a way to systematize aspects of ceremonial rhetoric (Aristotle, 1991). As James Jasinski explains, Aristotle combined three types of oratory into the one category of epideictic: "the encomium (speeches of praise or blame for a person or institution), the panegyric (the 'festival oration'), and the epitaphios logos (the eulogy or funeral oration)." Since this time (roughly 350 BCE), the epideictic genre has been the subject of "conceptual discussion and theoretical reflection over the centuries" (Jasinski, 2001, p. 210). For this study, it is the more useful branch for generating and maintaining communal identity in religious ceremony. As Laurent Pernot (2006) explains in "Rhetoric of Religion," "Rhetoric itself possesses a religious dimension in the power of words, the effectiveness of speech, and the magic of persuasion" (p. 235). Consider for example, the rhetorical force to a witnessing public in a ceremony held on 9/3/1996 at the Church of the Lord Jesus, Coots celebrates the power of Jesus to help folks lay their burdens down: "Glory Glory Hallelujah, When I lay my burdens down, I'll go home to be with Jesus ... Thank you, Lord! ... We got to rejoice for the courage ... we've got to rejoice." Here a type of epideictic rhetoric does not argue in any formulaic fashion for the ideas or ideals that bind people into a community so much as it displays them performatively to a witnessing public.

Typically, according to most accounts, serpent-handling churches meet at least once weekly, and sometimes more to worship God and experience manifestations of the spirit. As Hood and Williamson explain, "at the opening of the worship ... the pastor or another designated person cordially welcomes everyone and encourages all to obey God as he moves in the service" (Hood & Williamson, 2007, p. 4). The leader then announces the presence of serpents that have been brought to church in specially crafted boxes[10] placed beside the pulpit: note that although it is usually men who bring and handle serpents, there are many women handlers. Next to the altar in some churches there is a jar of poison (lye, carbolic acid, strychnine) for drinking and sometimes a blowtorch made from a bottle with a kerosene wick for fire-handling. The pastor emphatically announces "there is death in these boxes, jars, etc." The congregants speak an initial prayer followed by a song with guitars, symbols, tambourines, and often even an electric guitar or keyboard and clapping of hands by all of the congregation. As observers such as Duin, Hood, and Williamson all explain in their various printed accounts and in my observations of countless of hours of video footage, at some point during song or sermon, believers begin to move around to celebrate the presence of God. Then someone approaches the boxes, unlatches the lid, and takes up a venomous serpent.[11] Other serpents are taken out and passed around and sometimes believers will swallow poison, some combination of water and strychnine (Hood & Williamson, 2007, p. 4). Participants are not in any way coerced to handle serpents to prove faith but they can be persuaded by the spirit to do so. As Carl Porter explains during a ceremony at Church of the Lord Jesus Sermon (Jolo, WV) on 8/31/96:

> We don't put no serpents on the new guys. We don't make nobody handle them. We just let every man who is persuaded in his own mind to join in. You feel like you want to handle one, that's up to you. We're not responsible for anyone that might handle them because you go in the box, you go on your own. You want to drink the strychnine, you go on your own.[12]

When the atmosphere of ecstatic worship moves on, the congregants then return the serpents to the box. Usually, these proceedings are then followed by songs sung by individuals, personal testimonies of praise, and sermons, all of which are meant exhort the righteous, praise believers, and admonish the backsliders and blame them for their sins with a message of doom and judgment for those who are unrepentant of heart.

The epideictic dimension of several sermons uses work imagery to capture the activities of both the Lord and the Devil and as a way to entreat congregants to accept their burdens and to strengthen their commitment to their own toil, both physical and spiritual. Perelman and Olbrects-Tyteca (1969) explain that the epideictic form "is less directed at changing beliefs than to strengthening adherence to what is already accepted" (p. 54). This strengthening of communal bonds takes place in the present, in order to shore up a future pay-off in the heavens. Consider the following example from the 9/1/1996 sermon at the Church of the Lord Jesus in Jolo, WV in which Bob Elkins uses imagery from the organization of the labor cycle to confirm the value of self-denial (of alcohol, the temptations of "illicit sex," etc.) for a future reward: "Get your time in, your time in, Heaven, Heaven, Heaven is a-comin' after a while. I said payday, payday, payday's comin' after a while."[13] Such language and imagery promote identification in the Burkean[14] sense in which the primary aim is not necessarily to win an argument but to make a connection, to identify shared grounds or interests. In this case, to defer earthly pleasure for heavenly pleasure in the form of a spiritual paycheck, waiting for that ideal Friday when laborers can cash that promissory note they have been holding for a heavenly payoff. This cycle of labor and compensation is one with which congregants are well familiar. Jeffery Walker (2000) further explains the role of the epideictic and identification: "Epideictic appears as that which shapes and cultivates the basic codes of value and belief by which a society or culture lives; it shapes the ideologies and imageries with which, and by which, the individual members of a community identify themselves" (p. 33). Consider further a sampling of another one of Bob Elkins' services at the Church of the Lord Jesus in 1989 in which he uses the common work imagery of the plow to evoke a type of physical labor with which his congregants were familiar and yokes it to shared spiritual labor with Jesus:

> Put your hand on the plow, hold on Walking, uh, pushing for Jesus Christ. Now I'm in the church of God, put your hand on the plow, hold on. Well, hold on, hold on, put your hands on the plow and hold on. Well, don't you turn back to bury the dead. These were his words that Jesus said. Put your hands on the plow, hold on. Well, hold on, hold on, put your hands on the plow and hold on.

Here, Elkins' rhetorical move is to use language that purposefully names something (or someone) according to specific properties, in this case a plow, and his congregants associate with this labor and disassociate themselves from others that don't take on a similar burden. Here subjects (people, ideas or things) share important qualities in common by disassociating with other people (sinners—even the sinner within that doesn't labor with the Lord); ideas (promiscuity, laziness, materialism); or things (alcohol, tobacco, etc.). This naming results in identification—in this case, the state of being consubstantial with others or the Other (Jesus/Lord/God). In one sermon on 9/1/96, Bob Elkins reminds congregants that the Devil himself is a laborer, working twenty-four hours a day, "he is always on his job." He uses this specter to admonish his audience to double-down in their epideictic praise and celebration of the Jesus, to "get your time in." The Lord works through you, you identify with the Lord, but you remain distinct from the Lord. This rhetorical identification, that which Burke calls "consubstantial," marks a relationship that is both a conjoining and a separation: "In being identified with B, A is "substantially one" with a person [entity] other than himself. Yet at the same time he remains unique, an individual locus of motives. Thus he is both joined and separate, at once a distinct substance and consubstantial with another" (Burke, 1969, pp. 20–21). Such immanent coupling, for Burke, is necessary to a way of life, an acting-together in which "men have common sensations, concepts, images, ideas, attitudes that make them consubstantial" (Burke, 1969, p. 21). Burke links identification's personal, cultural, and discursive dimensions (Ratcliffe, 2006, p. 54), leading to my claim that the epideictic religious rhetoric of serpent handling services is exemplary of this type of consubstantiality.

A mark of consubstantiality is found in the practitioner's burning desire to handle serpents, a desire which they explain results in the anointing. This type of affect is felt in the body, not in thought and representation, and the experience of being anointed is direct, immediate, linked intimately with the present. The experience also escapes discursive restraints. As Jaime Coots attempts to explain in an interview on 10/11/98 from UTC's archives, *"there is no way of describing it,* you just, you feel way down deep like you just want to bust ... it made me closer to the Lord ... I mean anything that God lets you do will make you closer to Him, but in taking up serpents ... you always have to remain as close as you possibly can" (emphasis added).[15] In this case, remaining consubstantial with the Lord God is key to survival, since, as Coots further explains: "Every time the Lord moves on me to take up one, just for a second I check my life and make sure there's nothing there ... standing in my way ... Anytime you handle one, it could bite you and any bite could be your last bite ... you want to make sure everything's right."[16] For Coots and his fellow believers, everything is right when they are closest to God.

This description of being close to God, "the Lord moving on you," is an affective transmission that moves the believers to an ecstatic adherence to specific communal values and the desire to handle deadly serpents as the sign of this anointing or God moving on me. Teresa Brennan explains such transmissions:

> the "transmission of affect" ... is social or psychological in origin. But the transmission is also responsible for bodily changes; some are brief changes, as in a whiff of the room's atmosphere, some longer lasting ... [it] alters the biochemistry and neurology of the subject. The "atmosphere" or the environment literally gets into the individual. (Brennan, 2004, p. 1)

Her description is strikingly parallel to the congregants explaining the anointing as a "getting in," "God moving on me," which often takes place during the extemporaneous sermons. These can range from a few minutes to over an hour, and inspire in listeners a feeling of God moving on the person, in an embodied way that causes participants to get up move around, handle serpents or drink poison. As Coots further explains in his interview with W. Paul Williamson:

> It's just like the whole service changes, the whole environment seems to change, everybody seems to want to get in when the Lord begins to move. The service may be a little tight, people may not have their minds together, but then the Lord begin to move just a little bit, everybody begins to get their minds together ... then you can begin to get in and you begin to feel things kind of loosen up ... like you take one person, maybe four in a row, you know, it's pulling a heavy object, screaming hard, but when you get to two or three or four or five or eight or ten more, well then obviously it'll get a little easier. So when everybody tries to press in, you know, it gets easier for you. (Hood & Williamson, 2008, p. 133)

The pastor here is not making a "rational" argument in the service that persuades the audience with cold logic to then handle serpents or join the anointing; rather, the rhetorical force is that of the spontaneous revelation of God or divine radiance in a collective "getting-together" or rather a "getting-in." Rosenfield (1980) explains the true function of orators in rituals of the epideictic: "far from forcing his idea on an audience with cold logic, the orator charms his listeners; he enchants them so that they, like him, are attracted to a mode of thinking" (p. 139). The function of epideictic is to reveal or disclose something, and, experiencing an authentic performance is akin to a religious epiphany—such as the revelation of the presence of God as serpent handlers take up snakes in service, through a type of enchantment.

Through such testimonials and sermons, we can see that the service includes at least three types of the epideictic: encomium (rhetoric of praise or blame), panegyric (meant as public assembly in honor of a god), even sometimes eulogies for those who have died as a result of being bitten or poisoned. Note the following exchange between interviewer W. Paul Williamson (WPW) and Jaime Coots (JC) who is keen to explain his views on those who get bit and survive and those who die:

WPW: What does it mean when people die from a serpent bite when they are manifesting signs?

JC: ... it's just from the time they were born, that's their time to leave. It's nothing to do with their being disobedient or not having the anointing, but a lot of times when you get bit and just swell up and hurt, you may have disobeyed the Lord or something. But when you get bit and die, you don't—it's a different thing ... most people that I've seen bitten that die was anointed when they got bit. It's just your time to go.[17]

So, the complex relationship of faith, belief, and rhetoric culminates in a primal desire to risk physical death for spiritual life. Ned O'Gorman (2005) tells us that "As a phantasmatic phenomenon, epideictic operates at the 'primal' levels of desire and/or emotion" (p. 30), and the relation to these primal levels is a condition of the genre itself. And let me point out that no handlers in the interviews I've been referring to believe in magical ability to handle without harm: they understand that handling serpents may mean bodily death. This understanding, the simultaneous attraction to and fear of a foundational object, is key to the epideictic nature of the anointing. The identification and consubstantiality emerge from a performance (preaching, singing, handling serpents) that passes into content (anointing), and vividly displays what affect theorist Brian Massumi (2002) explains as a mutual immanence that is "lived, experienced most directly and intensely" (p. xxiii).

Feeling a consubstantiality or transmission of affect with others who share the same values—and threats—is important for these people of rural Southern Appalachia. We need a more nuanced and empathetic understanding of the significance of such rituals to a cultural identity against reductive, rigid, and unimaginative conclusions about their plight as articulated by the National Review commentator. The desire to be saved, for the ultimate self-preservation, immortality, is perhaps the primary drive behind the rhetorical force of these rituals: rather than the desire for physical life or self-preservation, however, they are motivated by the desire for spiritual life or self-preservation. Their mind is on heaven, the ultimate payday.

Ultimately, this on-going project raises questions of attunements of rhetorical beings, paying particular attention to the material bodies that inhabit them, either as subjects or objects of evidence. Further approaches would take up the posthuman turn in intellectual inquiry that seeks to de-center the all-knowing universal humanist subject, and to disrupt the primacy of language to represent in any stable way the messy materiality of the world. In further disrupting distinctions between subject/environment/discourse or the personal/cultural/discursive or even between the human (the pastor/congregation) and nonhuman (the serpents, Lord/Jesus/God), what emerges is a singular rhetoricity, an underlying openness, a capacity to act and to be acted upon that is radically relational and exposed.

Notes

1. Usually rendered as white and male. Note that there is one African-American handler that has been documented and a notable number of women. Considering these issues would be key to any sustained investigation of these sects as the racism and sexism of the white working class has been assumed. See Elizabeth Faue's essay "Gender, Class, and History." Further, as David Roediger's (1991) *The Wages of Whiteness: Race and the Making of the American Working-Class* shows us, the category "working class" often is synonymous with white men (p. 3).
2. Zweig estimates that the working class is 62 percent of the workforce, and white men are only 46 percent of this figure (2001, pp. 30–31).
3. https://prospect.org/article/how-american-south-drives-low-wage-economy
4. From 2001 to 2013, workers at auto-parts plants in Alabama—the state with the highest growth rate—saw their earnings decline by 24 percent, and those in Mississippi by 13.6 percent. The newer the hire, the bleaker the picture, even though by 2013 the industry was recovering, and in the South, booming. New hires' pay was 24 percent lower than all auto-parts workers in South Carolina and 17 percent lower in Alabama.
5. Until now. See Julia Duin's work on social media and the new gen. of serpent-handlers.
6. As Duin explains, she doesn't expect Andrew to refrain from handling snakes for long (2017, p. 205).
7. This description is taken from the UTC library's webpage which has the largest archive of Pentecostal Serpent-handlers. The main scholar of such practices, Dr. Ralph Hood, is an integral part of our psychology department. As the premier scholar of serpent handling and mysticism, he has been allowed unprecedented access to these rituals and even the congregants in their private homes. My work in understanding the rhetorical dimension of these rituals would not be possible without his extensive research into these communities, along with that of his collaborator, W. Paul Williamson.
8. Along with Karen Barad, I want to move toward more performative alternatives to representational accounts of phenomena that emphasize doings/actions/practices rather than an over-emphasis on "linguistic monism." See her essay "Posthumanist Performativity: Toward and Understanding of how Matter Comes to Matter."
9. http://channel.nationalgeographic.com/snake-salvation
10. Julia Duin (2017, p. 2) tells readers that snake boxes are gift-box size contraptions with hinges and handles so one can see which reptile was inside.
11. Serpents such as Timbler rattlers, Canebrake, and Eastern Diamondbacks are often used.
12. https://digital-collections.library.utc.edu
13. https://digital-collections.library.utc.edu
14. Kenneth Burke, of course, is a major American rhetorician most famous for his theories of dramatism and his terms of the Pentad. His major works include *A Rhetoric of Motives, Language as Symbolic Action*, and *Counter-Statement*.
15. https://digital-collections.library.utc.edu
16. https://digital-collections.library.utc.edu
17. https://digital-collections.library.utc.edu

References

Aristotle. (1991). *On rhetoric: A theory of civic discourse* (G. A. Kennedy, Trans.). Oxford University Press.

Bataille, G. (1989). *Theory of religion* (R. Hurley, Trans.). Zone Books.

Beale, W. H. (1978). Rhetorical performative discourse: A new theory of epideictic. *Philosophy and Rhetoric, 11*, 221–246.

Beech, J. (2004). Redneck and hillbilly discourse in the writing classroom: Classifying critical of whiteness. *College English, 67*(2), 172–186.

Brennan, T. (2004). *The transmission of affect*. Cornell University Press.

Brown, F., & McDonald, J. (2000). *The serpent handlers: Three families and their faith*. John E. Blair, Publisher.

Burke, K. (1969). *Rhetoric of motives*. University of California Press.

Burton, T. (1993). *'And these signs shall follow': Serpent handling believers*. University of Tennessee Press.

Condit, C. M. (2009). The function of epideictic: The Boston Massacre orations as exemplar. *Communication Quarterly, 33*, 284–299.

Covington, D. (2009). *Salvation on sand mountain: Snake handling and redemption in Southern Appalachia* (15th ann. ed.). DeCapo Press.

Darwin, C. (2007). *The expression of the emotions in man and animals*. Filiquarian Publishing, LLC.

De Genaro, W. (Ed.). (2007). *Who says? Working class rhetoric, class consciousness, and community*. University of Pittsburgh Press.

Duin, J. C. (2017). *In the house of the serpent handler: A story of faith and fleeting fame in the age of social media*. University of Tennessee Press.

Faue, E. (2005). Gender, class, and history. In J. Russo & S. L. Linkon (Eds.), *New working-class studies*. ILR Press.

Harkins, A., & McCarroll, M. (2019). *Appalachian reckoning*. West Virginia Press.

Holt, J. (1940). Holiness religion: Cultural shock and social reorganization. *American Sociological Review, 5*, 740–741.

Hood Jr., R., & Williamson, W. P. (2008). *Them that believe*. University of California Press.

Jasinski, J. (2001). *Sourcebook on rhetoric: Key concepts in contemporary rhetorical studies*. Sage Publications.

Kennedy, G. A. (1998). *Comparative rhetoric: An historical and cross-cultural introduction*. Oxford University Press.

Lindquist, J. (2007). Conclusion: Working-class rhetoric as ethnographic subject. In W. DeGenaro (Ed.), *Who says? Working class rhetoric, class consciousness, and community*. University of Pittsburgh Press.

Mailloux, S. (1985). Enactment history, jesuit practices, and rhetorical hermeneutics. *Critical Inquiry, 11*(4), 620–641.

Massumi, B. (2002). Introduction: Like a thought. In *A shock to thought: Expression after Deleuze and Guattari*. Routledge Press.

Newitz, A., & Wray, M. (Eds.). (1997). *White trash: Race and class in America*. Routledge.

Nicotra, J. (2016). Disgust distributed: Virtual public shaming as epideictic assemblage. *Enculturation, 22*.

O'Gorman, N. (2005). Aristotle's 'phantasia' in the 'rhetoric': 'Lexis,' appearance and the epideictic function of discourse. *Philosophy & Rhetoric, 38*(1), 16–40.

Palmer, H. (2021). Epideictic rhetoric in Pentecostal serpent-handling rituals of the contemporary Appalachian South. *Southern Studies: An Interdisciplinary Journal of the South, 28*(1), 90–113.

Perelman, C. H., & Olbrechts-Tyteca, L. (1969). *The new rhetoric: A treatise on argumentation* (J. Wilkinson & P. Weaver, Trans. University of Notre Dame Press.

Pernot, L. (2006). Rhetoric of religion. *Rhetorica, XXIV*(3), 235.

Ratcliffe, K. (2006). *Rhetorical listening: Identification, gender, whiteness*. Southern Illinois University Press.

Rickert, T. (2013). *Ambient rhetoric: The attunements of rhetorical being*. University of Pittsburgh Press.

Rosenfield, L. W. (1980). The practical celebration of epideictic. In E. E. White (Ed.), *Rhetoric in transition: Studies in the nature and use of rhetoric*. Pennsylvania State University Press.

Russo, J., & Linkon, S. L. (Eds.). (2005). *New working-class studies*. ILR Press.

Timmerman, D. (1996). Epideictic oratory. In T. Enos (Ed.), *The encyclopedia of rhetoric and composition*. Garland Publishing.

Vance, J. D. (2016). *Hillbilly elegy: A memoir of a family and culture in crisis*. Harper.

Walker, J. (2000). *Rhetoric and poetics in antiquity*. Oxford University Press.

Welch, N. (2011). We're here and we aren't going anywhere: Why working-class rhetorical traditions still matter. *College English, 73*(2), 221–242.

Zweig, M. (2001). *O*. Cornell UP.

Williamson, K. D. (2016, March 28). The father-führer. *National Review*. https://www.nationalreview.com/magazine/2016/03/28/father-f-hrer/

CHAPTER 12

White Bread as a Working-Class Symbol

Kelli R. Gill

I can tell you the exact type of bread that sat, week after week, in our kitchen cabinet when I was growing up. Sunbeam, split top, white bread. It's the kind of sugar filled, overly processed, starchy white bread that people reference when they say, "white bread." It's the kind of bread my grandmother would quit when she was going off carbs and trying to lose weight. It's the kind of bread my mom was referring to when we were at the store and she needed to check bread off her list.

The white bread was located on the third aisle at our Walmart, right past the frozen items, next to coffee, jam, and peanut butter. It was the first stop we would make when grocery shopping. My mother would lightly squeeze different loaves to decide which was the softest. If you, too, walk down a grocery aisle and squeeze loaves of bread (a practice I've realized is not as common as I was led to believe when I was younger), you'll notice that some loaves are indeed squishier than others. The "good loaves" gave a little when you pressed your thumb on one side and the remaining fingers on the other. You had to do so delicately, or else you'd smash the bread. Sometimes, before I'd mastered the art, I would transform a good loaf into a bad loaf by pressing too hard. The "bad loaves" would not easily give. They were stiffer or already squished. They didn't *feel right* when you grabbed them. We left those on the shelves. Even now, if I have to buy white bread for some reason, I can't help but test them. Check for quality. It's more ritualistic than anything.

I realize now that the bread never tasted different. It was always the same squishy, pliable, air filled slices. It didn't look or taste like anything we'd ever made ourselves. It lacked the substance that I associate with a hardy wheat, rye, sourdough, or the yeast dinner rolls my family baked on holidays. The truth is that white bread, for my family, wasn't really valued for those reasons; it was for its potential for invention, experimentation, and transformation.

1   A Story Retold

I have chosen white bread as an object which best illustrates how stories are used to devalue food and the people who eat it. This chapter will be divided in four main sections.

The first section, "White Bread/White Trash," looks to media representations of white bread to explore implications of white trash stereotypes. The second section, "Shifting Narratives," will discuss the origin stories of white bread and how narratives have shifted to associate white bread with working-class people. Within the third section I will focus on the food myths that perpetuate working-class stereotypes and assign moral value to the food we eat.

Lastly, I narrow the focus to more specific food stories to demonstrate the versatility of white bread. I have arranged this chapter to illustrate the ways that broader narratives are implicated in the interpretation of localized experiences. Additionally, within these stories I will talk about transformation, both the transformation of stories and the transformation of white bread. By starting the chapter with current assumptions and narratives of foods and ending with a new definition and potentiality of white bread, I hope to construct a rhetorical transformation of the food narrative—to demonstrate the power of stories to reimagine, redefine, and reinterpret material objects for working-class people.

2   White Bread/White Trash: Exploring Media Symbols

As a cheap food found in most working-class homes, white bread is recognizable by many poor people. White bread is so associated with low-income households, that when I type the phrase "growing up poor" in Google's image search engine, the first result to pop up was Figure 12.1.

FIGURE 12.1
"Growing up Poor" (internet meme, public domain)

The image is but one of many memes which attempted to encapsulate the experience of "growing up poor" through the use white bread. Often referred to as "struggle meals," the meme captures a recognizable moment of making due with what was available. What makes white bread symbolic, though, is how recognizable it is to people who didn't grow up working-class.

As I have talked with people about this project, I have yet to meet someone who cannot identify the red, yellow, and blue circles of a Wonder Bread package or someone who doesn't understand the difference between "white bread" and the contrasting artisanal varieties. While conversational anecdotes might quickly show how other people identify white bread as a food symbol, I recognize that this type of sampling isn't representative of American culture. I want to demonstrate the identification of white bread as a working-class icon in the media. If we look to media representation, we can see how working-class people are associated with white bread. I want to also explore the types of working-class people that are represented through these associations—specifically the ways that white, rural, less educated folk are used to demonstrate the "white trash" stereotype of white bread.

White bread appears in the media notably through movies and television. Sometimes it is exposure of a certain brand and other times it is the use of white bread in a specific scene. Take, for example, the movie *Talladega Nights*, which features the brand Wonder Bread as a Nascar sponsor. In the movie, Will Ferrell plays a race car driver and Wonder Bread's logo can be seen on his car, suit, and helmet. What's interesting about this type of brand display is that it was not part of a product placement sponsorship. The writers of *Talladega Nights* chose to use Wonder Bread as a mock sponsor (Wonder Bread is not an actual sponsor of Nascar). Though we are unable to infer exactly why the writers chose Wonder Bread, looking at Nascar's demographics might give us a better understanding of how Wonder Bread appeals to working-class people. ESPN writer, LZ Granderson, argues that Nascar is undeniably associated with white, country culture and that the association leads people to stereotyping Nascar fans as "hillbilly, redneck or dumb." Demographics show that 94% of Nascar's fans are white, and they are twice more likely to be from rural areas (Nielsen's 2013 Year in Sports Media Report). The association of white bread and rural, white people manifests in *Talladega Nights*' Nascar Sponsor, Wonder Bread.

Other media representations involve scenes in which white bread is used as a prop. For example, in the movie *Benny & Joon*, Sam, an illiterate white man, is shown using the classic white bread to make grilled cheese sandwiches with a clothing iron. This scene is but one of the multiple quirky eating habits in the movie—but it's a telling one. Sam, though illiterate, demonstrates a different literacy skill in his use of an iron instead of a pan. In addition to the association of white bread with uneducated people, white bread is often used as a metaphor for blandness and whiteness. The Woody Allen film, *Hannah and Her Sisters*, has a scene where the character Mickey attempts to become Catholic. He is shown bringing home a crucifix, a bible, a jar of Hellman's Mayonnaise, and a loaf of Wonder Bread. The two latter items in the scene are used as symbols of goyish culture—representing blandness in contrast to the richness of Jewish rye. While many movie scenes involving white bread are funny because they demonstrate seemingly peculiar eating habits, other scenes use the image of white bread as the icon of just a few qualities, namely "cheap" and "devoid of nutrition." When you extend those ideas to the stereotypes of the people who eat white bread, those people become reduced to the same, few qualities—"poor and bland."

Piet Defraeye, producer of the play *White Bread* (2016), argues that white bread is, "an iconic cultural symbol in our taxonomy of physical and spiritual nourishment, of which there typically is precious little in the case of white bread" (p. 102). In his play, white bread symbolizes a lack of substance and depth. Though these metaphors may seem harmless, they are ideas that are expressed through deeper misconceptions about white, working-class people.

In the book *White Bread: Weaving Cultural Past into the Present*, Christine Sleeter (2013) explores a phrase she noticed white teachers using in the classroom—"I'm just plain white bread American" (p. 3). She argues that variations of this phrase are often perceived as a strategy by white teachers to "shrug off implications that racial and ethnic identity might matter," but that they are really an indication that many white people are unsure of where they fit. They do not know if there are any collective identities to which they belong. Sleeter's commentary points to the danger of reducing white bread to qualities such as poor, white, bland, empty, "only air," or of no value. When white, working-class people are equated to white bread, we assign those same qualities to them. If media representations affirm those stereotypes, we raise generations of people who think they have "no culture" or identity. Though many poor, white people might not want to associate or identify with working-class culture, we should seek to understand culture in more nuanced ways. This chapter seeks to demonstrate that nuance.

3 Shifting Narratives: How Stories Shape Food Icons

As we start to unravel the narratives of white bread it is apparent that the story about white bread has not always been the same. While white bread is currently understood as a symbol of working-class people, it was not *always* so.

That shift in narrative demonstrates how a culture can reassign value to a food through stories.

When white bread was first invented it was anything but a symbol of the poor. The phrase "the best thing since sliced bread" is a remnant from previous narratives that painted white bread as a symbol of industrialization. Whereas today many people would argue that homemade bread is healthier, in the 1920s, homemade bread was more associated with poor people and poor diet. Many people became suspect of homemade bread due to overcrowding and lack of sanitation laws for food prep. Aaron Bobrow-Strain, a professor of food politics, in his book *White Bread: A Social History of the Store-Bought Loaf* (2013), traces the history of white bread. He argues that white bread, while originally a solution to hygiene, quickly became a way to criticize poor people. White bread became part of a food purity discourse used against working-class people. He writes,

> In a fashion reminiscent of many community-garden and anti-obesity campaigns designed to teach the poor about "healthy eating" today, reformers poured into the country's urban tenements and rural hill countries. What they achieved was not an attack on the economic root causes of poverty, but the spread of a gospel of progress through healthy habits. (pp. 36–37)

Later, white bread became fortified with vitamins and acted as a staple food during the Great Depression. Ironically, white bread was touted as a solution to the poor person's diet and lack of resources and today it is often cited as the problem. In comparison to other foods or alternatives, white bread was a better option for many people. However, somewhere along the line reformers stopped associating white bread with health and shifted to a new narrative. This narrative is the one that is most common today, that white bread is devoid of nutrition—a "bad" food.

Bobrow-Strain argues that the history of white bread demonstrates the dangers of food purity discourses. While industrialization and health narratives that produced white bread also made for safer food preparation law and a better understanding of nutrition, these narratives served to benefit mostly wealthy, white consumers. Rather than *for*, these narratives were used against working-class people to criticize their eating habits and belittle them for being poor. Health fears "[combined] with larger social anxieties and [reinforced] other kinds of exclusion and distract from root causes" (p. 49). It's important to recognize this shift in narrative, because it demonstrates how a discourse surrounding a food changes. The value of white bread cannot be reduced to its genetic structure or nutritional value alone—because it is understood within a cultural context that defines those values.

The stories we tell about a food shape its meaning, but the meaning is not permanent. As Kristie O'Neill and Daniel Silver (2016) explain, "we can treat food as items of objective culture and laden with multiple possibilities of cultural meaning" (p. 100). This means that white bread can be eaten and understood without participating in working-class culture; it has the potential of taking on multiple cultural meanings. By tracing a shifting narrative, I hope to demonstrate how stories change our interpretation of food. Once a symbol of food purity, white bread is now a symbol of poverty. Its meaning and status as a symbol is rooted in that transformation.

4 Food Myths: Discourses of Health, Morals, and Shame

I remember once a moment when a friend was over to my family's house, and we were cooking something that called for butter. I went to our refrigerator and pulled out the tub of Country Crock to which my friend commented, "Oh, my mom only buys real butter." Now, I don't recall what age this happened or who was over. I don't even remember what we were making. But—I do remember how I felt at that time. It was the same feeling I got when my dad picked me up from school in his work clothes or when I was in class and everyone was sharing vacation stories. My family wasn't dirt poor by any means. We had plenty to eat, in the summers I'd go to church camp, and every once in a while we'd go to the movies. However, there were things my dad wouldn't buy, things I'd never known were "poor people" things until some middle-class friend of mine would toss the phrase "real butter" at me. I didn't realize at that point that there was such a thing as fake butter, the way I'd known I wore Walmart clothes, or knew my family couldn't afford a trip to Disney World. It was a new level of feeling different that didn't go away after I left the classroom or the grocery store. A sense of shame in my own damn kitchen.

I want to emphasize that there is nothing wrong with a food associated with a certain group of people. It's true that my family never bought "real" butter (i.e. the sticks made with dairy cream) and always had Sunbeam white bread. It's also true that many other working-class people eat those same foods. However, it becomes a problem when that food symbol is used to shame poor people or to reduce working-class people to the food they eat. My friend's comment about the butter didn't just make me feel bad because it made me feel poor; it also made me feel as though my family's food wasn't good enough. If you are what you eat, then what does fake butter make me?

To take the conversation back to white bread, there is nothing wrong with acknowledging that white bread is a food commonly eaten by working-class people. There is a problem, however, with judging people based on the foods that they eat. The issue, which Chimamanda Adichie (2009) explains well in her TED Talk, is that "the single story creates stereotypes, and the problem with stereotypes is not that they are untrue, but that they are incomplete. They make one story become the only story." Within this section, I will explore the ways food stereotypes are masked by health narratives in order to regulate, shame, and perpetuate stereotypes.

In the last section, I traced the history of white bread to demonstrate how narratives shift While white bread was once a symbol of industrialization and health, it is now viewed as unhealthy and cheap. Understandings of white bread that ignore the history and shift in narratives are food myths. Food myths are narratives that pretend to have always been true. Food myths appear stable through scientific rhetoric. By acting as a scientific authority, food trends appear as facts. However, history shows us just how inconsistent food trends are. Popular diets shift constantly all with a claim to be rooted in nutrition and science. Low calorie, high protein, low carb, no fat, non-gmo, organic diets shift from decade to decade (O'Neill & Silver, 2016, p. 21). Food myths evoke a sense of science, but are caused by historic, cultural, and economic influences. A food myth effectively ignores that nutrition and science is shaped by a culture—results of a power structure rather than raw data unaltered by human interpretation.

Food myths might appear harmless, but they are not. I share my personal stories to demonstrate that food discourses powerfully shape our understanding of our community, our diet, our bodies, and our worth. While food myths might hide beneath health narratives (*"It's bad to feed your children white bread, because it doesn't have nutrients!"*), rhetorically they participate in hierarchies where the poor person's diet must be regulated by the virtuous upper class. Myths are so powerful that individuals will come to regard themselves or their specific community as the "originator of all that is humanly good and true" (Calefato, 2016, p. 377). As Isabelle de Solier (2013) explains,

> These lowbrow processed foods are associated with the consumption practices of the lower classes. Moral consumption, for foodies, involves purchasing 'good quality' food from alternative shopping spaces—such as greengrocers, butchers, bakers, delicatessens, ethnic grocers, specialty shops, markets and farmers' markets—rather than supermarkets. The foodie's morality of quality, then, cannot be separated from matters of class. (p. 22)

There are serious consequences to assigning moral value to foods and authority to those who can afford what is "good." It creates a hierarchy of consumers where poor people are at the bottom; it creates a system where people who can't afford real butter or healthy bread are ranked as "bad." Most importantly, it ignores *why* people eat certain foods or *how* those foods come to be associated with certain groups.

While I have demonstrated in these last few sections how white bread landed in the homes of working-class people and how American culture understands and interprets white-bread as a working-class food, I want to explore why white bread continues to hold its place. A question I believe can be answered by looking at the material qualities of white bread as a versatile ingredient.

5   Defining Versatility in the Working-Class Kitchen

I believe that the affordability of white bread is what made white bread a working-class food symbol, but that its versatility is what makes it unique. While many people consider bread to be a finished product (and sometimes it is), I believe that bread is an ingredient that is utilized by working-class people at each meal of the day. With each recipe the story of white bread is retold. Much like paper or the blinking cursor in a word processor it is limitless with possibilities. It is not just that white bread is cheap or that white bread is versatile that lends to its working-class nature—it is just how quickly it can transform itself and just how inexpensive that transformation is.

To illustrate, last week I was baking a birthday cake for my husband. It called for chocolate frosting, which I made, ambitiously, by scratch. It called for simple ingredients: butter, powdered sugar, cocoa powder, and milk. Many cooks would agree that these are versatile ingredients that lots of people keep on hand, some are cheap, like milk, and others are pricey, like butter. They could be rearranged with a few other simple ingredients to become something entirely different (such as adding flour to create gravy, yeast to make bread, or eggs to make pancakes). The distinct difference comes at the moment I threw my first batch of frosting out, because it didn't look quite "right." What should have been a smooth, glossy, warm frosting looked exactly like coffee grounds mixed in oil. The frosting had separated, and, in my confusion, I tossed it. My experiment became a failure, but what upset me most was that I had wasted food.

After a quick call to my mother-in-law and a new batch thrown in the mixer I had my glossy frosting. This redo, though, would never had happened in my family's house growing up. We did not keep "real" butter on hand, but had we purchased some for a special occasion it would never have ended up in the trash. While butter is versatile it is not cheap. It would not be something we'd be allowed to experiment with in the kitchen. Had we been allowed to make a batch of frosting, there'd be no guarantee that there was another stick in the fridge or more powdered sugar to try with. My family lived quite a way from a grocery store and we did not take trips to pick up single ingredients. In a working-class kitchen, experimentation and play aren't necessarily discouraged, but what is up for grabs must be cheap, always available, and able to be transformed quickly. White bread fits the bill.

Referring back to the "Growing Up Poor" meme shared at the beginning of this essay, consider how this image demonstrates the power of white bread, rather than its shortcomings. Some people might look at that meme and see four slices of white bread, but a working-class person like me envisions many potential variations. A loaf of Sunbeam had all the potential of being dipped in egg to make French toast in the morning, slathered with peanut butter and jelly to make lunch or used as a sponge to soak up the last of dinner's gravy. My favorite thing to make with white bread growing up was cinnamon toast. After many trial and errors I came up with a method that was not only tasty but didn't require using the oven (making it quick without wasting gas). I would place white bread and put it in the toaster. Next, I would butter it with my fake butter,[1] and sprinkle cinnamon and sugar on top. Last, I would microwave it for about 15 seconds. Ta-da! Cinnamon toast. We always had these things in the kitchen, so even if my mom hadn't been grocery shopping that week it was a reliable snack.

What these stories (the meme and my reflections) illustrate are the transformative nature of white bread. While an outside perspective of white bread sees its qualities (squishy, air-filled, lacking substance) as negative—the working-class person sees those qualities as virtues. Imagine trying to make a hotdog bun out of sourdough bread—nearly impossible. Its firm structure prevents it from being bent to a new shape. Alternatively, imagine if your eight-year old child took the last of your brioche to make an after-school snack. The very things that other people perceive as "bad" are what makes the transformations of white bread possible.

I see these transformations embraced not just in my childhood, but also in recipes online. Recently on Facebook a friend shared a video of a recipe for "French toast roll ups" (Williams, 2017). The video shows white bread being rolled flat, smeared with sweet ingredients like peanut butter and strawberries, rolled up, battered, and fried. I can see this recipe embodying working-class qualities even if it is a dish a working-class person may not make. The use of white bread rolled into a portable fried snack reminds me of my cinnamon toast. If you watch the video, you will also notice both adult and children's hands. *Tasty Junior* is a cooking vlog that creates recipes that children would want to make (and eat). The smashing of bread and hand-held dippable nature of the roll-ups might be child-like, but that does not mean it is only a child's food. I feel, though, that a child's perspective of white bread might be the most enlightening. My childhood perspective didn't regard white bread as poor people's food, but rather just my family's food. Of all the stories Bobrow-Strain provides in his book about white bread, the one I find most perceptive is the first paragraph where he writes:

> Supermarket white bread can pick up difficult bits of broken glass, clean typewriter keys, and absorb motor oil spills. Squeezed into a ball, it bounces on the counter. Pressed into my palate and revealed in a big gummy grin, it gets giggles from my kids, who can also use it to sculpt animal shapes.

So often in our discussion of working-class foods we focus on cost or nutrition alone, but when we look beyond the limits and start thinking about the possibilities it's easy to see how white bread holds nostalgia even for those of us who have moved on to different loaves.

Note

1 The interesting thing about Country Crock spread is that much like white bread, its virtues are demonstrated most in its differences from "real" butter rather than its similarities. Unlike stick butter which must sit out at room temperature for it to be spread, margarine and other vegetable spreads are easily scraped across a piece of bread. Thus "fake" butter is quicker and easier to use—especially when applied to white bread which is much softer and more easily torn if too much force is used.

References

Adichie, C. (2009). *Chimamanda Adichie—The danger of a single story* [TEDTalk].
Bobrow-Strain, A. (2013). *White bread*. Beacon Press.
Calefato, P., Fortuna, L. L., & Scelzi, R. (2016). Food-ography: Food and new media. *Semiotica, 211*.
Defraeye, P. (2016). White bread. *TranscUlturAl: A Journal of Translation and Cultural Studies, 8*(1), 101. doi:10.21992/t9jh0d

De Solier, I. (2013). Making the self in a material world: Food and moralities of consumption. *Cultural Studies Review, 19*(1), 9–27.

Granderson, L. Z. (n.d.). *NASCAR fans must be rednecks?* ESPN. www.espn.com/espn/page2/story?page=granderson%2F070118

O'Neill, K., & Silver, D. (2016). From hungry to healthy. *Food, Culture & Society, 20*(1), 101–132. doi:10.1080/15528014.2016.1243765

Sleeter, C. (2015). *White bread: Weaving cultural past into the present.* Sense Publishers.

Williams, H. (2017, February 25). *French roll-ups four ways.* BuzzFeed, Tasty Junior. www.buzzfeed.com/hannahwilliams/french-roll-ups-four-ways?bffbtasty

CHAPTER 13

"Put Some Flowers in the Graveyard"

The Gloomy Fate of the Working Class in George A. Romero's Land of the Dead

Philip L. Simpson

A key plot point in George A. Romero's film *Land of the Dead* (2005) centers on the defensive use of fireworks, one of American's most recognizable symbols of national pride and celebration of political independence, to distract the mindless undead long enough for the living to move unharmed among them to take supplies from infested zones. The human survivors refer to the aerial explosions as "sky flowers." To expand this metaphor, the first command heard in the film to launch them at the beginning of a supply run is the phrase "put some flowers in the graveyard." When the fireworks begin to fail in this purpose, it is a plot turning point which signals the dead are gaining enough self-awareness and deliberative collective force to defeat their human adversaries once and for all. In terms of the allegorical dimensions of the film, "putting flowers in the graveyard" becomes convenient shorthand for the collapse of American class structure itself. In fact, the plight of the working class in an inherently corrupt capitalist society has seldom appeared as hopeless as it does in *Land of the Dead*. Essentially trapped on an urban peninsula, these human survivors are surrounded by hordes of the undead who will devour them without mercy should the electrified fences separating the living from the undead ever fall. At the same time, in their daily lives the citizens at the bottom of the class hierarchy of Pittsburgh are oppressed by an elite minority at the top of that hierarchy.

The lord of the ruling class is a ruthless post-apocalyptic businessman named Paul Kaufman. Styling himself as a nattily dressed Fortune-500 CEO type benignly providing the community with not only a safe haven from the undead but goods, services, and much-needed entertainment in a uniquely depressing and bleak world, Kaufman represents predatory American late-stage capitalism at its worst. He commands such power—including the ability to evict from the community that in this savage world equates to a death sentence—that no one dares oppose or resist him. Well, almost no one.

Enter Riley Denbo, Cholo DeMora, Slack, Mulligan, and Big Daddy: the five lead characters who represent different aspects of the underclass and the relationship of each of these aspects to the ruling capitalist class. Cholo and Riley are supply runners who regularly venture out from the relatively safe borders of the city on raids to locate, collect, and bring back necessary commodities from the zombie-infested suburbs and rural areas around the city. Slack and Mulligan are members of what may be called the "Kaufman Resistance," with Slack being a foot soldier in that movement and Mulligan leading it. Finally, Big Daddy is a zombie who was a member of the blue-collar class in his human life but after death/reanimation has now evolved a functional intelligence, including conscious self-awareness of humans as an existential threat to his people. He represents the leadership of the "Zombie Revolution" that ultimately succeeds where the human resistance could not by itself: overthrowing Kaufman's regime and the stratified class system he represents.

Usually discussed as a parable of life in the post-9/11, post-Iraq war American dystopia of the George W. Bush era, *Land of the Dead*, released three years before the Great Recession of 2008, reads the societal trend lines accurately and from there presciently forecasts the increasing economic divides and the racist, anti-immigrant movement that would accelerate through the presidency of Barack Obama, attend the rise to political power of the far-right Tea Party and its disguised corporatist agenda, and reach a fever pitch in the election of uber-capitalist, ersatz populist Donald Trump as the 45th President of the United States in 2016. Kaufman resembles Trump much more than he does Bush, the president at the time of the film's release. The film's narrative presents the end result of American late-stage capitalism in the case study of Fiddler's Green as a functionally binary system—the oppressive minority upper-class and the oppressed majority working class, with any functional middle class largely eliminated and divisions within the underclass rendered effectively meaningless. While the film ends with a superficially utopian happy ending (perhaps contributing to the perception it is the most "Hollywood" Romero zombie film) in which Riley and his small band of allies leave the shredded corpse of capitalism behind and Big Daddy and his zombies do likewise, the insistence of Mulligan and his followers to stay behind to recreate Pittsburgh as a democratic, anti-capitalist society does not portend well for the future. Mulligan's idealistic vision, the film implies, will inevitably fail at some point in the future, with the implication being the future of the American experiment itself is equally terminal.

1 American Class Structure and the Living Dead

Class is a notoriously slippery concept to define. One will search in vain among the various academic disciplines most directly relevant (history, sociology, economics, anthropology, and the like) for a consensus definition. For example,

Karl Marx and Max Weber, the two most foundational analytical theorists on the subject during the nineteenth century, approach it with different emphases and intellectual predispositions. In essence, the Marxian view is that class structure is economically determined through one's relationship to what he famously called "the means of production." Class conflict then emerges between the capitalists who own the means of production (supported by a petty bourgeois class who carry out the commands of the capitalists) and the working class, or wage workers, who, if organized enough, carry the power to overthrow the elite to create a more equitable society. The Weberian approach, by contrast, argues for the importance of social status and power as cultural influences determining class stratification, in addition to economic position.

Throughout the twentieth into the twenty-first century, class theory has tended to focus on the primacy of three kinds of classes: the upper class, which while having the fewest members holds the vast majority of wealth and power; the middle class, which is comprised of professional workers and lower-end managerial types; and the lower class, which consists of low-income, low-job security types and is often subdivided into an underclass of the unemployed and homeless, or what Marx called the *lumpenproletariat*. Michael Zweig (2011) is one contemporary Marxist theorist whose book, *The Working Class Majority*, offers a basic definition of class that has relevance in deciphering the binary economic structure dramatized in *Land of the Dead*: "When I talk about class, I am talking about power. Power at work, and power in the larger society. Economic power, and also political and cultural power ... I will be describing the contours of power that operate in every aspect of society, to the benefit of some, to the burden of others" (p. 1). He elaborates on this definition in respect to American class structure, defining class as:

> based on the power and authority people have at work. The workplace engages people in more than their immediate work, in which they create good and services. It also engages them in relationships with each other ... that are controlled by power. A relative handful of people have great power to organize and direct production, while a much larger number have almost no authority. In a capitalist society such as ours, the first group is the capitalist class, the second group is the working class ... The great majority of Americans form the working class. (p. 3)

The capitalists, then, are those in the minority who give the orders and control and move the social levers of power.

As Zweig's academic work demonstrates, concern about class conflict and the domination of one class over others persists among contemporary scholars of and writers about American culture. Another such author is bell hooks, who frequently critiques through her idiosyncratically unconventional, non-academic personal style how capitalism perpetuates oppression, particularly of a racial and gender nature. One of the most striking features of American class consciousness is that it consciously denies the reality and prevalence of class hierarchies and conflict, though minimally thoughtful observation would prove irrefutably otherwise. This is where Zweig and hooks intersect, given Zweig's contention that the American ideal of the "middle class" and the level playing field where ambitious and hard-working individuals may rise to wealth based on merit is alive and well but does not admit the reality of more defined, practically insurmountable class barriers. One of the signature aspects of recent American economic life, according to hooks (2000), is that "there is no organized class struggle, no daily in-your-face critique of capitalist greed that stimulates thought and action—critique, reform, and revolution" (p. 1). Concurrently, as a byproduct of this kind of willful indifference or refusal to acknowledge openly class differences, hooks insists that "our nation is becoming class-segregated. The poor live with and among the poor ... the victims of predatory greed. More and more poor communities all over the country look like war zones ... No one safeguards the interests of citizens there; they are soon to be the victims of class genocide" (p. 1). At the same time, she observes, wealthy people "live in gated communities where they zealously protect their class interests—their way of life—by surveillance, by security forces, by direct links to the police, so that all danger can be kept at bay" (p. 2). One of the most insidious aspects of American class structure, then, is how the oppressed majority are in one sense perpetuating and even participating in their own oppression by refusing to see, let alone acknowledge, the walls placed between them and their oppressors by their oppressors.

One way oppressors facilitate this kind of useful social blindness, Zweig points out, is the scapegoating of an Other, such as foreigners, specifically immigrants, to blame for the economic stresses faced by the working class (p. 78). Justifiable anger over social inequity, then, is redirected away from its proper target toward a relatively defenseless and small population of foreign Others. One does not have to look very far or hard—at all—to find instances of this Othering of immigrants in contemporary political rhetoric. President Donald Trump's 2016 election campaign and subsequent election was based in large part on immigration policy reform, which he claimed was necessary because of the large number of criminals and terrorists among illegal immigrants. A signature promise of this campaign rhetoric against a foreign Other included the construction of a substantial wall between the United States and Mexico, which as of this writing in 2019 has not been built to any great extent but remains an ongoing political passion for the President and the many American citizens who support it. What is the Border Wall, really, but an extension of the concept of the American gated community as hooks described it and the exclusion of a social element or class perceived to be dangerous? In *Land of the Dead*, excluding the rivers as a natural barrier, what is Fiddler's Green and Pittsburgh surrounded by to protect them from the hordes of the living dead? A fortified Border Wall.

2   Class Structure in *Land of the Dead*

Land of the Dead is probably Romero's most full-throated indictment of American economic disparity and class conflict in a film series noted for doing so. As Robin Wood (2018) writes, the film is "Capitalism itself, with the brilliant casting of Dennis Hopper [playing Kaufman] as its supreme embodiment, Easy Rider maturing into its most monstrous tycoon" (p. 378). Long before Wood wrote these words in 2018, a truism had already emerged in critical appraisals of Romero's cycle of zombie films, stating that each represents an allegory of problematic dimensions of American political, cultural, and/or economic life. Excluding the countless number of media portrayals of zombies directly influenced by Romero, the original cycle spans five decades and includes six films: *Night of the Living Dead* (1968), *Dawn of the Dead* (1978), *Day of the Dead* (1985), *Land of the Dead* (2005), *Diary of the Dead* (2007), and *Survival of the Dead* (2009). The one consistent thematic through-line in all of the movies has been class conflict.

Land of the Dead not only serves as the transitional film between Romero's original trilogy and his latter, more self-referential zombie films; in many ways, it is the concluding chapter in one epic chronicle of zombie apocalypse told in an episodic format that Romero began decades before in *Night of the Living Dead* and even before that, according to Paul R. Gagne (1987), in an unpublished story called "Anubis" told in three distinct parts or movements (p. 24). The story, inspired by Richard Matheson's contemporary vampire novel *I Am Legend*, ultimately became the basis for the first three *Living Dead* films. The class consciousness informing the narrative of "Anubis" is encoded into the DNA of all of Romero's zombie films. In this regard, the final episode in "Anubis" is especially telling. Essentially, it depicts a world governed by a new zombie society, evolving from mindlessness to rudimentary consciousness and while so doing overthrowing through sheer numbers the previous human society. But the secret at the heart of the zombie society is that the zombies have been trained (through being fed human remains) to carry out the will of the small, elite group of humans who actually rule the post-apocalyptic world.

When it came time for Romero to turn this final chapter into the film *Day of the Dead*, budgetary constraints forced him to remove many of its more ambitious elements to focus only on the conflict between the military and the scientists, told in parallel to the training and "rehabilitation" of one gradually self-aware zombie named "Bub." The resulting film, while satisfying enough on its own limited terms, had always felt incomplete to Romero and his fans, who were keenly aware the original first two drafts contained so much more material. According to Tony Williams (2003), some of these excised elements included the depiction of a tropical island community of human "undesirables," comprised primarily of blacks, Irish, the disabled, and political dissidents, called Stalag 17. The upper classes of the tropical island society regard the residents of Stalag 17 as a pool of menial laborers. The island's middle class consists of scientists and other professionals. Sitting atop the upper class of this cross-section of post-apocalyptic American society is former Florida governor Henry Dickerson, who rules over the island from his luxurious abode surrounded by an elite few wealthy men and women and enforces his rule with a private army (pp. 129–130). It is not difficult to see how this treatment became the final screenplay of *Land of the Dead*, given the equivalences drawn between Stalag 17 and the underclass of Pittsburgh as well as that between Dickerson and Kaufman.

As befits a final chapter in an epic, *Land* has a grander scope. It clearly has a bigger budget than any of the other films, with the technology and elaborate special effects both practical and computer-generated to show for it. Given that technical polish and the presence of well-known names among the cast—Simon Baker in the lead role of Riley, the aforementioned Dennis Hopper as the villainous Paul Kaufman, John Leguizamo as the outlaw/terrorist Cholo DeMora, and Asia Argento as the heroine Slack—the film looks and feels more like a mainstream Hollywood epic than any of Romero's other films, albeit with more gross-out gore (especially so in the unrated cut, which remains truer to Romero's independent, guerilla filmmaker spirit than the theatrical release). But ironically enough, given the amount of capital paradoxically spent upon this denunciation of capitalism, the social consciousness that informs the first three movies is more pronounced than ever in *Land of the Dead*. For example, Steven Zani and Kevinx Meaux (2011) succinctly characterize the film "as allegory for George W. Bush's United States, with the walled-off community an allegory for his administration's support for building a wall across the entire U.S.-Mexico border" (p. 113). Brian Wilson (2006) maintains the film "contains the most complex social and political schema of any of the director's previous zombie films" because it "may be seen as a necessary reaction to the present atmosphere of terrorist threat, political disillusionment and George W. Bush."

Several critics have explored the class and economic metaphors of *Land of the Dead* in separate analyses. John Lutz (2010), for example, argues that the "economic system depicted in *Land of the Dead* has a remarkable parallel with Marx's representation of capitalist society," characterized by "unremitting conflict between classes with antagonistic and irreconcilable interests" (p. 121). He then lays out how the film presents "a complex, sustained allegorical treatment of class conflict in America and exploitation on a global scale" (p. 122) and analyzes in detail how the zombies of the film "signify not only the countless individuals impoverished by the system and the disruptive potential of their unrest, but also the commercial crises that periodically threaten the prosperity of the privileged classes" in a system modeled upon America's economic imperialistic hegemony in the world order (p. 125). In this system, the zombies' state of miserable undead existence, reflected in the title of the film, "represents the living death experienced by the brutalized and exploited worker" (p. 125). The climactic zombie uprising against the privileged residents of Fiddler's Green and Big Daddy's targeted killing of Kaufman, then, "effectively abolish the economic system [of the city] as well as the classes it supports" (p. 134). R. Colin Tait (2007) notes the film is built upon "class antagonism ... as there are two sets of under-classes (in short, the proletariat and the *lumpenproletariat*) in addition to the reconstitution of a post-apocalyptic bourgeoisie" (p. 69). Leah Richards (2018) joins the general consensus that the film is an expansion of Romero's "earlier films' indictment of the toxicity of capitalism" while emphasizing that in the end "it remains skeptical about ideologies that reconstruct one system from the ashes of another" (p. 657). While some may view the film's climax as an unqualified success for the rise of the working man (or zombie) against the lords of capitalism, Richards cautions those viewers to bear in mind that a "rebuilt Pittsburgh cannot become a utopia" (p. 672).

The present study concurs in general with these prior critical assessments but extends the film's assessment of the post-9/11 Bush era to the post-Great Recession Trump era. When viewed through the theoretical framework provided by Michael Zweig, Romero's allegory of class struggle places the hapless residents of the survivors' community in Pittsburgh in the majority working class and Kaufman and his inner circle in the capitalist class. Though the larger society collapsed during the zombie plague, Kaufman has recreated the inequities of the old order to an absurd extreme in his new order, eliding any sub-distinctions between the poor and working and middle class into what Zweig would call the working class majority that the aftermath of the Great Recession has only expanded. The oppressed occupants of this class depend upon Kaufman in his capacity as the overlord of Fiddler's Green to provide them with a bare minimum of shelter, food, water, protection through his own version of a Border Wall, and gladiatorial-style entertainment that diverts popular attention from economic inequity. In turn, Kaufman and his elite make money off the masses while otherwise essentially ignoring them except when needed as a labor pool, as Richards observes (p. 664). The film's quintet of protagonists as lumped into the working class all play a part in Kaufman's downfall. Each undergoes a kind of consciousness raising or awakening, which then unites them in a common revolutionary cause. Romero obviously draws the same kind of conclusions as hooks does about American class, which he dramatizes in *Land of the Dead* with his characteristic sharp critique of the American gated community. In fact, hooks could not have provided a better synopsis of the class conflict represented in Romero's film.

3 Robber-Baron Capitalism

The theme of class conflict is established at the beginning of the film with the opening credits sequence, which is shot in sepia-toned black-and-white and establishes the setting as "some time ago." As told by a panoply of sound bites from news broadcasts, the quick spread and reach of the zombie plague has led to a global societal collapse into lawlessness. The opening sequence sketches in the broad strokes of what post-apocalypse human society looks like, setting the stage for the class warfare parable to come.

Outi J. Hakola, noting the reporter's audio statement that "people are said to be establishing outposts in big cities and raiding small and rural towns for supplies, like outlaws" in the opening sequence, argues that *Land of the Dead* is a kind of post-apocalyptic Western. According to Hakola (2012), the resulting juxtaposition, between the zombified rural spaces and the human strongholds in the cities, not only calls back to the geographies established in *Night of the Living Dead* and *Dawn of the Dead*, but directs the viewer to the Western trope of the frontier and its demarcation between the wilderness and the city (p. 134). Following on this narrative logic, Hakola then argues how the zombies have colonized the wilderness and the surviving humans have created a city with three distinct zones surrounded by a fourth "lawless" zone, which for the purposes of this study can be called class enclaves: "the tower where the elite live, the surrounding areas of the city where common people live, and the front, which is inhabited by soldiers who defend against zombies attempting to infiltrate the city and suppliers who make incursions into the zombified territory in order to fetch supplies for the city" (pp. 138–139). Hakola characterizes the society that exists within this geography as a "two-tiered community where the classes are separated by lifestyle and future prospects, as well as concretely, by fences. Thus, reactions to the zombie threat have not unified the people but intensified their divisions; as their inequality grows more visible and the elite's imposition of fences and other methods of control cause tensions to grow" (pp. 139–140). Hakola's observation that the class structure in *Land of the Dead* is binary in nature is important to keep in mind, given that it parallels Zweig's assertion that American class structure is binary.

The degraded city surrounding the brightly lit tower of Fiddler's Green does indeed resemble a war zone, to use hooks's (2000) analogy: block after block of crumbling buildings; black-out conditions in which crime and underworld activity flourishes; overcrowded tenements; residents whose shabby clothing and generally unhealthy physical appearance attest to a hardscrabble life of poverty and deprivation. The city sits on a peninsula surrounded by filthy river water on three sides and an electrified gate (aka Border Wall) on the other side that serves a dual purpose of barring an ever-threatening enemy from entering from the mainland while preventing the residents from leaving. It is he home of the film's working class, as represented by Riley, Cholo, Slack, and Mulligan.

In sharp contrast to its squalid surroundings, Fiddler's Green is the high-rise condo equivalent of a gated community. As described in a promotional video that plays when Riley and Charlie return to the city from the supply run that opens the films, Fiddler's Green "offers luxury living in the grand old style" (Romero, 2005). It is fitted with all the materialistic trappings of late-capitalist decadence: luxury apartments high above the city; high-end department stores and gallerias and six fine restaurants in the ground-level shopping mall (which in itself is a callback to Romero's *Dawn of the Dead*, largely set in a suburban shopping mall). On the face of it, the building's name is a reference to a legend of a rather cheery afterlife with endless dancing and laughter. In context, however, the name reminds one more of the legend of the Roman emperor Nero fiddling while Rome burned, a suitably apocalyptic overtone here. The opulence of Kaufman's luxury high-rise also suggests echoes of Prince Prospero's abbey in Edgar Allan Poe's 1842 short story "The Masque of the Red Death," similarly walled off to avoid a plague blighting the outside world. The association is reinforced when a public address system in Fiddler's Green issues a party invitation only for residents of the Green (in other words, working class not welcome!) to attend "a masked ball on the eve of Allhallows. It is strictly forbidden to come as you are" (Romero, 2005). Kaufman and a small inner circle of wealthy elites physically and economically exclude the impoverished from living in the tower. He employs a private police and security force to protect himself and the wealthy high-rise dwellers from both the living and the dead. He maintains an elaborate electronic and human surveillance network to monitor his fiefdom for any signs of uprising or opposition, which his security forces oppress as quickly and brutally as necessary.

Ultimately, Kaufman's attempt to keep a wall between himself and the working class and the undead ends about as well as Prospero's did to keep out the Red Death, and in much the same way, with Death literally touching each room in the palace (or high rise). The film foreshadows this fatal outcome early, when Cholo on the way up to see the boss destroys the reanimated corpse of one of Kaufman's neighbors (who has committed suicide) in Fiddler's Green. When hearing of this incident, Kaufman is forced to admit to Cholo that "death intrudes on us even here in the city, I'm afraid" (Romero, 2005). When Big Daddy's zombie army begins devouring the shrieking privileged residents of the Green at the end of the film, Kaufman is outraged, yelling "You have no right"—but that just means he wasn't really believing the implications of his casually offered platitude to Cholo. Like Prospero, he just can't believe Death would even dare.

In his tailored suits and with his carefully coiffed hair, Kaufman may look and dress the part of a wealthy captain of industry—the CEO of Fiddler's Green, as it were. He prides himself on building a safe haven for the human survivors. However, he is really a robber-baron in the nineteenth century mode, engaging in predatory acquisition of goods and services built by other people. He ruthlessly presides over an urban underworld, his methodology accurately summarized by the character Slack who is intimately familiar with the vice empire of the man she calls Mr. K: "He's got his fingers in everything here. If you can drink it, shoot it up, fuck it, gamble on it, it belongs to him" (Romero, 2005). He uses whatever unscrupulous practices he must to amass further riches through crime. Romero's human antagonists in the *Living Dead* films tend to aspire to criminal power and resource acquisition at the expense of others as a means of survival while the world falls apart during the zombie plague. However, of these antagonists, Kaufman is by far the most powerful. He has been the most successful in acquiring and maintaining resources, showing just how much smarter, visionary, and ruthless he is. He has contingency plans in case the worst happens, as illustrated when he reassures his rich associates when Cholo's threat against the city begins to worry them: "I want to assure you that if anything goes wrong, measures have been taken. I've established outposts with food and supplies that will support us on our way ... Alternative sites have been chosen for us and our families as well as necessary support personnel ... All the others can be replaced" (Romero, 2005). His complete contempt and disregard for Pittsburgh's working class could not be more blatantly expressed.

In the end, it's all about Kaufman and his own colossal yet fragile ego and a related need to control others. When one of his elite friends questions his judgement, Kaufman's temper flares and he delivers a scathing rebuke that makes clear how the World According to Kaufman operates:

> You're interrupting me, Bill. It's bad timing. Just when I was talking about how people can be replaced. A day may come when you earn yourself some responsibilities. But right now the responsibilities are mine. They're all mine. It was my ingenuity that took an old world and made it into something new. I put up the fences to make it safe. I hired the soldiers and paid for their training. I kept the people off the streets by giving them games and vices, which cost me money. But I spend it because the responsibility is mine. Now, do you understand the meaning of the word responsibility? (Romero, 2005)

Kaufman's narcissism is on full display in this monologue. According to him, the only reason the people of Pittsburgh are still alive at all are because of his genius and money. But he didn't do it for anything resembling an altruistic reason. He did it to acquire more wealth and to quell any working-class discontent about his predatory capitalism through bread-and-circus distractions. However, his power, like money in a post-apocalypse world, is illusory. Cholo's threat profoundly destabilizes his perceived clout among even his business associates, who recognize through Kaufman's own words about "replacement" that the only person who matters to Kaufman is Kaufman.

4 The "Woke" Resistance

Among the film's five primary working-class protagonists who take on Kaufman's evil capitalist empire, Riley exhibits the most conventionally heroic traits. According to Kim Paffenroth (2006), he is "probably the most hopeful and optimistic character" in any of Romero's canonical Living Dead films (p. 129). In a violent world, he only reluctantly uses violence as a necessary tool for survival. Though he is quite proficient at violence when need be, even going so far as killing his own brother to prevent him from turning into one of the undead, Riley does not embrace or enjoy violence as so many other degraded characters in the film do. He is still capable of love, as demonstrated by his long-standing friendship with Charlie, a man with both intellectual and physical disabilities who in spite of these challenges is a proven warrior and survivor. Riley also retains empathy, shown in his rescue of Slack, a woman he does not know, from the zombie cage. Riley is also quite selfless; for example, when given a chance by Kaufman to be freed from imprisonment, he will only agree to the bargain if Charlie and Slack are also released. Though it is implied Riley has lost religious faith during the zombie apocalypse because of all the horrors he has seen and/or perpetrated to stay alive, he loves his friend Charlie for the latter's simple belief in Heaven. All of these examples attest to Riley's basic decency.

Nevertheless, he is not a moral innocent. However reluctantly or of necessity, he works for Kaufman and thus in a practical sense helps to perpetuate Kaufman's social evils. In the pre-plague world, a man of Riley's specialized skills would likely be a member of the professional middle class. Here, he is one more member of the working class who answers directly to Kaufman. While the origin of Riley's urban anti-zombie vehicle, *Dead Reckoning*, is uncertain, it seems likely that he was only able to execute his design with Kaufman's financial resources. Although he uses the vehicle in zombie-infested zones for the express purpose of keeping its human crew alive so they can retrieve supplies and bring them back to the city for all of its inhabitants, in so doing he nevertheless helps ensure the survival of Kaufman's capitalist empire. For the majority of the film, Riley continues in this role by taking on, however reluctantly, a mission sanctioned by Kaufman to recapture *Dead Reckoning* from Cholo, who is threatening to turn its guns on the city.

While his white heterosexual male identity would tend to mark him as less Other than the female/black/Hispanic characters in the film, Riley is still Irish, an ethnic and national group which itself has experienced historical discrimination, for example during the 19th century as refugees/immigrants to the United States. As such, he is acutely aware of the class prison in which Kaufman has placed him and other working class people. For instance, he scoffs at Cholo's insistence that the latter's insistence he has earned enough capital for Kaufman to be given an apartment in Fiddler's Green: "You're dreaming, Cholo. They won't let you in there. They wouldn't let me in there. We're the wrong kind" (Romero, 2005). In contemporary parlance, Riley is "woke." That said, he is no reformer struggling to correct the wrongs of an unjust social system from within. He accepts Kaufman's employment terms just long enough to acquire his (and his small circle of companions) long-held dream of freedom to escape north to Canada where there are no people.

This is certainly the kind of dream that many disillusioned, disaffected, or disenfranchised people in the era of George W. Bush could relate to and takes on even more poignancy now in the era of Donald Trump, a U.S. president surely even more in the Kaufman mold (right down to the urban skyscraper lair at the center of a financial empire) than Bush II. Riley endures Kaufman's exploitation only as long as he needs to so that he can arrange his escape. As the film opens, he is commanding his last supply run with Cholo as his second-in-command. Riley wants to bring everyone back home safely so that he and Charlie can leave town without incident in a car he bought the day before. Foiled when Cholo's greed kills a team member and then when Riley's car disappears into Pittsburgh's seedy underworld, Riley's primary motivation for going after Cholo is because Kaufman in return has promised him another car he can use to go north. However, for the first time that Charlie can remember, Riley is going to renege on a deal. He is going to take *Dead Reckoning* to Canada instead of returning the vehicle to Kaufman's control. Betraying one of his core principles illustrates just how much escaping in safety to Canada far from other people means to him.

Riley certainly represents one reaction to a corrupt and oppressive capitalist system: to live within the system only long enough to flee its reach entirely and live elsewhere in isolation with a few close allies. Nevertheless, he exhibits what Leah A. Murray (2006) labels the communitarian ideal of making "the world a better place for people immediately around him" by bringing "goods to the poor people" and saving "as many people as possible while putting his own life at risk" (p. 217). To the extent that Riley resists Kaufman's reign, Riley is at best an alternative constructionist. His solution to Kaufman's urban capitalist system is not to fight it, but to escape it by fleeing to a new rural frontier and creating a small communitarian utopia. Hakola specifically identifies Riley as an "iconic frontier figure: the hero ... who works as a mediator between society and wilderness ... [but] does not want to be part of [the community], preferring to find refuge in solitude ... Like the classic Western loner-hero, Riley recognizes that the independence he values is incompatible with the civilization he has protected" (pp. 144, 146). So, like most Western heroes, Riley lights out for the Territory (in this case, Canada) after the society he champions proves unworthy of him.

Cholo, Riley's second in command aboard the *Dead Reckoning*, is representative of the exclusively individualistic social class climber, attempting to leave the underclass against all odds by currying Kaufman's favor to obtain a coveted luxury apartment only for himself in Kaufman's high rise. Cholo's blind embrace of capitalism is on full display when he says to a compatriot that he doesn't "care about love. All I care about is money." As Richards (2018) astutely diagnoses Cholo, he "has been infected by capitalism" (p. 665) as surely as any zombie infection—his ultimate fate in the film—but does not recognize that Kaufman's hoarding of cash in greater amounts than anyone else is purely symbolic in an economy based more on service labor and goods. When first introduced, Cholo deviates from Riley's orders on the supply run on an ill-fated side mission to a liquor store to bring back Kentucky whiskey to sell on the street for his own gain. Cholo's greed results in the death of a rookie supply runner under his command. Unfazed, Cholo upon his return to the city that day brings a bottle of whiskey up to Kaufman's penthouse suite to ask to buy his own place in the Green with the money he has acquired through his solo entrepreneurship, but Kaufman denies the petition: "This is an extremely desirable location. Space is very limited ... I do have a Board of Directors and I have a membership committee. They have to approve."

This scene constitutes Cholo's own "woke" moment. He understands instantly what Kaufman is telling him: "You mean restricted, don't you?" Cholo presses his case for admittance past Kaufman's carefully erected class barriers with a plaintive plea that quickly turns to threats as he loses his temper:

> Don't do this to me. Don't. How long have I been working for you? Three years? Taking out your garbage, cleaning up after you, and then you're going to say I'm not good enough? Let me tell you something, you're going to let me in because I know what goes on around here. Do your committee members know what the fuck is going out with the garbage? So you're gonna let me in, you hear me? (Romero, 2005)

However, Cholo's "woke" status does not extend to revolution on behalf of the working class suffering under Kaufman. When Kaufman has him escorted out by security to be imprisoned or assassinated, he breaks free to commandeer *Dead Reckoning* to threaten to shell the city unless Kaufman pays him a $5 million ransom. While stealing Dead Reckoning, he ignores evidence that the zombies have started to invade the city through its no-man's-land perimeter. He shows no hesitation in preparing to bombard the city when it appears that Kaufman has not met his demand; only Riley's retaking of *Dead Reckoning* prevents that. So even though Cholo turns against Kaufman like the other main characters, he does not care about the city or its inhabitants like Riley does.

Whatever his individual motives, however, Cholo's hatred of Kaufman as the representative of the class system that has oppressed him is a powerful force for change. Any discussion of Cholo's agency in taking power away from Kaufman must take race into account. As a character, he embodies what hooks emphasizes in her analyses about American class structure's disproportionate negative impact on people of color and what Zweig says about the power elite using nationalist xenophobia about immigrants as a tool to divide the interests of the working class against itself. For one thing, as most critics of *Land of the Dead* recognize, his name "Cholo," which in the United States is typically used as a derogatory appellation for a Hispanic young man belonging to a street gang, coaches the viewer to regard him in terms of his race, and a specific subculture within that race perceived as threatening to white interests.

Cholo recognizes his own station in the class structure ruled by whites, as he expresses in wistful self-reflection to his friend Foxy: "I know I'm never gonna be great. I'm never gonna be on the list of names of people who done great things because I don't do anything. Not one thing. If it wasn't for [*Dead Reckoning*], I wouldn't be any different than that poor Mexican bastard [zombie] out there." He finishes by invoking the threat of foreign terrorism that so terrifies American white power structure: "Kaufman's gonna pay, man. But if he doesn't, he knows I'm gonna do a jihad on his ass" (Romero, 2005).

Not even death can stop Cholo's class- and race-based hatred for his oppressor. When he is bitten by a zombie after Riley releases him, he refuses the merciful bullet-to-the-brain remedy to prevent his reanimation because, he wryly jokes, he always "wanted to see how the other half lives" (Romero, 2005). On the surface, it's a bit of gallows humor about becoming a zombie, but what he really means is that he wants to continue his vendetta against Kaufman if he can somehow retain enough of his living consciousness after he turns.

Which, in fact, Cholo does just that. Like Big Daddy, he is motivated enough by rage to join forces with the other zombies to invade Fiddler's Green and he remembers enough about its inner geography that he can track Kaufman down to the underground garage to attempt to kill him. However, Cholo has been so compromised by his life choices he is denied this bit of posthumous vengeance against Kaufman—that honor falls to Big Daddy, whose improvised gas explosion wipes out both Cholo and Kaufman in a fitting end for the story's biggest capitalists. For his part, Kaufman's hatred of Cholo is definitely based in large part on racism. Like many a ruling-class white politician when faced with a foreign threat to white privilege and power, Kaufman immediately invokes the "T" word when dealing with the ransom demand: "We don't negotiate with terrorists" (Romero, 2005). At the end, when confronted by zombie Cholo right after his black chauffeur has abandoned him trapped inside his car, Kaufman resorts to racial insult and foregrounds what has been implied all along: "Fucking spic bastard" (Romero, 2005). These are the last words Kaufman says before his death at Big Daddy's hands. Kaufman's terminal undoing at the hands of two black men (the chauffeur and Big Daddy) and one Hispanic (Cholo) leave no doubt how much primacy racial prejudice has in the film's indictment of class structures.

Slack, a young woman who was previously forced into prostitution serving the city's upper class, represents those members of the working class who join Mulligan's organized resistance against the ruling class. Compared to the other lead characters, she is a secondary character in terms of allotted lines and screen time, but even that disparity reinforces how as a woman of the working class she suffers gender-specific exploitation. When first seen in the film, she is clad in stereotypical, highly sexualized hooker-fashion: black leather and fishnet with lots of exposed cleavage, thigh, and mid-riff. Though clearly capable of fighting, she is at a serious survival disadvantage in a cage match against two ravenous zombies for the amusement of the gamblers in the underworld of Pittsburgh: the "games and vice" Kaufman is so proud of as a means of keeping the masses occupied. When Riley and Charlie rescue her from the cage, all three are arrested, providing an interlude during which Slack explains to Riley how she ended up in her current plight: Kaufman's security forces "found out I was helping Mulligan and his people, tired of eating bones while he's having steak." She explains her background in more detail: "I had training. I was going to join the army, help the Green, till somebody figured out I'd be a better hooker than a soldier" (Romero, 2005). Exploited for her sexuality rather than her combat skills, Slack's fate is typical of that of a certain subsection of the working class female population of Pittsburgh under Kaufman's crime-based capitalism.

Though her preliminary introduction in her fetishized sex costume could easily have been exploited by a lesser director for the sole purpose of audience titillation, Romero takes her character through a story arc that proves her worth as Riley's ally, right alongside his long-term friend Charlie. She learns to trust Riley, even though he initially rebuffs her attempt to share her personal history with him, because Riley includes her in his deal to escape Kaufman's reach. To demonstrate her loyalty, she fights ferociously and capably by his side (in much more suitable soldier's garb that signals her reclamation of her proper professional identity) in the recapture of Dead Reckoning and the return to the city to save its people from the zombie assault. Though the film hints at some degree of romantic interest between Riley and Slack throughout, Slack's real purpose in the story is to demonstrate how she is one of the smartest members of the Kaufman working class resistance in switching her allegiance from Mulligan's vision of a democratic society to Riley's vision of it. Though already "woke" to class reality when the film begins, by the time it ends she is "woke" again to join Riley's isolationist campaign.

Mulligan is another secondary character in terms of the screen time he is given, but nevertheless he serves a critical function in the class consciousness established by the narrative. A fellow Irish kinsman to Riley, he is the face of the Kaufman resistance, a "woke" socialist firebrand who recruits revolutionaries like Slack from the city's working class with the intent of rising up against the capitalist class personified by Kaufman when they have enough of an army. When the film first introduces Mulligan, he is orating his social gospel on the street of the slum to a small but engaged group of listeners: "How long are you going to let Kaufman push you around? You like shining his shoes, pressing his pants? He didn't build that place. He just took it over. Kept the best for himself, and left us with a slum to live in. But if there's enough of us, if all of you would join up, we could make this a fit place to live in." Taking notice of Riley and Charlie coming toward him, Mulligan announces he used to work with Riley, "bringing in toothpicks for the bastards to pick at their gums" (Romero, 2005). Charlie, ever playing the part of the wise fool assigned to him by the narrative, tries to correct the full record by saying Riley and Mulligan also brought in "food and other stuff, for all of us," but Mulligan does not or will not hear a more nuanced view of class relationships.

Subtly, through Charlie, Romero cautions the viewer that Mulligan's worldview, while superficially more sympathetic when compared to Kaufman's predatory one, is just as binary and ultimately just as dangerous in terms of potential for suppression of dissident thought. Mulligan's next words reinforce his inherent messianic tendency: "Come in with us, Riley .... Together, we'd be unstoppable." Riley rejects the offer with a prophetic observation: "No one's unstoppable, Mulligan. You're worried about being locked out ... I can't help but think we're all locked in. I'm looking for a world where there's no fences" (Romero, 2005). Riley ends the conversation by handing Mulligan antibiotics for his sick son.

The film's final exchange between Riley and Mulligan, after Kaufman's death and the tearing down of the literal and metaphoric barriers between the working class and Fiddler's Green, reprises the offer/rejection dynamic of their first scene together. Mulligan asks Riley, "Why don't you stick around? We could turn this place into what we always wanted it to be." Riley implies refusal in his reply: "Maybe. Then what we will turn into?" Mulligan smiles in a decidedly non-reassuring way: "We'll see, won't we?" (Romero, 2005). His son, now fully recovered with the help of the antibiotics Riley brought in from the outside for him, pumps his shotgun for ominous dramatic effect. Unsettled by Mulligan and son's triumphal air, Riley and crew load up into *Dead Reckoning* and head toward Canada. The film's concluding stance on the potential for a human socialist utopia to rise from Pittsburgh's ashes is decidedly pessimistic.

Finally, Big Daddy, who is one of the zombie horde outside the city but has evolved enough intelligence and consciousness to understand who the human enemy is that keeps slaughtering his people, is representative of the power of organized labor to overthrow the capitalist system, as most critics of *Land of the Dead* have already argued. Significantly, as seen on a sign as the film opens, the name of the small town where Big Daddy "lives" is called Uniontown. Big Daddy commands a much bigger "union" army than Mulligan and essentially starts and completes the revolution that Mulligan could never quite pull together.

Big Daddy is the most evolved of the zombies in Romero's Living Dead films, outpacing even Dr. Logan's star pupil "Bub" in *Day of the Dead*. Bub, named by Logan after his father, can remember some details from his previous life, such as how to shave, listen to music, read a book, and salute a superior officer; he also learns to restrain his aggressive instincts around someone he feels affection for (Logan) and unleash them against his enemy (Captain Rhodes), going so far as to figure out how to fire a gun at Rhodes. However, Bub had to be trained by Logan (essentially, given vocational rehabilitation to overcome the nearly insurmountable cognitive deficits that afflict the reanimated dead) to get this far. Big Daddy (interestingly, also given a patriarchal nickname on screen in lieu of whatever his name in life was) achieves all Bub did and more, all on his own. Big Daddy demonstrates from his first introduction on screen the ability to remember details of his past life, such as responding to the station's signal bell when a zombie randomly steps on the hose by the gas pumps. He further realizes that the "sky flowers" are exploded by human enemies to distract the zombies and guns pose a mortal threat to his people. He possesses the cognitive and motor skill to turn human-manufactured weapons (a meat cleaver, a rifle) against the living. He displays empathy for his own kind's suffering by mercy killing one zombie who has been decapitated and another who is burning.

Most importantly to the film's class theme, he demonstrates the ability to marshal his fellow zombies into a unified community that follows his lead past formidable obstacles to slaughter their human tormentors. The most significant barrier they have to overcome is crossing the river separating them from the city. In one of the film's most striking visuals, Big Daddy and his army emerge from beneath the water to march up the river bank toward the city. One cannot help but make the association of this imagery to one that is commonly used to demonize immigrants: supposed swarms of illegals crossing the Rio Grande under the cover of darkness to enter the United States.

Once inside the city, Big Daddy and the other zombies ally with Mulligan's forces to kill (in Romero's signature gory fashion) the capitalists who inhabit Fiddler's Green. Such an alliance makes thematic sense, given the film's focus on the majority working class. The zombies are simply one more subclass who suffer under Kaufman's rule. As K. Silem Mohammad (2012) points out, the undead are "indistinguishable from the living poor: they are hungry, unruly, and unattractive, and no one wants to become one of them" (p. 94). As the hostilities cease at the film's end, however, the zombie army has collectively evolved to the point that their nascent society appears preferable to human civilization. As Simon Clark (2012) argues, "the evolved zombies ... seem to be drafting the plans for a non-repressive marriage between civilization and the instincts. As a manifestation of the dissenting repressed, the zombies have broken through the barriers, cages and chains that used to keep them imprisoned ... Instead of pursuing their appetite for flesh, the zombies have turned their backs on humans and are stumbling towards their new collective existence together" (p. 208). Yet this reading of the film, accurate to a point, must still keep in mind Romero's extreme skepticism about any kind of society. The zombie collective still retains vestigial signifiers of its pre-plague work occupations and class statuses in the form of their distinctive costuming (gas station uniform, butcher's apron, cheerleader's uniform, band uniform, clown garb, etc.). To the extent that a binary class system parallel to the human one is evolving among the zombies, Big Daddy and others like him who grow more cognitive awareness than the rest of the horde will control and direct the others. Class conflict is so endemic to the human condition, Romero insists, that not even death can conquer it.

5 Conclusion

To the extent that the film gives Riley and his friends the celebratory last word, showing them driving off to the border and firing off the last of *Dead Reckoning*'s now useless fireworks, Romero himself seems to privilege the escape solution as the best of the limited options to resist the pernicious influence of capitalism, which may have been temporarily defeated by the *deus ex machina* of Big Daddy's zombie army but will no doubt rise again as the inevitable outcome of revolutionary Mulligan's best intentions. There will always be another capitalist overlord, Romero implies: another Kaufman, another Bush, another Trump. Best to chuck the whole enterprise in an exhilarating moment of "fuck it, we're out of here."

We've seen Romero end his zombie films this way before. In *Dawn of the Dead*, Peter and Fran escape the shopping mall, but where are they going in a small helicopter with only a few supplies and a low tank of aviation fuel? In *Day of the Dead*, Sarah, John, and McDermott escape the underground hell of the science/military outpost to a deserted tropical island (maybe—was it all a dream?). Riley's escape is the most victorious of them all. But even this most hopeful of conclusions is haunted by the shadow of ambiguity. The fireworks, so evocative of America's Independence Day and coded in this film as an impotent failure of that utopian promise, do not portend well for Riley's future. Further, Romero leaves the future hard work of Riley and friends off-stage. Though preferable to what Mulligan is proposing, what Riley's communitarian utopia will look like, how it will be established, and whether it will escape the devilish temptations of material culture and capitalism are all open questions.

Frankly, given humanity's track record, it's not looking good. Maybe the best we can hope for, Romero's ambiguous conclusion suggests, is temporary escape/victory before our current heroes become the next generation's old guard to be dispatched and the whole doomed cycle repeats itself. Those fireworks bursting in the sky at the end of the movie are flowers in the graveyard for all of us.

References

Clark, S. (2012). The undead martyr: Sex, death, and revolution in George Romero's zombie films. In T. Fahy (Ed.), *The philosophy of horror* (pp. 197–209). UP of Kentucky.

Hakola, O. J. (2012). Colliding modalities and receding frontier in George Romero's *land of the dead*. In C. J. Miller & A. B. Van Riper (Eds.), *Undead in the west: Vampires, zombies, mummies, and ghosts on the cinematic frontier* (pp. 133–149). The Scarecrow P.

hooks, b. (2000). *Where we stand: Class matters*. Routledge.

Gagne, P. R. (1987). *The zombies that Ate Pittsburgh: The films of George A. Romero*. Dodd, Mead & Company.

Lutz, J. (2010). Zombies of the world unite: Class struggle and alienation in the land of the dead. In T. Fahy (Ed.), *The philosophy of horror* (pp. 121–136). UP of Kentucky.

Mohammad, K. S. (2012). Zombies, rest, and motion: Spinoza and the speed of undeath. In T. Fahy (Ed.), *The philosophy of horror* (pp. 91–102). UP of Kentucky.

Murray, L. A. (2006). When they aren't eating us, they bring us together: Zombies and the American social contract. In R. Green & K. S. Mohammad (Eds.), *The undead and philosophy: Chicken soup for the soulless* (pp. 211–220). Open Court.

Paffenroth, K. (2006). *Gospel of the living dead: George Romero's visions of hell on earth*. Baylor UP.

Richards, L. (2018). This land was made for you and me: The rise of the oppressed in George A. Romero's land of the dead. *The Journal of Popular Culture, 51*(3), 657–73.

Romero, G. A. (Director). (2005). *Land of the dead* [Film]. Universal Pictures.

Tait, R. C. (2007). Revolution at the gates: The dead, the "multitude" and George A. Romero. *Cinephile, 3*(1), 61–70.

Williams, T. (2003). *The cinema of George A. Romero: Knight of the living dead*. Wallflower Press.

Wilson, B. (2006, February 10). Edifying horror: Brief notes on "land of the dead." Filmcure. filmcure.blogspot.com/2006/02/edifying-horror-brief-notes-on-land-of.html

Wood, R. (2018). Fresh meat: Day of the dead. In B. K. Grant (Ed.), *Robin Wood on the horror film: Collected essays and reviews* (pp. 377–383). Wayne State UP.

Zani, S., & Meaux K. (2011). Lucio Fulci and the decaying definition of zombie narratives. In D. Christie & S. J. Lauro (Eds.), *Better off dead: The evolution of the zombie as post-human* (pp. 98–115). Fordham UP.

Zweig, M. (2012). *The working class majority: America's best kept secret*. ILR Press.

CHAPTER 14

Working Class on the Small Screen

Sarah Attfield

1 Introduction: Watching TV

Most people can remember television shows from their childhood vividly, and can recall how those shows might have shaped what they knew about people and events. It might have been *The Brady Bunch* (1969–1974), that offered a happy picture of a blended family. While this show was ground-breaking in its depiction of two divorcees finding love a second time around and recognition of the growing phenomena of blended families, it also presented a picture of white middle-class respectability and affluence. The Brady family lived in a big house and had a car and a housekeeper. They wore nice clothes and took vacations. For many working-class kids, this was a fantasy that couldn't possibly match their own experience, but despite this, they may have considered the Brady family in an aspirational way and possibly devalued their own family experience or circumstances. I know from my own experience that the nice middle-class families on television seemed appealing. They didn't have to beg for more time to pay the rent, shop in thrift stores or wear ill-fitting hand-me-downs. Television families enjoyed excursions and there always seemed to be an endless supply of cookies and other treats. If there had been a family like mine on television, I think it would have made me less embarrassed about my circumstances (embarrassment that later turned to pride in my working-class family and community).

In 1974, cultural critic Raymond Williams published his study on television—a cultural form that had not been subject to much scholarly analysis at that time. Williams understood the significance of television in people's lives, and his ideas became very influential in the subsequent field of television studies. But much has changed since Williams' time, and viewing habits have been affected by the development of internet-based television such as subscription-based models and catch-up TV. Viewers today are no longer restricted to watching what has been programmed in sequence—Williams' idea of "flow" (p. 97)—and can choose when, and where, they watch television (rather than at specific times and in their living rooms where the television set was located). Despite these new ways of watching, television is still plays a big part in people's lives. Shows still generate a buzz and water cooler discussions (think *Game of*

Thrones, 2011–2019), and there are still television events that are watched synchronously (such as the Olympic Games, the Super Bowl and royal weddings).

To see the influence of television on people's lives, we can look at the ways some television shows not only spark discussion and debate, but firmly embed themselves into popular culture. It is still common to jokingly refer to a blended family as akin to the Brady Bunch, or for people to say 'D'ho!' in Homer Simpson style. Character catch phrases can outlive the run of a series and become part of common lexicon. *Sex and the City* (HBO 1998–2004) made the high-end brand names of shoes such as Manolo Blahnik well known and in the 1970s, the hairstyle of Jill Munroe (Farrah Fawcett) in the ABC's Charlie's Angels (1976–1981), was a regular request in hair salons. More recently we see how stars of reality television have huge followings on social media and sign lucrative contracts to promote products to their fans. Kim Kardashian has used the fame gained from appearing on *Keeping up with the Kardashians* (E! 2007–present) to build her business, sell her own brand and advertise other brands such as Uber Eats.

Television is not only important as entertainment, or as a communal cultural experience or to deliver audiences to advertisers, but it is also responsible for shaping the world we live in due to the media's ability to frame things in certain ways. This framing tends to serve those with the most power in society, and framing can operate to maintain certain status quos and protect the interests of the dominant classes. As Kendall (2011) states, "media products … have the symbolic capacity to define the world for people and to limit the terms of debate if someone challenges ideologies" (p. 6). Television is never neutral, and the ways in which certain people and communities are portrayed reveals much about how class works. This essay attempts to explore the representation of working-class people on the small screen in the US (including a brief overview of the history of representation), but with a focus on the contemporary scene.

2 Representation Matters

How does working-class rhetoric play out on the small screen, and why might it be important? If we understand rhetoric as modes of communication intended to persuade and influence (Casey, 2002, p. 202), then we could suggest that the messages embedded in television shows have this potential effect—to persuade viewers to think about working-class people in certain ways. If those messages are negative and portray working-class people via stereotypes, then the audience may believe that working-class people are inferior to people with higher socio-economic status. This is why representation is so important.

We spend a lot of our time consuming popular culture—it is a daily habit. We watch television, movies, listen to popular music, follow sports and so on (Holtzman, 2000, p. 5). Much of what we know about our societies comes from popular culture and, according to Holtzman, television is the "most pervasive form of contemporary media" (p. 34). Casey suggests that an understanding of how representation works is an essential aspect of television scholarship because we understand the world through representations (p. 201).

Representation shapes our knowledge of various groups in society. Hall (1997) states that meaning is attributed due to "how we represent" things (p. 3). And much of the meaning that is produced occurs in "the modern mass media" (p. 3). If we don't see a certain group represented at all, we might know nothing of their existence (if we don't have personal connections with people from that group). If we only ever see negative representations of a particular group, we will tend to think of them disparagingly. This can mean that we just don't care about certain groups of people, or that we are even openly hostile towards them. Television itself has been described as "a particularly salient instrument of hegemony" because the public obtains "images of social reality" from television shows (Press, 1991, p. 17). There is the potential for television to produce "norms and rules" (D'Acci, 2004, p. 373). It is possible then that class on the small screen can reinforce class-based inequality (Butsch, 201, p. 20)?

For members of certain groups, representation is important because seeing yourself represented in popular culture means a validation of existence, and a potential sense of empowerment. The significance of sympathetic and nuanced representation cannot be underestimated. Despite the endless possibilities of what could be represented on television, scholars point to the narrowness of representation of certain groups, particularly women, people of colour, queer people and the working class (who do, of course, also occupy all categories of gender, race, sexuality, and so on).

With this in mind, how have working-class people been represented on the small screen in the US? Casey (2002) suggests that American television has been dominated by representations of white, middle class people (p. 27), and hooks (2000) states that television has been instrumental in promoting "the myth of the classless society" (p. 71). But are there particular genres where working-class people are more visible? Does television reflect the diversity of the working class? What are some of the potential effects of this representation or lack thereof? And who has the power to decide who and what is represented? How do "patterns of ownership" reveal the power over images wielded by the "economically dominant class" (Casey, 2002, p. 24)? Who are the producers, who decides on programming? Who are the writers and the intended audience?

3 Working-Class Representation in Situation Comedies

A comprehensive survey of the history of American television is beyond the scope of this essay, but it is useful to consider the history of working-class representation on the small screen. Have working-class characters or working-class subjects been featured consistently? In the early days of American television, working-class characters did appear, mostly in sitcoms. The sitcom genre has been around since before television and has its origins in radio comedy serials (Holtzman, 2000, p. 123), and some radio serials such as *Hancock's Half Hour* (1956–1960) were adapted for the screen (Casey, 2002, p. 29). The early American sitcoms tended to portray working-class people. *The Goldbergs*, which ran from 1949–1956 was centred around a Jewish family living in the Bronx and *The Honeymooners* (running from 1955–1956), featured a working-class married couple who lived in a low-rent apartment in Brooklyn. There were a number of other working-class sitcoms through the 1950s, but the working-class settings began to disappear by the 1960s, although each decade has seen at least one or two working-class sitcoms, such as *All in the Family* (1971–1979), *Sanford and Son* (1972–1977), the original series of *Rosanne* (1988–1997), *The Simpsons* (1989–present), and *The King of Queens* (1998–2007). Butsch (2016) suggests that working-class families have only constituted 10% of television families in American sitcoms (p. 21). He also claims that the majority of US working-class sitcoms have reinforced working-class stereotypes (p. 21), and suggests that the majority of male working-class protagonists in US sitcoms have been represented as "buffoons" (p. 21)—incompetent men who do not operate as good role models. They are created for laughs rather than to represent working-class life accurately. Working-class women in US sitcoms tend to be portrayed as possessing middle class sensibilities and values which operate as the antithesis of the men's uncouthness (Butsch, 2016, p. 23).

Different types of working-class stereotypes in sitcoms are identified and described by Pepi Leistyna in his 2005 documentary, *Class Dismissed: How TV Frames the Working Class*. Leistyna claims that there are five stock working-class characters in US sitcoms that reinforce the stereotype of working-class failure. By this he means a perceived inability to rise from a working-class position, represented as a self-inflicted lack. Such characters tend to appear throughout the history of sitcoms and assist in reinforcing the media owners' power through the endorsement of "principles of capitalism" (Scharrer, 2010, p. 28).

The first of the stereotypes is "bad taste"—the way working-class characters display bad taste through their choices of clothing, make-up styles, music, and so on. Characters might be portrayed as "trashy" or "tacky," lacking sophistication and the ability to distinguish between kitsch and things that are "classy."

This is a quite common characterization but this lack of cultural capital is particularly evident when a working-class character is present in a middle or upper-class world. Think about the class faux pas as *The Beverly Hillbillies* (1962–1971) characters negotiated a middle and upper class world, or individual characters such as Mimi from *The Drew Carey Show* (1995–2004), who is ridiculed for her excessive make up, tacky clothes and brash manner. Clothes, lack of middle-class manners or ignorance of middle-class etiquette, and "course" speech make characters like Mimi stand out in a completely negative way.

Secondly, there are the working-class characters who display a lack of intelligence—they are often loveable buffoons (and generally male, but not always). Their lack of intelligence renders them unable to aspire to a middle-class life. This is Homer Simpson, or Al Bundy from *Married with Children* (1987–1997)—often stupid or ignorant. A classic example is when Homer Simpson discovers that "gym" is not pronounced "gime."

A third stereotype consists of working-class characters who display reactionary politics—they are bigoted, sexist, racist, homophobic which is a common assumption held about the white working class. A classic example would be Archie Bunker from *All in the Family* (1971–1979) who makes sexist, racist and homophobic comments. This is not to suggest that working-class people can't be bigoted, but that it is rarer to see such reactionary politics in middle or upper-class characters.

Fourthly are the working-class characters who are lazy, have a poor work ethic and unambitious. They fail to adhere to the myth that hard work and determination are all that is needed for people to move away from their lower social class. Louie from *Lucky Louie* (2006) fits this stereotype—he drinks too much and doesn't seem to have any motivation for hard work. And Homer Simpson also displays laziness—he is often seen avoiding work or sleeping on the job.

Lastly, there is the dysfunctional family. While they do also appear in middle-class sitcoms, they tend to be more exaggerated in working-class shows. The Bundy family from *Married with Children*, or Joy and Darnell's family in *My Name is Earl* (2005–2007) are good examples and it should be noted that the "trailer trash" characters tend to come off worst in these shows. Joy is particularly stereotypical—she has children from different fathers and has lied about their paternity. She is a petty criminal and only just manages to avoid prison and she comes across as selfish and neglectful of her children.

The continued use of stereotypes is arguably what made *Roseanne* stand out when it was first aired. The show depicted a believable scenario—a white working-class family who struggled to make ends meet. A simple premise that contained an air of authenticity, helped with the choice of furniture for the set that was sourced from retailers popular with low-income people (Holtzman, 2000, p. 129). The titular character, Roseanne, is a tough and uncompromising working-class woman who tries to do her best as a mother but does not adopt middle-class styles of parenting. Roseanne is also often seen at her place of work and the show depicts her confrontations with her employers over her working conditions and pay. Roseanne also celebrated her class status and would affectionately refer to herself and her family as "white trash" which challenged the media's negative framing of poor white people (Kendall, 2011, p. 142). The show was very successful and its discontinuation in the 1990s was met with disappointment from viewers. When the 2018 reboot was announced, there was a wave of nostalgia from mostly white fans for the original show and its representation of white working-class life.[1] Commentary from scholars, viewers and critics indicated that there had been a dearth of working-class representation since *Roseanne*.

There have been a number of working-class sitcoms since the 2000s, but working-class characters still remain in the minority in this genre. Some notable shows include *My Name is Earl* (2005–2007), *Malcolm in the Middle* (2000–2006) and *Everybody Hates Chris* (2005–2009). Of these shows, it could be argued that *My Name is Earl* reinforces class stereotypes, particularly around the "white trash" figure. The characters are caricatures—Earl is a petty criminal, his ex-wife Joy lives in a trailer and is represented as unintelligent but constantly scheming for ways to get money. Earl's brother, Randy, is a loveable idiot. These are characters to laugh at due to their class—they are funny because they have working-class accents, and wear "trashy" clothes and are generally unsophisticated.

In *Malcolm in the Middle* the family's financial struggles are realistic but Malcolm's mother is overbearing and his father is generally incompetent. The conceit of the show is that Malcolm is academically gifted—which marks him as different from the rest of his working-class family. Malcolm eventually wins a scholarship to attend a prestigious university (which could be interpreted as the character finding a way out from his working-class and dysfunctional family). While there might be aspects of *My Name is Earl* and *Malcolm in the Middle* that are recognizable to some working-class viewers, it's difficult to imagine many working-class viewers being able to identify with the majority of the representations in these shows.

Everybody Hates Chris is very different. While funny, it is set in a reality for a Black working-class family living in a housing project in Brooklyn. The show depicts racism and classism and defies the stereotypes of other working-class sitcoms, particularly through the character of Chris' father who is an efficient and attentive parent (the humour is created as a result of his elaborate ways to make wages go further). Wright (2018) suggests that "images of blackness" on television have been filtered through a "white perspective" (p. 13) due to the industry being white-dominated, and despite some increase in portrayals of Black people on the small screen, that Black stories and representations of Black people are still "limited" in terms of "variety" (p. 15).

More recently, from the 2010s, there have been some interesting working-class sitcoms that have resisted the stereotypes and they do have the potential to offer more nuanced portrayals of working-class life. By doing so, it's possible that they might persuade non-working-class viewers to be more empathetic towards working-class people. They also showcase the ways in which working-class people communicate. *On My Block* (2018–present) is a coming-of-age sitcom set in a working-class neighbourhood of Los Angeles. The show follows four teenagers, Monse, Cesar, Jamal and Ruben as they navigate high school and overcome obstacles along the way. The characters and the setting are believable and while still a sitcom, the show clearly represents the social and political reality of life in an inner-city poor neighbourhood. This is conveyed in the very first episode of the show as the four protagonists spy on a party hosted by older kids – a party that ends when gun shots can be heard. As the four run from the area, they jokingly argue about the type of gun that was used and there is no comment on the shots or why they might have been fired. This everyday portrayal of social issues continues as they walk along the street on their way to their high school orientation day. There are police cars constantly patrolling or sitting on street corners and the friends come upon gang members and a group of men beating another man. Apart from comments to each other, to "keep walking" and "don't look," there is no commentary—this is just their everyday reality and they have found their own ways to survive in this environment (through solidarity and collective action). The show also represents the racially diverse working class—all the main characters are people of colour.

The ABC sitcom *The Middle* (2009–2018) is centred around an Indiana family with two parents who work, but often struggle financially. While the family in the show are described in some reviews and promos as middle class, they are a working-class family who live in the mid-west and their money worries are a feature of the series. They are the kind of family who are only one or two paychecks aways from economic hardship and their house is cluttered in a permanent state of disrepair. The humour doesn't rely on class stereotypes, rather the characters are well-developed and the butt of the jokes is the circumstances that lead to the chaos that occurs in the family's lives. *The Middle* also features a strong female working-class character in the protagonist Frankie Heck (Patricia Heaton) who tries to hold her family together, and provide a future for her children with more options than her own.

Another recent ABC sitcom that challenges working-class stereotypes is *The Goldbergs* (2013–present), which is set in a Pennsylvanian town in the 1980s and based on the creator, Adam F. Goldberg's, own childhood. While the family are loud, both in speech and in their choice of fashion and décor, they show how working-class rhetoric can operate and how abrasiveness doesn't necessarily mean a lack of care. The father, Murray (Jeff Garlin), is often tired and over-worked and he shouts at his children. But he also displays moments of tenderness and is trying to do his best for his family.

What's interesting when considering the continuing dearth of working-class characters in sitcoms is the actual absence of a reason for their invisibility. As Butsch (2016) points out (p. 21), a sitcom can be set in any kind of situation—there really are no limits, so the lack of working-class families and characters reveals discrimination against working-class people on a structural level in terms of the television industry. Producers are not interested in working-class stories and writers employed by the networks are not writing working-class stories which points to the middle-class domination of the media and creative professions.

4   Drama

If working-class characters are generally thin on the ground in sitcoms (which is one of the most prolific television genres), do they appear in other genres such as drama? For the most part, television dramas are dominated by middle-class professionals. Numerous dramas feature legal and medical professionals and while some are interesting in their inclusion of gender issues, and some do tackle racism, they rarely feature working-class central protagonists. According to Baron (2016), working-class women in particular, "remain invisible," appearing "in the background … as hotel maids, nannies, waitresses, sales clerks, factory workers and welfare mothers" (p. 185). This invisibility of working-class women is even notable in so-called "quality" television dramas—the complex serial dramas such as *The Wire* (2002–2008). "Quality television" is a contentious term used to describe television shows with complex narratives and certain stylistic features such as "high production values, naturalistic performances … careful camera work … and a sense of aural style" (Cardwell, 2007, p. 26). *The Wire* features a number of working-class characters and was critically acclaimed as a realistic depiction of life for marginalised communities in Baltimore, but it is not without some problematic elements such as the representation of working-class Black women who are mostly relegated to stereotypes or exploited as victims (Kennedy, 2016, p. 207). The series is focused on male working-class characters, who, according to Kennedy are attempting to "salvage American working-class masculinity in an era of global capitalism" (p. 207). Other dramas featuring working-class characters include *Ozark* (2017–present), which has middle-class central protagonists in the characters of Marty and Wendy Byrde, but includes white working-class characters such as the Langmore family who live in trailers and have a history of crime and violence. The Langmores are portrayed as hillbillies who spend a lot of time drinking and scheming, even though the character of Ruth Langmore is played as an independent and intelligent young woman, she is still untrustworthy and prone to criminal behaviour. She is outsmarted by the middle class, formally educated and sophisticated Marty.

Police dramas do feature working-class characters, but they tend to focus on detectives rather than the regular police working traffic duties or patrolling neighbourhoods. The detectives are often portrayed as sophisticated and possessing high levels of cultural capital which keeps them well equipped for questioning white collar criminals. Although some crime dramas do feature uniformed police, such as *Chicago P.D.* (2014–2017), contemporary crime shows are not usually very realistic when it comes to depicting the reality of police officers supporting families on their modest salaries.

Nurses do feature in medical dramas, but often in juxtaposition to the doctors, who tend to be the ones portrayed as brilliant and life-saving, or as love interests for the handsome surgeons. Popular medical dramas such as *Grey's Anatomy* (ABC 2005–present), have focused almost exclusively on doctors, and there is little sense of the work of nurses and other auxiliary staff in the hospitals. NBC hospital show ER (1994–2009), fares a little better in its inclusion of nurses and other staff, with some characters such as nurse Carol Hathaway (Julianna Margulies) becoming a regular character. Hathaway is often depicted having conflicts with doctors who treat the nursing staff badly and is an advocate for the nursing teams and is involved in labor disputes with hospital management. The audience is also privy to Hathaway's financial situation and her struggles to pay her mortgage. But despite these realistic aspects of Hathaway's life—she does fall for the handsome doctor and her final act as a character is to leave the hospital and join him in another city.

Some genre-blending shows have offered much more interesting representations of working-class life and these include *Atlanta* (2016–present) and *Jane the Virgin* (2014–present). *Atlanta* is a comedy drama with surreal and absurdist elements and depicts the life of Earn as he tries to make his way in Atlanta's rap scene by managing his cousin Alfred who performs under the name of Paper Boi. In a similar way to *On My Block* (with a much more adult vibe), *Atlanta* shows the everyday realities of working-class people of colour and represents hardship and financial struggle, the racism of the police and the discrimination experienced by people of colour when interacting with official institutions. *Jane the Virgin* is a romantic comedy drama that uses some of the genre conventions of Latin telenovelas. The central character is a Latina single mother whose own mother was a teenager when Jane was born. Before she accidentally falls pregnant, Jane is working in a hotel and studying to become a teacher. The show has many telenovela elements, such as complex plot lines and characters experiencing many highs and lows—but although it doesn't have the gritty edge of a show like Atlanta, it does provide some representation of the struggle faced by single parents and counters stereotypes of young, single mothers.

5 Reality Television

It is in reality television that the majority of working-class representation appear, but these representations are not always positive. Reality TV has become a dominant form and according to Kavka (2012), it has "transformed" the way television is produced and led to a "celebrity industry" (p. 2). Kavka states that the ubiquity of reality TV has also made viewers very astute in their ability to understand the "mechanics of television production" (p. 2). Reality TV is not a completely new genre—it has its origins in the *Candid Camera* shows (1948–2004) and family documentaries such as *An American Family* (1973) (p. 13). But it developed from "ride along" shows such as *Cops* (1989–2020) (p. 54) to the fly-on-the-wall style documentaries "docusoap" form (p. 64), to the "surveillance and competition" form of *Survivor* (2000–present) and *Big Brother* (2000–present) (p. 75) and makeover shows such as *Extreme Makeover* (2002–2007) (p. 126).

While reality TV shows often feature working-class people, it has been suggested that overall, reality TV displays middle-class sensibilities that are often hidden (Grindstaff, 2011, p. 197). This is particularly the case in lifestyle and makeover shows such as *What Not to Wear* (2003–2013) which present the participants (who are almost exclusively working class) as requiring middle-class interventions to improve their health, their looks, their homes, relationships and so on (p. 201). The "transformations" that occur are on middle-class terms, and according to Grindstaff they "legitimate normative middle-class aspirations" (p. 201). On these kinds of shows, working-class people are deficient— unable to make the right kinds of choices to improve their lives (ie, present as middle class). Middle class "experts" provide "guidance" for the working-class subjects who are "failing in the skills of self-work and self-development" (Skeggs & Woods, 2011, p. 15).

There is also a sense of exploitation of working-class people in some reality TV shows (Skeggs & Woods, 2011, p. 1), not just because subjects can be vulnerable due to their low-income status and lack of cultural capital (Grindstaff, 2011, p. 205), but because there are working-class participants who agree to participate in reality TV in order to earn a fee—this arguably leaves them open to economic exploitation (they are paid much less than professional actors). Possibly due to their lack of power in the relationship, working-class reality TV participants are often represented in overly negative ways, and there is an emphasis on the abject in terms of their behaviour. They are course, loud, aggressive and "uncultivated" (Grindstaff, 2011, p. 199) characters, such as the subjects of shows such as *Jersey Shore* (2009–2012), where they are also depicted as drinking too much and being over-sexed (mostly on heterosexual terms). This is represented as particularly negative for female subjects who are seen as rejecting respectability and "violating...the codes of hegemonic femininity" (p. 199). This notion of rejecting respectability can also be seen in the popular show *Here Comes Honey Boo Boo* (2012–2017) which follows the family of child beauty pageant contestant Alana Thompson as they go about their daily business in their small home town in Georgia. According to Rennels (2015), the family rejects notions of neoliberalism and therefore "ideal whiteness" (p. 271) and as a result become both subjects for ridicule and spectacle for the middle-class viewer but I would argue they also represent authenticity for some working-class viewers who might identify with them. Rennels (p. 274) suggests that the family do not adhere to "ideal whiteness" because they display a lack of aspiration that might manifest in self-improvement and self-control (they are not concerned about losing weight, changing eating habits or supressing bodily functions for the sake of the cameras). In fact, the subjects of the show—Alana and her mother, Mama June, delight in this rejection of so-called good manners. While the uncouth behaviour of the characters is intended to be laughed at by audiences who might look down on "redneck" characters—the unself-conscious nature of their behaviour can also be seen as refreshing and empowering for audiences who might identify as members of the white poor or working class. Along with their generally uninhibited behaviour on camera, the family also displays a sense of unity and collectivism and Mama June in particular, is a strong female head of the family and it's possible that working-class viewers enjoy such shows and build connections with the on-screen characters (some of whom have enjoyed celebrity status outside of the show's life).

Other reality TV formats feature working-class people. The competition-based shows sometimes include details of contestants' working-class occupations or backgrounds, particularly when the contestant is being packaged as an underdog, with a story of resilience and survival to create sympathy from judges or the audience who might be voting for them to remain in the competition. This can be seen in talent shows such as *American Idol* (2002–present) when, for example, contestants such as Lee DeWyze (season 9, 2010) reveal their day jobs (in DeWyze's case, the job was in a paint store). Or in the long-running show *Survivor*'s (2000–present) 30th Season version, *Survivor: Worlds Apart* (2015) which divided participants based on their occupation (and therefore class) status. The winner was a member of the blue-collar group—Mike Holloway, a former oil worker.

Numerous home renovation shows include working-class people, albeit on the periphery, and also reveal the ways in which class intersects with race and ethnicity. *Flip or Flop* (2013–2017), *Masters of Flip* (2015–present), *Fixer Upper* (2013–2018) consist of mostly white couples who buy homes in need of renovation. We watch the couples design the new layouts, choose the fixtures and fittings and start the renovation work, but in the background an army of tradespeople who are often Latino or African American men actually carry out the construction work. On occasion the host couple will speak with a representative of the workers, such as a building foreman, but rarely do the tradespeople or labourers get a chance to speak or introduce themselves to the audience.

I would suggest that there is a genre of reality TV shows that offer interesting representations of working-class people—those that show working-class people at work. This type of show began with the original *Cops* which, despite being clearly structured in ways that present the police as the good guys, does at least show people doing their jobs. *Homeland Security USA* (2009), featured workers responsible for border protection at US airports and mail centres and depicted people in their daily work. Other shows, such as *Deadliest Catch* (2005–present) and *Ice Road Truckers* (2007–2017), feature workers engaged in dangerous working-class occupations, workers who have been described as "hyper-masculine blue-collar heroes" (Grindstaff 202). These programs are edited to create high drama with cliff-hangers between advertisement breaks as the viewer is left wondering whether the workers will make it across the ice or survive a storm. There is a sense of tension and excitement linked to the jobs which are mainly targeted at young male viewers (Kendall, 2011, p. 140). This mostly masculine presentation of manual work is also seen in *Dirty Jobs* (2005–2012), which includes a host, Mike Rowe, performing jobs such as sewer inspector or garbage collector along with workers to provide commentary on the skills needed for the jobs. In this show, the workers are presented as highly skilled and their work is valued. Rowe is always impressed with the workers' ability to perform their duties under very difficult and often dangerous conditions.

6   Soap Opera

Soap operas have existed since the early days of television and according to Ford (2010) are one of the "longest-running genres" (p. 11) and as a result a "cornerstone of American popular culture" (p. 14). But American soap operas differ from those of the UK, which tend to feature working-class communities. The most popular soaps in the UK are *Coronation Street* (1960–present) and *EastEnders* (1985–present). *Coronation Street* is set in a working-class town in the north of England and the main characters are predominantly working class. *EastEnders* is set in the east end of London, a traditionally working-class area and the show maintains a majority ensemble of working-class characters. Popular soaps in the US though tend to be centred around middle and upper-class characters. *The Bold and the Beautiful* (1987–present) is set in the fashion industry in L.A. and features glamorous and rich characters. A thoroughly middle-class family is the centre of *Days of Our Lives* (1965–present) and the main characters of *General Hospital* (1963–present) are brilliant and glamorous doctors (there are nurses too, but they also tend to be glamorous and married to doctors). And of course, the hugely popular *Dallas* (1978–1991) and *Dynasty* (1981–1989) focused on rich oil families. Why are there no American soaps that centre around working-class communities? It is possible to create a soap that includes drama and intrigue while set in an everyday reality for working-class people. The absence of such a show doesn't necessarily mean that audiences aren't interested—it does mean that television writers and producers are not creating such opportunities.

7   Conclusion

The potential of representations of working-class people on the small screen to reinforce stereotypes and therefore maintain the power of those from the dominant economic classes shouldn't be underestimated. Television is ubiquitous and has the ability to shape opinion and understanding of groups of people and to reveal the ways in which structures of oppression, such as class, operate. It is also possible for television to create new realities for people—to demonstrate the nuance of working-class life and to create sympathy and understanding for working-class people and to value working-class experience. Despite a small number of television shows that do represent working-class life in interesting and authentic ways, the majority of television shows have relied on negative stereotypes of working-class people, or have excluded working-class experience altogether. The working classes make up the majority of the American population, and the only reason working-class people do not see themselves on screen very often, rests with those who control its production. Until there are more working-class background people working as writers and producers, this is unlikely to change, so the few shows that do display working-class life and include sympathetic working-class characters should be celebrated and shared.

Note

1 The 2018 reboot of Roseanne was cancelled after the show's creator, Roseanne Barr, posted racist comments on social media. A spin-off series, *The Conners*, starring most of the original cast (minus Roseanne Barr) took its place the same year.

References

Baron, A. (2016). Vanishing act: The sexualization of the workplace and disappearance of class in American television dramas (1990s–2010s). In N. Cloarec (Ed.), *Social class on British and American screens: Essays on cinema and television* (pp. 184–203). McFarland.

Butsch, R. (2016). Six decades of social class in American Sitcoms. In N. Cloarec (Ed.), *Social class on British and American screens: Essays on cinema and television* (pp. 18–33). McFarland.

Cardwell, S. (2007). Is quality television any good? Generic distinctions, evaluations and the troubling matter of critical judgement. In J. McCabe & K. Akass (Eds.), *Quality TV: Contemporary American television and beyond* (pp. 19–34). I.B. Tauris.

Casey, B. (2002). *Television studies: The key concepts*. Routledge.

D'Acci, J. (2004). Television, representation and gender. In R. Allen & A. Hills (Eds.), *The television studies reader* (pp. 373–388). Routledge.

Ford, S. (2010). *Survival of soap opera: Transformation for a new media era*. University of Mississippi Press.

Grindstaff, L. (2011). From Jerry Springer to Jersey Shore: The cultural politics of class in/on US reality programming. In B. Skeggs & H. Wood (Eds.), *Reality television and class* (pp. 197–209). Palgrave Macmillan.

Hall, S. (1997). Introduction. In S. Hall (Ed.), *Representation: Cultural representations and signifying practices* (pp. 1–13). Open University.

Holtzman, L. (2000). *Media messages: What film, television, and popular music teach us about race, class gender and sexual orientation*. M.E. Sharpe.

hooks, b. (2000). *Where we stand: Class matters*. Routledge.

Kavka, M. (2012). *Reality TV*. Edinburgh University Press.

Kendall, D. (2011). *Framing class: Media representations of wealth and poverty in America*. Rowman and Littlefield.

Kennedy, A. T. (2016). The gender and class politics of social realism in the wire. In N. Cloarec (Ed.), *Social class on British and American screens: Essays on cinema and television* (pp. 204–217). McFarland.

Leistyna, P., & Alper, L. (2005). *Class dismissed: How TV frames the working class*. Media Education Foundation.

McCabe, J., & Akass, K. (2007). Introduction. In J. McCabe & K. Akass (Eds.), *Quality TV: Contemporary American television and beyond* (pp. 1–11). I.B. Tauris.

Press, A. L. (1991). *Women watching television: Gender, class and generation in the American television experience*. University of Pennsylvania Press.

Rennels, T. R. (2015). Here comes Honey Boo Boo: A cautionary tale starring white working-class people. *Communication and Critical/Cultural Studies, 15*(3), 271–288.

Scharrer, E. (2010). From wise to foolish: The portrayal of the Sitcom Father, 1950s–1990s. *Journal of Broadcasting and Electronic Media, 45*(1), 23–40.

Skeggs, B., & Woods, H. (Eds.). (2011). Introduction: Real class. In *Reality television and class* (pp. 1–29). Palgrave Macmillan.

Williams, R. (1974). *Television: Technology and cultural form*. Fontana.

Wright, J. K. (2018). *Empire and Black images in popular culture*. McFarland.

CHAPTER 15

#ActorsWithDayJobs

Geoffrey Owens, Job Shaming, and the Ideology of Work

William DeGenaro

> Perhaps it's time to stop differentiating what kind of work we think is 'real'—whether it's acting, bagging groceries, writing (hi!), governing a state, or tilling the fields—and start valuing hard work in whatever form it comes.
> MICHAEL SCHULMAN

∴

During much of the 1980s, no hour of television exemplified the decade's capitalist ethos quite like the first hour of NBC's Thursday night primetime schedule. The hour began with the hugely successful *The Cosby Show* (1984–1992) and continued with *Family Ties* (1982–1989), two sitcoms made possible as much by President Ronald Reagan as any member of the respective creative teams. Reagan preached tax cuts, the deregulation of private industry, the dissolution of labor unions, the values of personal responsibility and individual achievement, and the gospel of trickle-down economics—and enacted public policy supporting all of the above. From his firing of striking air traffic controllers in 1981 to his rehearsal of the racist rhetoric of the "welfare queen," Reagan valorized the accumulation of wealth as the apotheosis of American values and he dismissed collectivism and New Deal notions of the "common good" as the antithesis of those values.[1] A telegenic former actor, he owned the airwaves during the evening news, and this was an era when Americans got our news from network television.

Reagan owned the airwaves during primetime, too. *The Cosby Show* focused on an idealized family led by an obstetrician and an attorney with lots of kids, lots of disposable income, and an expensive New York townhouse full of love. Their blackness was lightly underlined by signifiers like the music the parents listened to and the Afrocentric art in their home, but certainly didn't impede their mobility or their navigation of the world. *Family Ties* reversed the version of the generation gap that had dominated the baby boom era with its middle-aged hippies clashing with their politically conservative, materialistic, but good-hearted son. Alex P. Keaton embodied and explicitly voiced his idol Ronald Reagan's ideology, mocking his dad's employment at a public television affiliate and dreaming of a future on Wall Street. "Family ties" doubled down on Reagan's photogenic charm with a teenaged avatar of the president who was ready to be splashed on the locker doors and bedroom walls of teen fans.

Television programs have long reflected and refracted dominant values about social class, and they've likely *influenced* those values throughout the television era, too.[2] Media and working-class studies scholar Pepi Leistyna has pointed out, for instance, that the earliest examples of tv families included large numbers of working-class immigrants (think "Mama" which debuted in the late 1940s), but as the medium became a means to market products geared toward upwardly mobile suburbanites, families representing professional-managerial classes became the norm (think "Leave it to Beaver" in the 1950s). Although class mythology had long been a motif of family tv, rarely had programs so vigorously and overtly promoted the broader culture's beliefs in meritocracy, individualism, wealth, and consumerism than the lead hour of "Must-See TV,"[3] the evening of primetime television programming NBC was to dominate for at least two decades.

So it was perhaps fitting that a co-star of that storied hour of Reagan-era tv starred thirty years later in another story—this time as protagonist—of dominant culture's ideology regarding social class. Geoffrey Owens, who played one of Dr. Huxtable's sons-in-law on "The Cosby Show," returned to the spotlight in August, 2018, when a fan spotted Owens working at a New Jersey grocery store, snapped an unflattering photograph, and provided the picture to the media. Several news outlets picked up the story and tweeted out the photo, which showed Owens working as a cashier, his Trader Joe's uniform stained from having just bagged potatoes. A protracted conversation across social and traditional media about Owens's career trajectory and what it means to be successful unfolded during, coincidentally, Labor Day weekend. The views expressed during that conversation suggest that many of the myths preached explicitly by Reagan and supported implicitly by popular culture during his presidency still circulate, albeit via new platforms that many of us who grew up during the Reagan era never imagined. Though many pundits and Twitter-users expressed surprise that Owens was working at Trader Joe's, the narrative itself was not surprising—at least insomuch as conversation participants largely rehearsed familiar values and sentiments. The media happening that trended on Labor Day weekend, 2018, suggests that as a culture we still struggle to discuss social class in nuanced ways and still largely rely on the same commonplaces. After all, many responses to the Geoffrey Owens moment on both old and new media largely fit into existing myths and narratives.

1   The Myth of Meritocracy

Meritocracy means that achievement is based on merit, but of course "achievement" and "merit" are abstractions. Do hard workers get ahead? Do the most worthy reap the most reward? Capitalist systems rely on the myth of meritocracy to establish some sense of justice, i.e., to *just-ify* why some folks do better than others. Achievement and getting ahead are defined in both material and social terms. To do better means to do that which earns monetary and cultural capital: making more money, living in places and taking part in pursuits that signify caché. Likewise, merit is defined as the possession of individual qualities like work ethic, initiative, and creativity. People who pick themselves up by their bootstraps and work hard will obtain success. People who lack those qualities will find upward mobility difficult. An invisible hand, this myth suggests, decides who wins and who loses. When spun positively, this mythology has a great deal of appeal. Reagan knew how to turn on the charm as he told stories of hard-working Americans who got ahead thanks to the values that mythically comprise this notion of "merit" and so it made sense when he argued that forms of government intervention like social welfare programs were crutches that led to codependency, weakened individual will and work ethic, and rewarded those who lacked the merit required to be successful. If you aren't achieving, you aren't working hard enough. The "meritocracy" ignores the roles that luck, circumstance, and systemic injustices like racism and sexism play in deciding who gets ahead. Meritocracy does not allow for the possibility that one might work very hard and display a great deal of merit and nonetheless not climb upward, materially or culturally speaking.

In the initial versions of the Owens story that circulated in late August and early September, 2018, the fan who took his picture is quoted as saying, "Wow, all those years of doing the show and you ended up as a cashier" (*From Learning Lines*, 2018). Owens is working a job with little cultural caché, i.e., a working-class job in the service sector. Further, his trajectory looks like a kind-of reverse American Dream—having gone from a job with maximum cultural capital to the service sector, a site of minimum cultural capital and, often, relatively low pay (though Trader Joe's prides itself on paying a living wage unlike many service jobs). The original news story in particular has, as BET (*Black Entertainment Television*) acknowledged in its critique of the Owens story, a gotcha tone, singling out specific aspects of Owens's employment including his wage, the fact that he's wearing a Trader Joe's t-shirt, and the fact that the t-shirt is soiled. The story quotes the fan who took the photo observing that Owens has gained weight since his tenure on "Cosby." She says, "It was a shock to see him working there and looking the way he did" (*From Learning Lines*, 2018). The fan/photographer voices many of the most judgmental sentiments about Owens, but the story itself, attributed only to the news outlet and not a specific reporter, contextualizes her words with its own sense of wonder that the actor is working at a grocery store. The implication is that Owens's stained uniform and paunch, for instance, are newsworthy, if only because both are signifiers of a non-Hollywood caste. Owens has transgressed the upward trajectory of the meritocracy, these stories suggest.

Fox News notably tweeted out Owens's photo with a link to its "Celebrity News" story (also sans attribution to a specific writer) about his employment at the store, but so did other news outlets. Fox's tweet placed the image of Owens in his Trader Joe's uniform next to a photo from his "Cosby" days in which he wears a suit. Their news story contains three side-by-side iterations of the same photo (Owens at Trader Joe's), the two outermost photos darkened and the one in the middle fully lighted; the three identical but differently shaded images look like a Warhol silkscreen. Fox made the decision to emphasize the imagery—not an uncommon choice for news outlets in the digital age in which we live, but at the same time notable in the way they highlight the *gotcha* aesthetic and the gaze toward.

Owens's body. Other news outlets followed suit. Twitter in particular became the public sphere for circulating rhetoric that shamed Owens for his lack of achievement, for working an allegedly unmeritorious job. The images prominently featuring his body and his uniform, the stories quoting the fan-photographer's surprise, the revelation of his salary—all of these repeated details hammer away at the idea that Geoffrey Owens did something wrong, transgressed (or, rather, reversed) the American Dream. It was like the media collectively felt justified commenting on his body, his shirt stains, and his wage because—as the myth of meritocracy suggests—Owens himself was at fault. Like the medium of prime-time television hour thirty years prior, Twitter now served as the arena where the myth of meritocracy was on display.

Celebrities in particular are flash points for the power of the myth of meritocracy—and the paradoxes of that myth. The general public enjoys "rags to riches" stories about celebrities, but also sometimes consumes "take-down" stories that gaze at falls from grace and other alleged failures. It becomes essential for celebrities to maintain both status and the appearance of status. As Sophie Gilbert (2018) wrote in her analysis of the Owens story, for stars "to admit financial failure is to somehow break a contract with fans by bringing yourself back down to earth, by dulling some of the sheen of stardom." But that desire to project status and success is also true, oftentimes, for non-celebrities as well. Few want to seem downwardly mobile because if success equals merit then non-success must equal a lack thereof.

The myth of meritocracy maintains our collective ambivalence toward working-class persons and working-class jobs. If we truly believe that the best "get ahead," where does that leave the working class? Working-class studies scholar and economist Michael Zweig is a leading theorist on working-class identity, labor, and culture. Zweig (2011) suggests the working class occupy "a place of relative vulnerability—on the job, in the market, in politics and culture" (p. 13). Zweig explains that unlike the professional (think: lawyers, doctors, professors) and managerial (think: those who manage and supervise the labor of their employees) classes, the working-class have little control over the pace and the nature of their jobs. The working-class, then, includes those who work "rank and file" jobs in manufacturing, service, and information sectors. Myths of meritocracy generally suggest that such workers can and should work hard in order to demonstrate their merit and "get ahead," which often means moving upward into another social class. But scholars like Barbara Jensen describe and theorize the cultures and lifestyles of working-class identity—the varied ways of being in the world that define "working class" as a meaningful marker. Though she writes about her own passing from a working-class childhood to a professional-managerial class adulthood (she is a counselor and academic), Jensen's descriptive and personal look at working-class life challenges the notion that working-class is something to escape through individual merit. There are, after all, meritorious individuals who stay working class and express pride in who they are.

2   The Myth of the Nobility of Hard Work

Although working-class jobs across manufacturing, service, "pink collar," and information sectors generally possess less cultural caché, individuals who hold these jobs are often placed on a pedestal and even fetishized for their hard work. We have a romantic attitude toward the idea of working with one's hands, of getting sweaty, of putting in a long day on an assembly line or in a field, and we have an abiding affinity for those who perform such jobs. In her *On Point* segment after the Owens story broke, National Public Radio's Meghna Chakrabarti urged her listeners to consider the disconnect between how we value low-wage workers, but with equal enthusiasm devalue the kind of work they do. Witness colloquialisms like "salt of the earth" and "an honest day's work," the popularity (across class lines) of Bruce Springsteen's anthems of hard work, country music's countless odes to "working to nine to five," and pictures of workers on inspirational Franklin Covey posters. It's clear that we collectively view those who work in these jobs as pure, morally upright, honest, and necessary. Getting sweaty at work is a purer embodiment of the protestant work ethic, the myth suggests, and a person who holds one of these jobs is doing something noble and virtuous.

The day after the Owens story broke (or "blew up," in Twitter parlance), the backlash began. A combination of celebrities, pundits, and everyday social media users came to Owens's defense and criticized the news outlets and tweeters who had *job-shamed* him. This represented something of a feel-good moment, as appalled individuals offered support to Owens and critiqued the cruel stories that, they collectively argued, were wrong to suggest Owens was a lesser person for working at a grocery store. On Twitter, hashtags like #actorswithdayjobs and #noshame trended in the days that followed the initial story (Labor Day weekend, natch), as users suggested not only that Owens should be left alone, but also that he was doing something noble by supporting his family at a physically demanding job. The specific messages included sentiments such as the idea that all work has dignity, that Owens is hard working, but most prominently that Owens is noble for working a low-caché, working-class job.

Mainstream media gave Owens a platform to respond to being "job shamed," a term that circulated widely that weekend. "I was really devastated [by the personal attacks] ... Every job is worthwhile and valuable," Owens said on a morning news program while wearing his Trader Joe's name tag (Pelletiere & Ghebremedhin, 2018). Celebrities shared their own experiences with second jobs, side-hustles, and low-prestige employment. Actor and retired football player Terry Crews tweeted, "I swept floors AFTER the NFL." Actor Blair Underwood: "#NOSHAME in good, honest, hard work. He's being a man in doing what he needs to do to provide for himself and his family. Much respect to you Sir!" *Family Guy* creator Seth McFarlaine: "Fox News making a sideshow out of a guy just minding his own business and doing honest work." And Actress Pamela Adlon's supportive tweet stated, "Work gives you pride and purpose." Many of the celebrity tweets in support of Owens singled out the nature of the labor Owens was performing, not only urging the media and Trader Joe's customers to leave him alone but also suggesting his employment at the market was morally good (e.g., "honest"). None of this is to critique the individual Owens supporters. On the contrary, the point is that it would be far less likely touse the word "honest" to describe Owens's labor as an actor or to suggest one of his television gigs is "noble" because it allows him to support his family.

The discourse around hard work is often masculinist (note Underwood's suggestion that Owens was "being a man") and can sometimes even avert the possibility of systemic critique. Instead of fostering critical discussions of the materiality of work, rhetoric supporting the myth of hard work's nobility operates at a primarily affective level. We *feel* supportive of the idea of manual and wage labor, but what do we do with those feelings? What does it mean to rally around first responders but disparage the unions to which they belong and the levying of taxes that pay their salaries? Often, talking about hard work as an *abstraction*—as something dignified, honest, purposeful, masculine, etc. – prevents us from talking about wages, wealth inequality, and workplace harassment, for instance. It's worth noting that Owens also emphasized in his interview after the incident that the Trader Joe's gig was a necessary stopgap between his acting jobs; so while he articulates a belief in the value of "all" work, he also makes sure the audience knows that his primary job is acting.

3   The Myth of the Benevolent One Percent

The myths of the meritocracy and the nobility of hard work are pervasive and visible. Though just as powerful, the myth of benevolent elites takes a little more unpacking. The U.S. has a long history of valuing charity and charitable giving and a collective belief that the wealthiest among us can solve social problems through their benevolence. We place industrialists and barons on a pedestal and tell stories of their generosity—from Andrew Carnegie funding libraries and universities to Bill Gates creating a foundation with a diverse and ambitious mission. There is a sense that the philanthropy of the wealthy is the best way to progress, the best hope of solving our greatest problems. Charity feels good, whereas activism and political engagement, which are distinct modes of civic engagement, can feel confrontational and risky. ACT UP disrupting a Catholic Mass in an act of protest against the church's stance on condoms *feels* frightening or wrongheaded to some, but far fewer would feel or express negativity toward the prospect of Bill Gates spending millions of dollars on AIDS research, to use a perhaps stark set of examples. Nevertheless, charity has problematic implications, as it can sometimes cloud our understanding of systemic injustice, foster a top-down/us-and-them attitude, and even militate against more lasting forms of social change.[4]

Collectively, we feel positive regard toward charity, and we have particular affinity toward those who can write the largest checks. The elite benefit from this positive regard, which at times stops us from questioning income equality. It's easy to support CEOs and the rest of the one percent when we tell stories about their generosity and their giving. Their amassing of large amounts of wealth looks like a good thing (even if it happens on the backs of overworked laborers) to us if we focus on their philanthropic endeavors.

What ought we do about the judgmental attitudes toward working-class jobs like grocery store clerk? How should we solve that systemic problem? Those are complex questions. But there's nothing complex about feeling happy that

Tyler Perry offered Geoffrey Owens an acting job days after the Owens story trended (Corinthios, 2018; E. Jensen, 2018). It is a reflexive happiness. Tyler Perry offering Owens an acting job evokes "good" feelings and reinforces the idea that the benevolence of the rich can deliver the working class from their lot. Perry is an actor and filmmaker whose films and television programs about African-American family and culture are tremendously popular. He is an influencer, a rainmaker, a kingmaker. If the culture reveres CEOs who "give back," so too do we elevate celebrities who project a philanthropic ethos. Tyler Perry also employs scores of African-American performers (and crew members too), so his "giving back" arguably occurs at more systemic levels, too.[5]

This is not to say that Tyler Perry did anything wrong in offering Owens an acting gig; on the contrary he is by most accounts an ethical, reflective, and socially conscious professional. Nor am I suggesting Owens does not merit the job. The point is that Perry—like other bosses—manages and profits from other people's labor, benefits when the public regards him positively, and projects the kind of benevolence that elites from other sectors (e.g., one-percenters in the corporate world) use to cultivate positive public relations. To be sure, Perry's job offer occurred in the very public sphere of the twitterverse and came with accompanying pomp: "#GeoffreyOwens I'm about to start shootings OWN's number one drama next week! Come join us!!! I have so much respect for people who hustle between gigs. The measure of a true artist." Hashtagging Owens's name days after his story trended assured even wider circulation. Indeed, less than one year later, at the time of writing, Perry's message has 9,401 retweets and 55,102 likes. Major news media outlets ran stories on Perry's offer, and generally focused as much on Perry as on Owens (see for instance Corinthios and E. Jensen).

Many tweets in response to Perry's tweet commented on Perry's character. Words like "kind," "godsend," "respect," "heart of gold," "class act," "compassion," "support," "hero," and "integrity" appear in those responses, as do Bible verses and religious testimonials praising Perry. The overwhelming take-away is that Perry used his wealth and influence for good, and that is indeed what happened. But like a charitable act, Perry's job offer was an act without the potential to change the larger cultural value system that devalues particular types of employment. As a culture, we need individuals to act with compassion and grace, but we also need political action and broader solutions for systemic injustices. It takes more than benevolence from the upper echelons to progress as a society.

4   What Did the Narrative Overlook?

It matters that there's nothing new under the sun when it comes to how we talk about work and the working class. Aristotle acknowledged the central role that commonplaces have in civic discourse, but when those commonplaces negate the possibility of generating new ideas and new solutions to problems, then not only is the discourse weak, but so too is the broader culture in which that discourse circulates. This is especially true of discourse about social class. For instance, few pundits seemed to connect Owens to the story of the neoliberal "gig economy." We might have looked at Owens and seen an example of the gig economy in play and cutting across multiple sectors. We might have seen an example of how the gig economy is operative for members of both the working classes and professional/managerial classes. Indeed, Owens had been working as a character actor in various television programs (mostly guest roles), teaching acting in both academic and community-based settings, doing theater, *and* working at Trader Joe's. His story is not the story of failure, nor downward mobility, nor even the nobility of labor as much as it is a story about working multiple gigs.

In this way, his story should inspire solidarity across class lines. Who are the players in the new millennial gig economy? Creatives who we normally associate with wealth as well as struggling members of the working poor who are working at least two service jobs. Absent in much of the Owens reporting are calls for stronger unions for members of the creative arts or certainly calls for greater public support for performers (à la the vision of the New Deal). Too often, we accept the tenets of the gig economy as a done deal. University students are taught to prepare for such an economy. Boomer and Gen-X comedians and pundits dismiss the work ethic of millennials while ignoring the erosion of job security that has occurred since they were in their twenties. We barely even notice the "gig economy" aspect of Owens' story. We fail to challenge the way this paradigm often results in an overworked work force. We ignore the negative implications of the gig economy by either mocking those who engage in "gigs" that lack cultural capital (bagging potatoes at a grocery store) or glorifying the "work ethic" of the person hopping from gig to gig. According to blogger, entrepreneur, and job coach Vanessa Parker (2017), "Job shaming is making someone feel bad for working a 9–5." Parker offers advice to women who have started small businesses or wish to be entrepreneurs and emphasizes that there is nothing wrong with having a "side hustle," especially if said hustle provides benefits and prevents one from accruing debt, and even if that hustle involves a "gig" like driving for Uber or making telemarketing calls from home.[6] Parker's advice is helpful in its emphasis that individuals should not be shamed for the labor they perform, but is notably geared toward entrepreneurs who are working other jobs. Parker doesn't state the imperative to respect the labors of those who strictly work "side hustles" as their sole sources of income.

Though one might look at the rhetoric surrounding the Owens story and recognize familiar, mythic, uncritical patterns of talking about work, some of the conversations offered historical and social context. Several outlets pointed out in think pieces[7] that Owens was also doing stage work and teaching acting (Gilbert, 2018; King, 2018; Schulman, 2018). Unlike the "gotcha" celebrity reportage and the reflexively abstract support for Owens as a "noble" laborer, BET (*Black Entertainment Television*) published an opinion piece that explored the ways the entertainment industry is less supportive of African-American actors, who often have to secure multiple non-acting jobs to earn a living. In the *BET* article, Aliya S. King also speculates that fewer "Cosby" airings in the wake of Bill Cosby's conviction for sexual assault likely have a material impact on Owens' bottom line. King's analysis is an example of more reflective discourse about "work"—discourse that engages deeply with material realities instead of just abstractions and myths. And in *The New Yorker*, Michael Schulman (2018) helpfully distinguishes between "celebrity" and "working actor" and the accompanying material conditions of each, arguing that the Owens story illustrates why we need to think of creatives as "laborers." Schulman was one of the only pundits to point out that Owens was taking part—as many actors do—in the "gig economy." National Public Radio's *On Point* segment on Owens was the site of an important conversation between King (who wrote the BET piece) and leftist critic Barbara Ehrenreich[8] (2001) in which Ehrenreich voiced a compelling call to value all work and workers and questioned the mentality of "escaping" the working class for life in the professional-managerial classes. King agreed with Ehrenreich on the imperative to think of all work and workers as dignified but pointed out that as an African-American woman, her family's urging her not to return to service jobs has an added urgency. It was a critical and *intersectional* conversation that put multiple women in conversation with each other about the complexities of mobility and social class.

These more robust, contextualized discussions of Owens only occurred in media outlets (e.g., BET and National Public Radio) with less circulation than the outlets prone to "gotcha" journalism that are more likely to uncritically reproduce cultural myths. Still, it's heartening to see alternative and public media offer deeper engagements. And although Twitter was a site of the reproduction of these myths during the Owens affair, it's also true that Twitter brings together the elite and the everyday. It's the corner of social media that pulls back the curtain on the elite and so presents opportunities to de-mystify, opportunities to engage across class lines, and by extension can be a place to forge solidarity and start thinking about all work and all workers as worthy of dignity and value. In his study of the cognitive and rhetorical skills that blue-collar and service work require, Mike Rose (2004) suggests we pay attention to "the presence of mind up and down the ladder of occupational status" (p. xxxiv). Rose points out that the complex thinking and sophisticated forms of communication required by restaurant workers and hair stylists,[9] for example, challenge our culture's mind-body binary and the notion that there is such a thing as "unskilled labor." Respect for workers is already built into our national mythology (if not our public policy); Rose's research reminds us that respect for the work itself, across sectors and class lines and including jobs that are often dismissed and devalued as "grunt work," is often missing from the national ethos. Our script is still informed by the Reagan 1980s and the pervasive rhetoric of bootstraps, meritocracy, and benevolent elites. What might it look like to make conscious efforts to flip that script? What might it look like to resist job shaming and have honest and open discussions about work and our work lives in the 21st century?

Notes

1. See especially Bates (2011) for a compelling analysis of Reagan's rhetorical appeal.
2. Based on Leistyna's work, the documentary *Class Dismissed* (2007) offers a thorough and engaging critique of the medium's class politics in general and particularly its portrayal of working-class families through the decades.
3. NBC didn't unveil "Must-See TV" as an official slogan until the 1990s—an era when upwardly mobile, single, urbane New Yorkers (think "Friends" and "Seinfeld") replaced upwardly mobile suburban families as the staples of popular sitcoms. But the slogan established a through-line between the 1980s and 1990s wherein the network sustained its dominance in terms of both ratings and buzz-worthiness. By the way, that 1990s shift from the bourgeois family to the single "professional" as the default sitcom protagonist extended beyond NBC; Fox's "Living Single" and ABC's "Spin City" also focused on New Yorkers with disposable income who were largely eschewing traditional family life in favor of careers and peer-to-peer relationships. Like "Cosby" in the prior decade, "Living Single" foregrounded images of African-American mobility. And "Spin City" essentially focused on an adult version of the teen protagonist of "Family Ties," winkingly played by the same actor, Michael J. Fox.
4. I often talk to students in my service learning classes about the possibly apocryphal story of the soup kitchen volunteer who says that he hopes the soup kitchen will always be there so that someday his children can have the experience of feeding the poor.
5. In the face of commercial success, Perry has continued to produce films and television programs with a distinctly African-American argot. Instead of laboring to "cross over," Perry seems to be committed to assuring that particular kinds of black stories are told.
6. Notably, most of Parker's examples of "side hustles" don't provide benefits.
7. In the information and social media era in which we live, "think pieces" have augmented the old media genre of the Op-Ed. Op-Eds (opinion columns published on the page "opposite the editorial page") consist of a columnist or knowledgeable community member opining about a current issue of public importance; "think pieces" often tend to adopt provocative stances to generate discussion of a current event as well as "clicks" (and the attendant ad revenue) for the outlet publishing the piece. See also the hot take.
8. Ehrenreich wrote the seminal critique of the treatment of low-wage workers *Nickle and Dimed*, which describes her undercover experiences waitressing and cleaning hotels.
9. Rose uses interview and observation data to discuss the intellectual and rhetorical dance involved, for instance, in waiting tables, where on-the-job success depends on quick thinking, procedural knowledge, interpretative skills, the ability to perform sophisticated forms of audience analysis, and constantly shifting modes of communication.

References

Adlon, P. [@pamelaadlon]. (2018, September 2). *I had been a working actor for years. Jobs stopped, as they do. I worked in retail. At a flower* [Tweet]. Twitter. twitter.com/pamelaadlon/status/1036267335303147520

Alper, L. (Director). (2007). *Class dismissed: How TV frames the working class* [Film]. Media Education Foundation.

Bates, T. G. (2011). *The Reagan rhetoric: History and memory in 1980s America.* Northern Illinois UP.

Corinthios, A. (2018, September 7). Geoffrey Owens reportedly accepts Tyler Perry's TV offer after Trader Joe's job-shaming. *People.* people.com/tv/geoffrey-owens-accepts-tyler-perry-job-offer

Cosby Show Actor Geoffrey Owens Spotted Bagging Groceries at NJ Trader Joe's. (2018, August 31). *Fox News.* foxnews.com/entertainment/cosby-show-actor-geoffrey-owens-spotted-bagging-groceries-at-nj-trader-joes

Crews, T. [@terrycrews]. (2018, September 1). *I swept floors AFTER the @NFL. If need be, I'd do it again. Good honest work is nothing to be* [Tweet]. Twitter. twitter.com/terrycrews/status/1036105596041228289

Ehrenreich, B. (2001). *Nickel and Dimed: On (not) getting by in America.* Metropolitan.

Fox News [@FoxNews]. (2018, August 31). *Cosby show actor Geoffrey Owens spotted bagging groceries at NJ Trader Joe's* [Tweet]. Twitter. twitter.com/foxnews/status/1035663476180615168

From Learning Lines to Serving the Long Line! The Cosby Show Star Geoffrey Owens Is Spotted Working as a Cashier at Trader Joe's in New Jersey. (2018, August 30). *The Daily Mail.* dailymail.co.uk/news/article-6116357/The-Cosby-star-Geoffrey-Owens-spotted-working-cashier-Trader-Joes-New-Jersey.html

Gilbert, S. (2018, September 4). What the shaming of Geoffrey Owens reveals. *The Atlantic.* theatlantic.com/entertainment/archive/2018/09/geoffrey-owens-and-the-paradox-of-fame/569218

Jensen, B. (2012). *Reading classes: On class and classism in America.* Cornell UP.

Jensen, E. (2018, September 7). After job shaming, Geoffrey Owens lands Gig on Tyler Perry's 'The Haves and Have-Nots.' *USA Today.* usatoday.com/story/life/tv/2018/09/07/geoffrey-owens-tyler-perry-haves-and-have-nots/1222077002/

Job Shaming of 'Cosby Show' Actor at Trader Joe's Renews Dignity of Work Debate. (2018, September 11). *National Public Radio.* wbur.org/onpoint/2018/09/11/trader-joes-geoffrey-owens-cosby-show-work

King, A. S. (2018, September 4). *Geoffey Owens—And how Black Artists are expected to survive.* BET. bet.com/celebrities/news/2018/09/04/geoffrey-owens-and-how-black-artists-are-expected-to-survive.html

Parker, V. (2017, March 13). *Stop the job shaming.* Pink Boss. pinkboss.com/stop-job-shaming

Pelletiere, N., & Ghebremedhin, S. (2018, 4 September). Cosby show star speaks out after being 'job shamed' for working at Trader Joe's: 'It Hurt.' *ABC News.* abcnews.go.com/GMA/Culture/cosby-show-star-speaks-job-shamed-working-trader/story?id=57587525

Perry, T. [@tylerperry.] *#GeoffreyOwens I'm about to start shootings OWN's number one drama next week! Come join us!!! I have so much respect* [Tweet]. Twitter. twitter.com/tylerperry/status/1036944072836034560

Romano, A. (2018, September 4). Geoffrey Owens, actor and Trader Joe's employee, sparked a debate about how we value work. *Vox.* vox.com/culture/2018/9/4/17818300/geoffrey-owens-work-job-trader-joes-actorswithdayjobs

Rose, M. (2004). *The mind at work: Valuing the intelligence of the American worker.* Viking.

MacFarlane, S. [@SethMacFarlane]. (2018, August 31). *Fox news making a sideshow out of a guy just minding his business and doing honest work. Unfortunately, it fits* [Tweet]. Twitter. twitter.com/SethMacFarlane/status/1035778913874505728

Schulman, M. (2018, September 2). The shaming of Geoffrey Owens and the inability to see actors as laborers, too. *The New Yorker.* newyorker.com/culture/cultural-comment/the-shaming-of-geoffrey-owens-and-the-inability-to-see-actors-as-laborers-too

Underwood, B. [@BlairUnderwood]. (2018, September 2). *#NOSHAME in good, honest, hard work. He's being a man in doing what he needs to do to provide for* [Tweet]. Twitter. twitter.com/BlairUnderwood/status/1036299642567372802

Zweig, M. (2011). *The working-class majority: America's best kept secret* (2nd ed.). Cornell UP.

Zweig, M. (2016). Rethinking class and contemporary working-class studies. *Journal of Working Class Studies, 1*(1), 14–22.

CHAPTER 16

(Literal) Self-Exposure

Celebrity "Activism" during Covid-19

Abby Graves

In late January, the World Health Organization officially announced a public health emergency of international concern after a new, unknown virus originating in Wuhan, China began rapidly spreading throughout the country. Not two weeks later, despite Chinese border closures and travel restrictions, France, South Korea, Iran, and Italy reported deaths from the now-named Covid-19, or "coronavirus." After quickly spreading through the entirety of Europe, the western hemisphere followed suit, and as of March 2020, the majority of the world was enforcing lockdown or stay-at-home orders, yet cases continued to rise, people continued to die, and fear permeated every aspect of people's lives. The virus had not only become a world health crisis, but has also served to reveal a great many of America's systematic failures. The necessary precautions in response to the pandemic, and resulting needs of the public, exposed glaring shortfalls and insufficiency of America's capitalist-based economy, healthcare, company regulations, public safety, individual liberties, and—affecting the vast majority of citizens—worker's rights. The situation revealed the Federal administration's inability (or unwillingness) to intervene on the worker's behalf as millions lost their jobs due to company closures and safety precautions. Major corporations and banks were bailed out of their resulting financial losses while families struggled to receive a $1,200 stimulus check, minimum wage employees were forced to endanger themselves, continue to show up to work, and given no time off, sick leave, or even masks to wear. Tensions rose, the cultural climate heated, as entire families were confined to small apartments. In the age of social media, however, people worked to expose these shortfalls online, and to offer one another moral support and advice, leading to much online activism, which has potential to bring awareness, prompt reforms, and help people in desperate situations.

The idea of "spreading awareness" by simply posting about a topic of concern, though, is a much-debated topic in terms of how much net "good" it actually achieves. Online activism in the form of social media posts has of late been criticised as "virtue signaling," or showing other people how good of a person one is by expressing opinions that appear righteous and moral. However, when Gal Godot recruited twenty-five other A-list celebrities to join her in spreading "awareness" and "support" during one of the most confusing and unstable times for the working class (a lack of information, lay-offs, sickness, death, lawfully enforced quarantine), the majority of America was unimpressed. Apparently inspired by a video of a singing, quarantined Italian man, and under the alleged stress of her own quarantine for six whole days, Godot and company's "activism" took the form of a video. Each celebrity (including the extremely famous actors Will Ferrel, Natalie Portman, and Mark Ruffalo) soulfully sang a few words of John Lennon's "Imagine" a song which rejects consumerism, materialism, bigotry, cultural separations, and overall, inspires a sense of class consciousness, essentially becoming a symbol to much of the American public. Each brief celebrity appearance included a look of contrived concern or self-assured grin, and featured some aspect of their privilege or wealth in the background (including spacious mansions and a luxury car). The irony of the lyrics coming from the singers was not lost on working Americans. Along with the celebrities' appropriation of a song that rejects wealth, their lack of genuine action, false concern, smugness, and glaring hypocrisy, the reaction of the working class audience was more than ambivalent—the audacity inspired bemusement and anger.

Immediately after Godot posted the video to her Instagram in late March, following quarantine orders, the working class internet users took notice—after all, they were either laid-off, quarantined at home, or perhaps on their lunch break as they put themselves in danger of death while they encountered the public because their billion-dollar corporate fast-food chain employer offered no time off for the international crisis. Whichever the case, these unsure, frightened working class Americans who were clinging to their social media feeds for updates about medical availability, case and death count, viral spread, business closures, lay-offs, were met with the video of uber-rich, privileged celebrities offering their "support" in the comfort of their private estates. Sandwiched between social media posts about poverty, illness, and death, the video displayed these elites saying with their transparent pained expressions, "I'm stuck at home, just like you—this sucks, but we can do this!" And as families lacked medical care, food, essentials, and confined to tiny apartments, the tide of working class Americans' attitudes toward the elite tangibly shifted. This video offered a sort of revelation to the working class, that in fact, they really are not "just like you and me ..." while "you and me" might or might not get $1,200 to cover every need for unforeseeable future, "they" are unbelievably rich, disconnected from the reality the average American faces. The involved celebrities' disingenuous concern rubbed salt in the gaping, recent wounds. The video quickly spread to all other forms of social media, including Twitter, Facebook, and YouTube, prompting passionate reactions and responses from users.

Throughout February and March, workers were being laid-off by the millions, save those working in "essential" businesses, which includes grocery stores and many other restaurant-style businesses—positions of which are notorious for their shockingly low pay. According to Zweig (2001),

> In 2010, the labor force numbered 152.7 million people ... the working class was 63 percent of the labor force [and so] we live in a country with a working class majority ... Over 70 percent ... hold white-collar jobs in wholesale and retail trade, finance, insurance, and real estate, and a wide variety of business, personal, and health-related service industries. (p. 31)

With this in mind, the lowest-paid worker demographic, the least likely to have savings, insurance, or food and housing stability, was being thrown at the front lines of the virus, putting their lives in danger, while their billion-dollar employers refuse to pay them a livable wage, or allow them to take a paid leave. And more horrifying,

> In 2009 ... almost 15 percent of Americans suffered from food insecurity within the past year ... [and] another 8 percent of the poor were 65 years or older ... When poor people do not work, it is often because they are ill, disabled, or unable to find work, conditions that afflict the poor more frequently than the nonpoor. In 1990, nearly a quarter of all working-age poor people who were out of the labor force were sick or disabled ... Forty percent of poor working-age people who were out of the labor force stayed home to take care of family. (pp. 82–83)

This means that not only were the poor working class the ones who were put in most danger of the virus, but also that the workers forced to be exposed to the virus risked bringing the disease back home to their older or younger housemates who are naturally more susceptible to infection, and more likely to die if they do become infected. And considering YouTube alone "is now used by nearly three-quarters of U.S. adults and 94% of 18- to 24-year-olds. And the typical (median) American reports that they use three of eight major platforms," and that "88% of 18- to 29-year-olds indicate that they use a form of social media ... 78% among those ages 30 to 49, [and] 64% among those ages 50," i.e., the same demographic that makes up the workforce and is majority working class, it was they who were the video's primary viewers and spreaders and respondents (Smith & Anderson, 2018). This working class, being the American majority, was the audience, and the intended one, of Godot's virtue-signaling video. Her rhetorical appeals missed her mark completely—instead of portraying themselves as compassionate and caring, possibly actually intending to offer support, they insulted their viewers. The workers wondered if they could cash in the celebrities' "positive thinking" and "support" for food, medicine, or rent that was still due.

An overarching reaction by the working class audience was to retaliate back online, "calling out" the celebrities' detachment from reality, their lack of self-awareness, their satisfaction with themselves for doing the bare minimum in the face of a crisis, and portraying such as a good deed, a beacon of hope for the plebians to savor. The video served to enlighten the audience to the immense culture and wealth gap that lay between them and the rich, privileged elite. A few months before, America's "class comprehension gap [was] allowing the United States (and Europe) to drift toward authoritarian nationalism," with the even the poorest thinking of themselves as able to "work their way up" to similarly privileged lifestyles—if only they take on a few extra shifts, and work really hard (Williams, 2017, p. 16). The celebrities in Godot's video exhibit a class cluelessness that permeates the elite, having no clue what the working class needs are. Still, though, working class "resentment of professionals [did] not extend to the rich [as] there's an almost mystical desire among the working class to see a rich person from the upper class reach out to them" (p. 37). This attitude noticeably shifted when the cultural situation is saturated by an international pandemic, a health, housing, and food crisis, mass unemployment, and general public fear. Now, workers no longer cared about the elite "reaching out"—they needed provisions, money, food, medicine, and certainly could do without the serenading of a few half-interested celebrities.

American society has, for the past few decades, and even ever since the mainstream introduction of television, held distorted views of the lives of the rich and famous. "Daily life reinforces admiration of the rich," now especially, with devices in every hand, the working class has the ability to be connected directly to the people they see in movies and shows, their favorite pop stars, billion-dollar CEOs, let into their personal lives, and have formed a kind of one-sided relationship that allows them to, inaccurately, believe themselves to have similar struggles (Williams, 2017, p. 16). Online, "real life 'rich' people, usually celebrities ... talk about their lives—their problems ... viewers are not only able to imagine that they can rise to fame and fortune, they can have a sense of intimacy with the rich" (hooks, 2000, p. 73). The working class are connecting their struggles to the elite more than their fellow workers. The average American's contrived social media "connections" and "relationships" with the rich and famous, and the celebrities themselves portraying themselves as having working class struggles, has led to immense class disparity and loss of class consciousness by "altering the attitudes of poor and working-class people

... toward the rich largely through marketing and advertising, television promoted the myth of the classless society" (p. 71). The working class on social media became suddenly disillusioned with this image of a "classless society," because now, as they fearfully quarantined with their family and lost their jobs, they could finally clearly view with their own eyes, that the elite are not "just like them," cannot relate to their struggles, and are not in their class, on their side, working for the same goals.

The facade of relatability crumbled as working class people saw that while their worst fears were starvation, homelessness, sickness, and death, those of the elite class, with a condescending look on their face, showed on video, their worst fear was becoming bored in their mansions. Online, "the rich were and are fictively depicted as caring and generous toward impoverished classes," and before international crises, this front was believable—"They are portrayed as eager to cross class boundaries and hang with diverse groups of people ... that the rich are open, kind, vulnerable. And more importantly that they 'suffer' as much as anyone else" (hooks, 2000, pp. 71–72). Godot earnestly tells the audience "it doesn't matter who you are, where you're from ... we're *all* in this together." The Instagram video speaks to the exact opposite, though, portraying rich individuals singing about rejecting wealth while surrounded by lavishly expensive houses and cars, exposed their lie of pretend solidarity. The working class realized that the elite do not truly suffer as they do.

The social media celebrities have used to boost their fame, promote themselves, form "connections" to their fanbase, and instill false ideas of solidarity. In a sense of irony, is exactly what was the main medium for the spread of and reaction to the video, which, for the vast majority, consisted of tweets, reaction videos, articles, and even memes created to relentlessly to berate, criticize, and mock both their social and vocal tone-deafness (see Figures 16.1–16.3).

The spread of the memes across social media sites such as Twitter, Instagram, and Facebook turned the very same devices that celebrities used to

FIGURE 16.1   @joshgondelman Tweet, March 19, 2020
(https://twitter.com/joshgondelman/status/1240642905947148289)

(LITERAL) SELF-EXPOSURE

FIGURE 16.2   @writtenbyahmad Tweet, March 19, 2020 (https://twitter.com/writtenbyahmad/status/1240625861801447433?ref_src=twsrc%5Etfw)

bolster their fame, against them. The traditional western rhetorical climate had shifted: the kairos of the entire society had shifted in a few weeks from a comfortable normalcy of freedom, to fear, isolation, and feelings of being abandoned by one's own government. Therefore, the usually idolized celebrity "charity" and "relatability" had quite a different taste, when it was not accompanied by a comfortable normalcy. When this celebrity attitude was set against genuine crisis, the radically altered rhetorical situation elicited audience reactions quite unusual for a 21st century society. The audience of workers were now criticising and berating those to whom they once compared themselves, worshipped them, and aspired to emulate. This shift in kairos altered the medium of social media from something that maintained celebrity status and appeals, to one that hosted the tearing-down, and degradation of celebrity worship by the working class.

The video pictured situations that were so clearly unlike those of the twenty-six celebrities' intended working-class, consumer audience, who, now, no longer had mindless consumption of media and entertainment as their priority. In their normal, pre-pandemic lives, "The chaos of personal life in crowded quarters ... no money for regular health care and a host of illnesses that come with poverty ... sick children and elders to take care of ... unreliable cars or long bus commutes to work or school ...—these and other everyday life

214   GRAVES

FIGURE 16.3   "We're All in This Together." Offkey Comics (instagram.com/offkeycomics)

circumstances of the ... working poor," where the consumption of entertainment and vicarious living through the elite's updates on social media is their form of escapism from their own lives, and offering a beacon of hope for their own futures (Zweig, 2001, p. 93). But because "brashly wealthy celebrities epitomize the fantasy of being wildly rich while losing none of your working-class cred," by revealing they were certainly not working class, by being so carefree in a time of crisis, they officially lost this relatable "working-class cred," and the jig was up (Williams, 2017, p. 44).

"Despite their good deeds, [celebrity] silence maintains their class solidarity with those who exploit and oppress," and the working class noticed their failure to speak out against corrupt the government who bailed out banks instead of its working citizens, or greedy corporations who laid workers off instead of offering paid leave (hooks, 2000, p. 78). Instead, these celebrities maintained and exposed who they truly lay in class solidarity with: other elites, and certainly not the working class, so much as they would like to pretend on social media. The memes, criticisms, and snarky replies in response, though, through the means of social media, also functioned to promote working class solidarity. When the self-distracted working class of a consumer-capitalist society could not come together for their mutual benefit, they finally did in mutual disgust. The video meant to reify the high cultural status of the elite, maintaining their place on a high moralistic pedestal, instead clearly and explicitly exposed the hypocrisy and unfairness and inequality that exists between class lines. Working class Americans realized, as a result, how tired they were of being duped, exploited, and deceived.

References

hooks, b. (2000). *Where we stand: Class matters*. Routledge.
Smith, A., & Anderson, M. (2018, March). *Social media use in 2018*. Pew Research Center.
Williams, J. (2017). *White working class: Overcoming class cluelessness in America*. Harvard Business Review Press.
Zweig, M. (2001). *The working-class majority: America's best kept secret*. Cornell UP.

CHAPTER 17

Returning to Van Buren Street

A Photographic Essay

David Engen

> Many of us are confused about class and don't tend to think about it as consciously as we might our race, ethnicity, gender, religion, age, or sexual orientation. Nonetheless, our class identity has a huge impact on every aspect of our lives: from parenting style to how we speak, from what we dare to dream to the likelihood we will spend time in prison from how we spend our days to how many days we have.
> YESKEL (2014)

I grew up on Van Buren Street in Fridley, Minnesota. Friendly Fridley as it is sometimes called, a working-class suburb of Minneapolis. Dad a truck driver. Mom a home-maker. Dad and Mom lived in the same house for over 50 years: 7461 Van Buren Street NE. I was raised there. In that home. On that street. It's

FIGURE 17.1   7400 Block of Van Buren Street

a street where my old neighbor calls my craft beer Democrat beer and where I learned it's ok to be educated so long as you don't look, sound or act educated. Several things interest me about Van Buren Street, but maybe the thing that interests me the most is that it seems so uninteresting—even to those who live there. The homes are modest and plain, though sagging more these days under the weight of it all. Political signs never seem to appear in yards. Even the president after whom the street is named is said to have been boring. Springsteen would never write a song about this street or this suburb, but I think there is some beauty and some depth here.

I left Van Buren Street for college in 1988. I got one degree, then another, and then another, and at some point it seemed the only logical thing to do was become a professor, which I did. I've been teaching now since 1995. I'm 53.

Teaching. Whenever people ask me what I do for a living, I say I'm a teacher. That's Van Buren Street talking some. I assume I'll look arrogant if I say I'm a professor. Best to hide that fact as long as I can.

As a career academic, I'm exposed to sometimes subtle and sometimes overt cues that US social class issues—particularly involving the white working class—don't really matter or aren't worth exploring. I think they are. I've spent a good chunk of time studying this aspect of my life, and I'd like to walk you through my old neighborhood. Along the way, I hope to shed some light on the complexity of social experience that shaped me and many like me.

• • •

> Many people in the middle class, including people who were once working-class, get upset when they hear me present positive aspects of working-class cultures, warning me over and over not to 'romanticize' or 'glorify' the working class. It makes me wonder: Why are they upset? The middle class is glorified everywhere I look ... Why is finding good things about working class life considered glorifying it anyway?
> JENSEN (2012)

I'm sitting in the car with my mom. It's nearing Christmas, 2018. Dad is gone. Mom in assisted living. We're out in front of the old house on Van Buren Street. She is looking at the house and, I realize, at her entire life. I'm trying to keep quiet to see what she might say. She begins: "You know, our driveway is not too bad yet ... I'm sure glad your dad turned out to be right about that." I ask for some clarification. "Dick and your dad did their own driveways at the same time, right when we moved in. Dad thought you needed to put in six inches of

FIGURE 17.2   7461 Van Buren Street, Engen family home

concrete. Dick thought you only needed four. Said it was a waste to put in six. Looks like Dad won that one." Dick was mom and dad's next-door neighbor when they moved to Van Buren Street in 1960. He and dad worked together at the trucking company. Dick died in a work accident in the early 1970s, and in 2018 his driveway is indeed in terrible shape. There are cracks everywhere.

When you opened the front door to my childhood home you walked right into the basement. To the left a pool table. To the right stairs leading to the main living area upstairs. 11 steps up. It got a little smokier with each step. The house always smelled like a mixture of smoke and something. Smoke and pot roast when I was a kid. Smoke and Febreze in the later years when I'd come home to visit and mom was trying to please her preaching children who could not stop lecturing her about her smoking habits.

When I was little I used to look out the big picture window in our living room on the second floor and watch my dad shuffle back and forth on the driveway below. Right. Left. Right. Left. Up and down the driveway. In my memory he is wearing a maroon windbreaker and a white baseball hat. Left. Right. Left. Right. Left. It looked for all the world like he was dancing. His feet pivoting and twisting. You know what he was doing? Killing ants. He didn't like them on the driveway he built. Left. Right. Left. Right. He'd kill half an hour killing ants. Work. Order. Results.

∙ ∙ ∙

> And class happens when some [people], as a result of common experiences (inherited or shared), feel and articulate the identity of their interests as between themselves, and as against other [people] whose interests are different from (and usually opposed to) theirs. The class experience is largely determined by the productive relations into which [people] are born—or enter involuntarily. Class consciousness is the way in which these experiences are handled in cultural terms: embodied in traditions, value-systems, ideas, and institutional forms.
> THOMPSON ("The Making of the English Working Class," cited in Coles & Zandy, 2007)

FIGURE 17.3 Neighbor Pat's place

Van Buren Street sits one block to the East of *Melody Manor*—a collection of five tree-lined streets named after things that confused me in school—Tempo Terrace, Concerto Curve, Lyric Lane ... The homes were nicer in Melody Manor than on Van Buren. Doctors and lawyers didn't live in Melody Manor, but teachers and nurses and retail managers did. When I asked old friends and relatives to talk about Van Buren Street, it became clear the meaning of our street emerged in part from its relation to the symphony of streets next door.

> [Van Buren Street] is a bunch of middle-class houses and middle-class people. A richer group bought in Melody Manor. Dad never mixed with any of those people, but I did because of your sister being in baton. There was Scott Johnson's mom. She was a snob when I think back. (Mom)

It felt like we were not part of the neighborhood of *Melody Manor*. The times you could tell was at Halloween if you walked over to *Melody Manor* it was so crowded with kids. Our street was not. We were kind of left out. When they had those neighborhood garage sales our street was not invited to join in.

Do you think it had to do with Melody Manor being what might be called higher class?

Yeah—I do. (Neighbor)

Yeah, this neighborhood is working-class. You work from ground zero and you stay kind of just mellow. I'm out there with cheap beer and a bologna sandwich and laughing at everybody else. I don't have to be important. To me that's just arrogant. You just ... you got your own class. Ok that's fine. You keep your arrogant class to yourself. I'd rather be simple and do the things I do and laugh and joke. That's half of life. I won't never stop work. I'm not going to sit and retire. Most people you'll find in the working-class that grew up from nothing will never stop work. (Neighbor)

• • •

> We belong to a generation of working-class children propelled into the middle class by postwar prosperity ... We make our parents proud, yet also mystify them with our alien ways. Why haul your kids across town to play soccer when there's a park down the street? Why eat the paper-thin deli turkey when a frozen loaf is a much better buy? What's so funny about Garrison Keillor anyway? My dad once paid this great compliment to my brother-in-law: 'Rog is such a nice guy you'd never even know he was educated.'
> REGISTER (2000)

I want to share two stories about my father, Kenneth Engen. "Kenny."

Whenever I would come home from college I would walk up the eleven stairs and inevitably find Dad perched at his place by the kitchen table. To his right was the small back window he would look out for hours while sipping coffee, often complaining about the birds crapping on his patio. He hated birds, but he loved that view. We would talk for a few minutes after I got home and then, realizing talking was never all that easy for us, we would go downstairs and

FIGURE 17.4   Kenny Engen's garage

shoot pool. One year I was home from graduate school. I was working on my Ph.D. and had been in college for about seven years. As I recall our conversation during the pool game went like this.

Dad: "So, what are you majoring in anyway?"
Me: "Communication."
Dad [*chalking his stick*]: "Hmmm ... Seems to me like you communicate just fine."

That was, as I recall, our one and only conversation about what I was doing in college. This never bothered me, nor was it really something I thought about. Home for me was very separate from school. That's just the way it was.

The second story takes place several years before the first. In the eighth grade I started taking karate lessons. I was tired of getting beat up on Van Buren Street and everywhere else and thought maybe I should do something about it. After a year or so in karate I started competing in karate tournaments. I went to one tournament after another but never came home with a trophy. I simply wasn't very good.

Then one day I went to a tournament in Iowa. Dad and mom did not attend. I was fourteen. And I won. Not once but twice. I took third place in form (karate gymnastic routine) and first place in fighting. I was thrilled. We got back to the karate school in Minneapolis late on a Sunday night. I called home and dad told me he was on his way to pick me up. A few minutes later he arrived, and I walked out proudly holding two large trophies. Our conversation went like this.

Dad: "Whose are those?"
Me: "Mine!"
Dad [*growing slightly frustrated*]: "David, whose are those?"
Me: "They're mine, Dad. I got third place in form and first place in fighting."
Dad: "David, go put those back inside. I have to work in the morning. I don't have all night."

I don't recall exactly how the conversation ended. But somehow I convinced Dad they were mine. I imagine him smiling and feeling good. I've told this story to many over the years and most seem to find it sad. I don't find it sad at all. Dad never expected me to win—at karate or anything else. And for that I suppose it is ok to fault him. So long as he gets some credit for never caring if I lost.

• • •

> One guy says good morning to you and you say good morning. To another guy you say fuck you. The guy you say fuck you to is your friend.
> LEFERVE ("Steelworker," cited in Terkel, 1974)

Your dad and I, we got along good. He always called me a dumb ass, but other than that you know ... I'd give him shit and he'd say, 'you dumb ass.' The one time I'll never forget. We bought a new dishwasher and your folks were over having a beer. He says 'I'll help you put it in.' He went home and came back with his goddamn drills and shit, just laughing and said 'I just love drilling holes in other people's houses.' That was the first

FIGURE 17.5   Neighbor, Paul Kroska

time we did ever did anything together. We laughed like hell. It's different now. I don't talk too much anymore. (Paul Kroska)

When my dad was in a nursing home recovering from a stroke, Paul Kroska visited every day after work. He never missed a day, ever. Paul gives me a hard time. A lot. That's how I know he likes me. He says things like, "I don't know if I should call you a professor or an asshole" and he razzes me for my liberal political beliefs. I don't talk to Paul as much as I used to when I lived across the street from him. He's a tough guy in a lot of ways and a big softy in a lot of others. I think he looks like Bruce Springsteen, but he doesn't seem to care about that.

After my dad got pretty sick but was still at home he would fall down every once in a while. One time he fell backwards in the bathroom at 2 am and landed right in the empty bathtub. He was stuck and my mom couldn't get him out so she called Paul. Paul came over and gave him a hand. While helping him up he said, "Hey Kenny, it is my opinion that is not a great place to sit down." They laughed and had a drink after dad got out of the tub. Paul stood up and told this story at my dad's funeral. Paul and his wife Kathy were both always there for my mom and dad. First as friends and then as family.

I gave a eulogy for my dad. After my talk Paul walked up to me and said, "I guess all that education *did* pay off. You sounded real good up there. There's no way I could do that." His comment made me feel good. And proud. Paul works with steel. Owned his own shop for years. He can do a whole lot of things I cannot do and don't understand, but it was nice to have him notice something I could do.

• • •

> Fox News stokes fear. And the fear seems to reflect the audience it most serves—white middle—and working-class people.
> HOCHSHILD (2016)

I have not formally surveyed all residents of Van Buren Street but the ones I know best, the ones with whom I grew up, are kind of mad about a lot of things. They voted for Trump and they seem to feel less than hopeful about the future. An old neighbor from Van Buren Street talked to me recently about how girls now want to join the Boy Scouts. She also had heard that "girls" on college campuses are trying to join fraternities. She found both these ideas, well, kind of dumb. She also expressed concern about police having their guns taken away.

I have a couple stock arguments I use for these kinds of conversations. One is the McDonald's coffee lawsuit, the case where the woman sued McDonald's

FIGURE 17.6   Car on Van Buren Street

because she spilled the coffee and burned herself. I brought this up to my neighbor and she said in a tone of confusion, "yeah ... can you believe that?" Then I gently, and I'd like to think a non-arrogant academic sort of way, said "yeah ... but I watched this film, you know, and it turns out McDonald's had been told many times to cool their coffee and that they were serving it way too hot and the woman had really severe burns." The neighbor was listening. "I mean you should be able to spill coffee without really hurting yourself. They can't put something that dangerous in your hands."

The neighbor likes me. I like her. We respect each other. Which may be why she said "that's really interesting. I guess you get to look at things a lot of different ways in your job and that changes things." I do—get to look at things in different ways. It does—change the way you make sense of things.

It seems to me we need better information and media in this country, to be sure. But it seems to me we also need more cross-class relationships based on respect and collaboration and common destiny. The idea here is not that everyone everywhere should or will become progressive if only a good film is discussed. But I wonder how many individuals, working-class and otherwise, can come to see more complexity in the world if topics are discussed within relationships instead of presented between commercials. Although, to be perfectly honest, my old neighbor and I don't talk as much as we should.

• • •

> [working-class] Whites' moral standards center around a work ethic, responsibility, and the defense of traditional morality ('family values' and anticrime). Hence the 'disciplined self' is absolutely at the center of the rationale that leads white workers to view blacks as moral violators.
> LAMONT (2000)

My father dropped out of school in the 8th grade and yet managed to secure a good job driving truck for Midwest Motor Express. He lied about his education to get the job. I doubt he would have gotten the job were he not white. I doubt my parents would have gotten the loan to buy their house in the suburbs were they not white. I always felt out of place and disconnected from school, but I bet I would have felt even more so were I not white. The list of benefits my family and I received because of our whiteness is a long one.

I didn't talk much with my parents about what I was learning in college. But one time I was learning some things about race, and I tried to share my newfound knowledge with my dad. I explained to him that I didn't think he'd be where he was without being white. He was less than impressed with my analysis. See, Dad was a hard worker. He would drive from Minneapolis to Fargo, North Dakota five days a week. That's a ten-hour drive. He would get eight hours off between runs. I'm sure he could count on one hand how many

FIGURE 17.7   Home on North End of Van Buren

runs he missed. He drove a red Gremlin car and when it was bitter cold outside he would sleep for a couple of hours, go start the car to make sure it would start later, and then go sleep for a couple more hours. When he died one of the items on the table at his funeral was a letter to his boss complimenting how kind he had been to a stranded motorist. He was a worker. He thought everybody else should work as hard as he did and if things weren't going their way, well, that meant they weren't working hard enough and most likely had some kind of character deficit.

My father never seemed able to hold in his head two realities of his life. One reality was that he was indeed a hard and disciplined worker who provided for his family. Another reality was he was given the opportunity to work hard in no small measure because he was white. As a citizen, professor, and product of the white working class, I do my best to understand the connections between my story and American story. What I find is seldom pretty. One reality of my life is that I worked pretty hard. Another reality is that I started on second base; my children are starting on third. As a white male professor from a working-class background I do my best to understand my story as fully and honestly as I can, and I work to help students from backgrounds like mine create more complex stories about themselves, their communities, and our world. I'm not certain my actions are making all that much of a difference, but I am trying and learning.

• • •

> From an early age, middle-class people learn how to get along, using diplomacy, nuance, and politics to grab what they need. It is as though they are following a set of rules laid out in a manual that blue-collar families never had a chance to read.
> LUBRANO (2004)

I attended Woodcrest Elementary School on Van Buren Street. I was a Woodcrest Woodchuck. I believe it was in the third grade that I got sent home from school for saying the "F"-word. "What the fuck is wrong with saying 'fuck,'" I asked anybody who would listen. So funny was I. In music class, after we finished our unit on the recorder (think plastic flute), I took my recorder and put it under the tire of a school bus parked in front of the school. The music teacher was on bus duty and watched as I did this. The bus moved forward and the recorder burst into bits. I hated every level of school—elementary, middle, and high school. I don't know why. It felt like the teachers were talking in a different language. Nothing stuck.

FIGURE 17.8   Woodcrest Elementary School, Van Buren Street

Not long ago I was driving on Van Buren with mom and asked her, "so, did you ever have any hopes and dreams for your kids?" She replied, "no. I don't think so. I don't think we did. We just kind of did what we wanted to do and we figured the kids would do what they wanted to do." I followed-up by asking, "did you ever think about how your kids might get into college or anything like that?" "No," she said, "I don't think we gave that much thought until you went to college."

I graduated high school in 1986 and the college-for-all model was still in its infancy. On the one hand, I rather respect this approach to child rearing. Let your kid become what your kid will become. Mom and Dad where always there for me. I never wanted for a thing. On the other hand, this does seem to leave a bit up to chance.

• • •

> Social-class differences and the inequality they reflect now organize American society more than ever.
> MARKUS & FISKE (2012)

I'm not sure when or why I started reading about working-class life and culture. I believe it was at the tail end of my graduate studies, maybe even my first couple years as a professor. What I do recall is finding my family and my home on the pages of sociological and psychological texts I was reading. I couldn't believe we were there. I hadn't thought much about myself or my family up

FIGURE 17.9   Dick and Barb's old place, Van Buren Street

until that time. I really hadn't. I was not the reflective sort, at least not about my own life. But I started reading and it was as if the texts were written precisely about us, my family, my neighbors:

> Education is valued but more functional, emphasis on conformity and obedience, moral order extremely important, restricted codes and inside jokes, storytelling a prime way of communicating, hard work valued above creative expression, minimize size of self, a 'be home by dark' approach to parenting instead of finding activities to cultivate the child's unique self, solidarity, limited skill on the part of young people at talking with people in authority, a fondness for Ronald Reagan, a 'can't fight city hall' mentality, a 'culture of constraint,' white privilege.

For me anyway, up until I began reading about social class and culture, I was an individual with no culture or identity I could name. Zip. Reading and reflection have led me to realize I was and am still in some ways *"working-class."*

I feel lucky that formal education helped me realize I am a cultural being. I am shaped by my race and gender, to be sure, but also by my class. I know some who grew up on streets like Van Buren and look back on their families only to see a collection of deficits—all the ways their families were not professional middle-class. They didn't talk right or have the right taste in clothes or cars or food. That's not what I see at all. I see a culture with some good features and some not so good ones. And I see two versions of me—a working-class version and a professional middle-class one. I'm still on Van Buren Street, or perhaps better said, Van Buren Street is still on me.

This dual identity of sorts makes me something of a mess in some ways. I am not totally comfortable in a college faculty meeting, and I am not totally comfortable in a VFW. But I can hold my own in both places and for that I'm grateful.

• • •

> The professional elite values change and self-development; working-class families value stability and community.
> WILLIAMS (2017)

FIGURE 17.10   Driveway of Engen family home

Regrets

Regrets, I have a few

Never knowing what my car
got to the gallon

Taking a job you
couldn't understand

Becoming a person you
couldn't know

Yeah, I have a few

That Thanksgiving
when you slid out of
the Lazy Boy to the
floor and laid there on
soft carpet with
your picture window a
million miles away
I'm so worthless
I'm so worthless
You whispered

I regret not lying
down next to you
gently grabbing your
hand with tears rolling
down my face while we
stared up at the smoke
stained ceiling of our world
until we both saw stars and
light and whispering to you

she's getting about 31 to the gallon, dad,
and that's in the city

∙ ∙ ∙

Family Photos

Mom looked like Shirley Temple
Dad like Beatle Bailey
There in the hallway

Graduation photos and a
Brother-in-law who is no
More
There in the hallway

The family across the street
In a white frame from long ago
Three kids Mom helped raise as if
They were her two
There in the hallway

One Award
Driver of the Month
January 1978
Looks like it was awarded yesterday
There in the hallway

Grandpa and Grandpa too
A picture from the State Fair
Machinery Hill

They carried my father out of that house
Moved him from his blue recliner into
A black bag with a silver zipper
That was sad
But also what he wanted

The toughest thing of all
Was taking those photos
Off the wall

Knowing the center
Had shifted
And home was there
No more

References

Coles, N., & Zandy, J. (2007). *American working-class literature*. Oxford University Press.
Hochschild, A. (2016). *Strangers in their own land*. The New Press.
Jensen, B. (2012). *Reading classes: On culture and classism in America*. ILR Press.
Lamont, M. (2000). *The dignity of working men: Morality and the boundaries of race, class, and Immigration*. Harvard University Press.
Lubrano, A. (2004). *Limbo: Blue-collar roots, white-collar dreams*. John Wiley & Sons.

Markus, H. R., & Fiske, S. T. (Eds.). (2012). *Facing social class: How societal rank influences interaction*. Russel Sage Foundation.

Register, C. (2000). *Packinghouse daughter*. Minnesota Historical Society Press.

Terkel, S. (1974). *Working*. Pantheon/Random House.

Williams, J. (2017). *White working class: Overcoming class cluelessness in America*. Harvard Business Review Press.

Yeskel, F. (Ed.). (2014). *Class lives: Stories from across our economic divide*. Cornell University.

Index

Adichie, Chimamanda   154
All in the Family   183, 184
American Dream   18, 78, 89, 124, 197, 198
American Federation of Labor (AFL)   124, 125
American Idol   191
An American Family   189
Animal House   48
Anzaldua, Gloria   5
Appalachia   8, 134, 137, 138, 144
Atlanta   188, 189

Barthes, Roland   75
Beech, Jennifer   1, 31, 73
Benny & Joon   150
Berrey, Ellen   33
Big Brother   189
Blackman, Orville   28
Bourdieu, Pierre   4, 16, 20, 22
Bratta, Phil   6, 8, 33, 65, 69, 119
Burke, Kenneth   126, 129, 142, 145
Bush, George W.   160, 164, 165, 170, 177

Candid Camera   189
Chakrubarti, Meghna   199
Chavez, Minerva S.   29
Chicago P.D.   188
Clark, Simon   177
Class Dismissed: How TV Frames the Working Class (Pepi Leistyna)   183
Class in the Composition Classroom: Pedagogy and the Working Class   4
classless society   182, 212
Cloud, Dana   122
Coots, Jaime   138, 139, 142, 143
Coronation Street   192
Covid-19   10, 208
cultural rhetorics   26

Dallas   192
Days of Our Lives   192
de Solier, Isabelle   154
Deadliest Catch   191
Dirty Jobs   191
double consciousness   27
Drucker, Johanna   119

Duin, Julia   136, 140, 145
Dutch East India Trade Company   50

EastEnders   192
Edwards, Mike   74
Ehrenreich, Barbara   204, 205
ER   188
ethos   27, 195, 202, 205
Everybody Hates Chris   185
Extreme Makeover   189

Family Ties   195, 196, 205
Ferrel, Will   150, 209
Fixer Upper   191
Flip or Flop   191
Foss, Sonja   121
Foucault, Michel   7, 109
Fox News   198, 200, 223
Friends   16, 17, 22, 24, 26, 30, 45, 46, 52, 53, 55, 56, 63, 75, 79, 80, 82–84, 92–100, 102, 104, 106, 169, 177, 186, 219, 223

Gadot, Gal   10
Game of Thrones   181
Gates, Bill   20
General Hospital   192
gente educada   4, 26, 27
Grey's Anatomy   188
Gries, Laurie   122

habitus   4, 7, 16
Hakola, Outi J.   166, 167, 171
Hamilton, Alexander   17
Hannah and Her Sisters   151
Hardt, Michael   123
Here Comes Honey Boo-Boo   190
Homeland Security   191
Hood, Ralph W.   138–140, 145
hooks, bell   3, 4, 10, 76, 162, 163, 166, 167, 172, 182
hysteresis   23

I Am Legend (Richard Matheson)   163
Imagine (John Lennon)   10, 209
Immigration and Customs Enforcement (ICE)   41

INDEX

imposter syndrome   4, 6, 7, 62, 73
Industrial Workers of the World (IWW)   8, 119, 124, 131

Jane the Virgin   188, 189
Jefferson, Thomas   17
Jones Royster, Jacqueline   27

Keeping up with the Kardashians   91, 181
Knoblauch, Abby   121
Kornbluh, Joyce L.   125, 131

Land of the Dead (George A. Romero)   9, 159–161, 163–167, 172, 175
Learning to Labor: How Working Class Kids Get Working Class Jobs (Paul Willis)   6
Leave It to Beaver   196
Liminality   6, 7, 31, 65, 71, 72, 78
Lindqiust, Julie   135
Lucky Louie   184
Lumpenproletariat   161, 165
Lutz, John   165

Malcolm in the Middle   185
Married with Children   184
Marx, Karl   69, 161, 165
Massumi, Brian   123, 144
Masters of Flip   191
meritocracy   9, 114, 196–199, 201, 205
middle-class   1, 4, 6, 7, 19, 21, 23, 24, 79, 91, 92, 96, 102, 106, 153, 180, 184, 185, 187–190, 192, 219, 226, 228, 229
misogynoir   33
Morrison, Toni   35
multilinguality   24
My Name is Earl   9, 184, 185

NAFTA   40
National Public Radio   199, 204
Negri, Antonio   123
neo-Marxist   2
nepantla   31, 72

O'Neill (Kirstie)   153
Obama, Barack   160
Of Hospitality (Jacques Derrida)   43
On My Block   186, 188
Owens, Geoffrey   9, 10, 195–204
Ozark   188

Pernot, Laurent   139
Perry, Tyler   202, 205
Phenomenology   6, 66, 123
Portman, Natalie   209
Prelli, Lawrence   122
punctum   75

Queer Phenomenology (Sara Ahmed)   6, 66

Ragged Dick (Horatio Algers, Jr.)   17
Reagan, Ronald   195–197, 205, 228
Reflections from the Wrong Side of the Tracks: Class, Identity, and the Working Class Experience in Academe   4
rhetorical situation   3, 8, 10, 15, 23, 213
Roper, Edie-Marie   74
Roseanne   184, 185, 193
Rowe, Mike   191
Ruffalo, Mark   209

Samatar, Sofia   34
Sanford and Son   183
Seinfeld   205
serpent-handling   8, 134, 135, 138, 139
Sex and the City   181
Silver, Daniel   153
Social Class and the Hidden Curriculum of Work"/"Social Class and School Knowledge (Jean Anyon)   51
Sociolect   20, 21, 23, 24
Stadium   75
Sunbeam   148, 153, 156
Survivor   159, 165, 168, 169, 189, 191
Survivor: Worlds Apart   191

Talladega Nights   150
Tell Me How it Ends: An Essay in 40 Questions (Valeria Luiselli)   41
testimonio   29
The 300 Spartans   97
The Beverly Hillbillies   184
The Bold and the Beautiful   192
The Cosby Show   195, 196
The Count of Monte Cristo (Alexandre Dumas)   22
The Drew Carey Show   184
The Goldbergs   183, 187
The King of Queens   183
The Middle   186

INDEX

The Simpsons 183
    Homer Simpson 184
The Souls of Black People (W.E.B. Du Bois) 36
The Vanishing Middle Class: Prejudice and Power in a Dual Economy (Peter Temin) 30
The Wire 187
The Working Class Majority (Michael Zweig) 161
The Working-Class Majority: America's Best Kept Secret (Michael Zweig) 1
Thinking-Class: Sketches from a Cultural Worker (Joanna Kadi) 4
This Fine Place So Far from Home: Voices of Academics from the Working Class 4
Trader Joe's 196–198, 200, 201, 203
Tremouille 10
Trump, Donald 5, 40, 42, 136, 160, 162, 165, 170, 177, 223
Turner, Victor 72
Twitter 122, 196, 198, 200, 204, 209, 214

Weber, Max 161
Welch, Nancy 135
What Not to Wear 189
White bread 8, 9, 148–157
White Bread (Piet Defraeye) 151
White Bread: A Social History of the Store-Bought Loaf (Aaron Bobrow-Strain) 152
White Bread: Weaving Cultural Past into the Present (Christine Sleeter) 151
White Trash 149, 150, 185
Williams, Raymond 180
Wobblies 8, 121, 125, 130, 131
Women and Minority Faculty in the Academic Workplace: Recruitment, Retention, and Academic Culture (Adalberto Aguirre) 28–29
working class 1–11, 16, 18–24, 26, 27, 30–32, 34, 35, 40, 42, 47, 51, 52, 54, 63, 67–70, 74, 78–81, 89, 92, 94, 96, 98–100, 102, 105–110, 113–115, 121–125, 127–131, 134–138, 145, 148–157, 159–162, 165–170, 172–176, 180–193, 196, 197, 199–202, 204, 205, 209–217, 219, 220, 223–229

Yang, Guobin 72
Young, Vershawn Ashanti 27

Zembylas, Michael 63
Zorn, Dianne 63